Jesus,
King Arthur,
and the
Journey of the Grail

Jesus,
King Arthur,
and the
Journey of the Grail

THE SECRETS OF THE SUN KINGS

MAURICE COTTERELL

Bear & Company
Rochester, Vermont

Bear & Company
One Park Street
Rochester, Vermont 05767
www.BearandCompanyBooks.com

Bear & Company is a division of Inner Traditions International

Library of Congress Cataloging-in-Publication Data
Cotterell, Maurice.
  Jesus, King Arthur, and the journey of the Grail : the secrets of the sun kings / Maurice Cotterell.
    p. cm.
  Includes bibliographical references (p.   ) and index.
  ISBN 1-59143-053-4 (pbk.)
  1. Grail—Legends—History and criticism. 2. Ireland—Religion. 3. Jesus Christ. 4. Arthur, King. I. Title.

  BF1442.G73C68 2006
  001.94—dc22

                                                                    2006007784

Printed and bound in the United States by Lake Book Manufacturing

10 9 8 7 6 5 4 3 2 1

This book was typeset in Palatino

To send correspondence to the author of this book, mail a first-class letter to the author c/o Inner Traditions • Bear & Company, One Park Street, Rochester, VT 05767, and we will forward the communication.

Contents

Acknowledgements

With sincere thanks, as always, to G, and VH; to my wife Ann for her continuing support; to Eduardo Velasquez for German–English translation; to the team at Inner Traditions USA and to the staff of the National Museum of Ireland, Dublin.

Credits

Sources of illustrations and quotations
All illustrations, drawings, artwork and photographs by Maurice Cotterell, except those specified below:

Text Figures
3b, (55) American Museum of Natural History; 18a, 18b, 19, 21a AKG Images; 23a, 23b, 29 National Museum of Ireland; A27 (mask) after Vautier de Nanxe; 34, 35, 37, 38 (part), 62 (part); 52b, 53a Victoria & Albert Museum; 53b, after Augustus Villagra.

Colour Plates
Plate 1a, 1b, 1d Jeffrey Newbury / *Discover Magazine*, vol. 15, no. 4 (April 1994); 1c Prof. He Dexiu; 14a, 14b, 14c Werner Forman Archive; 15 Christies Images Ltd.; 17,18,19 AKG Images; 20a (20c and 21, detail), 20b, 24a, 24b National Museum of Ireland; 21g Wm. MacQuitty Collection.

Quotations
The Chinese Classics vols. I–V, James Legge, University of Hong Kong Press (1960); *Sacred Books of the East* vol. X, Max Muller (trans.) Oxford (1881); *The Popol Vuh*, University of Oklahoma Press (1947); *Holy Bible* (Special Command), Eyre & Spottiswode (1897). *The Geeta*, Swami Shri Purohit, Faber and Faber (1935). *The Annals of Inisfallen*, Dublin Institute for Advanced Studies, Ms Rawlinson B.503, ed. Seán Mac Airt (1988). *Treasures of the National Museum of Ireland*, ed. Wallace & Raghnall Ó

Floinn, Gill & Macmillan (2002). *The Treasures of Ireland,* Royal Irish Academy (1983). *Application of Science in Examination of Works of Art,* ed. William J. Young (1970). *Celtic Art,* George Bain, Dover Books (1973). *Hidden Wisdom in the Holy Bible,* vol. 1, G. Hodson, Wheaton, Ill., Theosophical Publishing House. *Bede's Ecclesiastical History of the English People,* ed. B. Colgrave and R. A. B. Mynors (Oxford 1969) IV. 4. Letter from Aluin to Ethewald, *The Annals of Ulster,* 793.

CHAPTER ONE

The Celts

The Mystery of the Blonde-haired Mummies

When Victor Mair, Professor of Chinese studies at the University of Pennsylvania, and archaeologist J. P. Mallory returned from China, they told their colleagues of what they had seen: perfectly preserved 4,000-year-old mummies, desiccated by dry desert sands. Tall white women with blonde hair, pigtails and tattoos; tall white men with brown beards; tiny white babies with blue eyes; woven fabrics of tartan and bonnets made of soft dyed wool. Everyone laughed. Mallory and Mair must have been mistaken, everyone agreed. Perhaps what they had seen were simply aberrations of the eye from wandering too long in the desert sun.

But a week later when the photographs appeared (plate 1), the laughing stopped and the questions began. What were Caucasians doing in the wastelands of China 4,000 years ago? How did they get there? Where did they get their knowledge of spinning and weaving? What process had preserved the bodies so perfectly? And why had it taken so long for modern man to discover them?

And the speculation began: Could these be the survivors of the legendary Atlantis that Plato says[1] sank to the bottom of the sea 9,000 years before Solon?[2] If so, how did they get from the eastern Mediterranean, the likeliest location of the fabled island, to the Taklamakan Desert of China? And why would they wish to settle there at all? Could the mummies be related to the mysterious tall, blonde, blue-eyed Philistines who came seemingly from nowhere in around

1000 BC to attack the Hebrews in Canaan, modern-day Israel? Could they have been the precursors of the legendary Aryans, the blonde-haired, blue-eyed, fair-skinned master race thought to be the genetic precursors of the Germans? Or were they the kin of the Celts,[3] the blonde-haired, blue-eyed, tartan-clad seminomadic herders who spread from Germany from around 1000 BC throughout Europe? Or, could all of these—thorns as they are in the side of history—owe their lineage to the mummies of Taklamakan?

Little is known of any of these peoples. The Celts, who feature most prominently and whose ancestors survive today, are difficult to define adequately. Attempts have been made to classify them by the language they spoke, but the picture is complex[4] with insufficient evidence to suggest that continental Celtic derives from a common source.

Attempts have been made to classify them biologically, as a race; a study carried out in 2001 by Professor Bryan Sykes of the Oxford Genetic Atlas Project compared the DNA[5] of a sample of Celtic Welsh people to an ancient central European Celtic bone sample and showed that Celts in the west of Britain share the same genetic lineage as those in Ireland, whereas the DNA of samples from the east of Britain is more closely related to the DNA of the later Anglo-Saxons[6] and the Vikings and Normans who came later.

Most historians do not believe that there was just one single influx of Celtic people that invaded the western parts of the British Isles. The consensus seems to be that the modern-day Irish, who describe themselves as Celtic, most likely evolved from several European incursions into the British Isles, the first in around 3113 BC, another in around 1500 BC, and others, later, all from Europe.

It seems that in around 3113 BC a single group of European-mainland migrants split into two, one settling in Wales and England—the builders of Stonehenge, in around 3113 BC—and a second that settled on the east coast of Ireland, the builders of megalithic Newgrange (close to the Neolithic barrows and ring ditches of Tara, northwest of today's Dublin).

'The Irish World Chronicles', a section in *The Annals of Inisfallen* that covers the historical period from the creation of the world to AD 432, says that the Tuatha Dé [Danann] were the mythical masters of

Ireland in around 1500 BC, before the arrival of 'the sons of Míl'.[7] The Chronicles then follow the flight of Míl from Scythia at some time between 1498 BC and 1029 BC.[8]

Entry No. 35 says that [following a failed attempt to secure the throne for himself] Míl killed Reflóir, the son of Némim, and fled into exile taking four ships each of which carried fifteen married couples and a mercenary soldier. The ships make landfall at an island called Taprobane where the exiles rest for three months before embarking on a ninety-day sea voyage that takes them to Egypt. In the eighth year of their stay Míl marries Princess Scotta, the Pharaoh's daughter. The Pharaoh subsequently drowned in the Red Sea.

> When Míl and his people found out [that the Pharaoh had died] they set out by sea with the same number as before and with Scotta the Pharaoh's daughter. They landed [again] in Taprobane Island and stayed for a month. After that they voyaged around Scythia near the entrance to the Caspian Sea. Then they anchored in the Caspian Sea for 27 days . . . until Caicher the Druid delivered them. After that they rowed past the promontory of the Riphaen Mountain, coming from the north, until they landed at Dacia where they stayed for a month. Caicher the Druid said to them 'until we reach Ireland we shall not halt'. They then rowed . . . and landed in Spain. They found it uninhabited on their arrival and dwelled there for 30 years and it was from it that 'Míl of Spain' was named; and there the two sons of Míl, Eremón and Ír, were born. And they are the two youngest . . .
>
> The 60 married couples and 4 mercenaries set out after that with the sons of Míl and Scotta, Pharoah's daughter, over sea to Ireland. . . . A great storm arose and parted the ship in which Donn[9] . . . was separated from the others. He and the crew of his ship were drowned in the sand dunes in the western sea . . . The sons of Míl divided Ireland between them after that, as the historians relate. (*The Annals of Inisfallen*, Trs. Ms Rawlinson B.503, ed. Seán Mac Airt, Dublin Institute for Advanced Studies, 1988)[10]

Later incursions into Ireland carried the tall blue-eyed blondes from France and Germany firstly to England and then on to Ireland c. 800 BC. If this is indeed what happened, then it at least explains away the ubiquitous presence of the blue-eyed ginger-blondes that live along-side the shorter black-haired types in Ireland today.

The orthodox view, augmented by the discoveries in the Takla–makan Desert, provides a simplified scheme (figure 1a) suggesting that the blonde-haired tartan-clad Celts first appeared in Chinese Turkestan in around 2000 BC. Commentators agree that they probably migrated north as the Tarim basin fell slowly to desertification. Tombs at the site of Qawrighul, near Loulan, where the 'Beauty of Loulan' (plate 1a) was found, are marked by semi-submerged log posts buried deep into the ground, arranged like massive circular henges in concentric circles with radiating arms, emulating the Sun and its rays—proving on the one hand that trees must have once grown in the region before it became desert and, on the other, that the people of Taklamakan revered the Sun and its rays, as did the Celts, who adopted the solar cross as their symbol (figures 2b and 2d). The surviving seminomads of the Tarim basin could then have migrated to central Europe, moving their cattle and sheep to ever-more fertile pastures northwards and westwards through the grassland steppes of Eurasia. At the same time, another splinter group may have moved westwards (figure 1b) through Sumeria to Turkey, explaining away the Philistine and Aryan enigmas. Having reached central Europe in around 1200 BC, some may have carried the Celtic language southeastwards to Turkey.

The fact is that no one knows for certain who the Celts were or where they came from. And, yet, we all seem to know to whom we are referring when we speak of them.

Later we discover that, colloquially, the Celts shared a common art form; their Druidic priests understood the super-science of the Sun—how it controls behaviour (astrology) and regulates fertility as it spins on its axis every twenty-eight days; they understood how the Sun brings periodic catastrophic destruction to Earth—erasing each civilization in turn from the annals of history; they believed in an after-life and they worshipped the bat god as the god of death and the stag as the god of fertility. They believed in a 'Son of God' who was born through an Immaculate Conception, performed miracles and who—when he died—became Venus, the morning and the evening star, the brightest and purest source of light in the heavens. And like the ancient sun-worshipping Maya of Mexico, and the ancient Peruvians,

The Celtic Highway

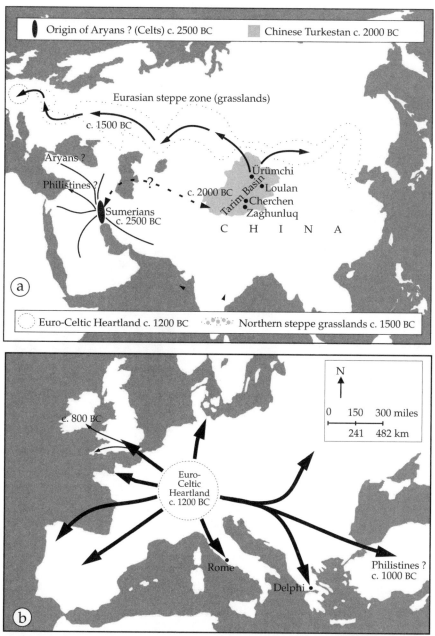

Figure 1. (a) First detailed reports of the Tarim mummies reached the West in 1994. The seminomadic precursors of the Celts followed their cattle and sheep across the fertile steppes arriving in central Europe in around 1200 BC. (b) From around 1000 BC they moved across Europe reaching Britain and Ireland by c. 800 BC.

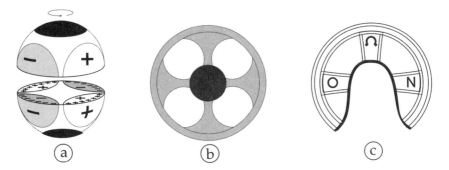

Figure 2. (a) Schematic of the Sun's magnetic fields. (b) Plan view of the Sun's equatorial magnetic field—[with the (black) polar field superimposed]. (c) The Celtic solar cross derived from (a) and (b) was later adopted by Christians. (d) and (e) Only Christ wears a halo containing the solar cross. (f) Lesser mortals wear other arrangements reflecting the degree of purity of the spirit.

Egyptians and Chinese, they encoded their secrets into their treasures for themselves to rediscover in a future incarnation—just in case they failed to make it to Heaven this time around.

The Euro-Celtic Heartland

By around 1000 BC the Celts had settled at the pre-historic salt-mining site of Hallstatt in the Austrian foothills at Saltzburg (figure 3).[11] The rock salt, sediment of an ancient sea, was important to the Alpine Celts as a source of iodine—used in the prevention of cretinism and goitre in mountain regions; as a meat preservative; and as a flavour enhancer, making it a valuable commodity that could be traded for luxury goods with other landlocked areas.

Mining first began by digging tunnels into the sloping hillsides and then continued deeper into the mountains. The 4,000 metres or so of disused mine shafts today contain a legacy of Celtic industrial activity, including the salt-preserved bodies of dead miners, fragments of woven clothing, leather boots, backpacks and tools.

In 1846 the archaeologist Johann Georg Ramsaeur discovered a

The Euro-Celts

Figure 3.

burial ground near the mines containing the bodies of 1,045 of the Hallstatt elite. Excavators unearthed a wealth of Celtic treasures including bronze urns decorated with spoked-wheel discs and birds [both of which are known Celtic solar symbols], bronze daggers and swords.

The style and decoration of artefacts found in the cemetery is distinctive, and similar-style artefacts have been found scattered across Europe.

This initial appearance of Euro-Celtic culture is named the Hallstatt period. Archaeologists later began to notice the emergence of differences in the style and content of grave goods and divided the period into four phases: Hallstatt A (c. 1200–1000 BC); B (c. 1000–750 BC); C (c. 750–600 BC) and D (c. 600–480 BC). For example, early Hallstatt C dis-

The Carving on the Hallstatt Scabbard

Figure 4. Detail of the engraving on the scabbard [from tomb number 994 in the Hallstatt cemetery c. 600 BC]. The centre circle represents the Sun. The top and bottom circles represent the planet Venus, as the morning star and the evening star. The characters either side represent the twins, a metaphor used by all of the sun-worshipping civilizations to represent the twin-star (planet) Venus (figure 5). The borders contain an interlaced vertical reverse-swastika pattern. The maze-like pattern that circumscribes the centre circle contains encoded secret information.

coveries include bronze and iron swords, whereas in the later period, D, daggers were more plentiful.

One sword scabbard from the Hallstatt cemetery is engraved with ostensible battle scenes showing warriors, some marching in formation, some on horseback carrying spears and other scenes that are duplicated—as though to emphasise their importance—showing two soldiers holding a wheel (figure 4).

The scene tells us a lot about the Hallsatt Celts. The central circle represents the Sun. The star inside the circle shows that the Celts were acutely aware that our Sun is, in the scientific sense, a star. Two circles, one above and one below the Sun symbol, represent the twin-star (planet) Venus in its various manifestations as the 'morning star' and the 'evening star' (figure 5) which for 292 days (viewed from the moving Earth) can only be seen in the dark morning sky, before the Sun rises. During the next 292 days Venus can only be seen after sunset, in

The Twin-star (planet) Venus

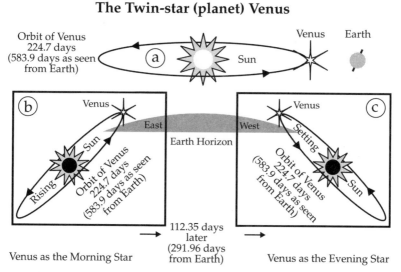

Figure 5. (a) The 224.7-day orbit of Venus falls between that of Mercury (not shown here) and Earth. The interval between successive identical appearances of Venus, as seen from the moving Earth, is 583.9 days. This means that Venus, in the position shown in (b), appears brightly illuminated in the dark morning sky. In position (c) the Sun sets before Venus which shines brightly in the darkening evening sky. Because of this, and because Venus is the brightest heavenly body, she is referred to as the morning star and the evening star, the twin-star.

the dark evening sky. Because it is the brightest and purest source of light in the sky, it was associated with love and purity of spirit by sun-worshipping civilizations. In the carving the two soldiers, positioned either side of the Sun, represent 'the twins', not only as the twin-star but also as a mirror image of each other. Whenever the ancients referred to the mirror image, they were referring to the soul, the mirror image of the body (figure 6).

The borders of the scabbard carving contain a vertical string of interlaced swastikas, a shape which is known to have been used by ancient civilizations as a solar symbol because it is derived from the pattern of the radiating solar wind (figure 7). This means that the Celts of Hallstatt must have known, as early as 600 BC, that the Sun spins on its axis and showers positively charged particles [the nucleus of the hydrogen atom] and negatively charged particles [electrons] towards the Earth. And they must have known about the 'sectored structure' of the radiating solar wind—how it changes alternately from positive to negative every seven days, in concordance with the underlying

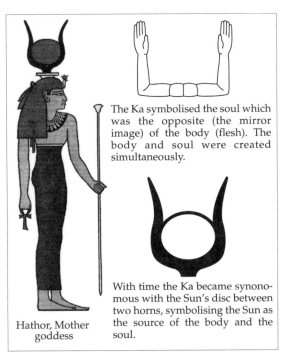

The Body, the Soul and the Sun

Figure 6. The ancient sun-worshipping Egyptians also believed that the soul was the mirror image of the body [that the left is the mirror image of the right] and that the Sun (God) separates the body from the soul.

The Ka symbolised the soul which was the opposite (the mirror image) of the body (flesh). The body and soul were created simultaneously.

With time the Ka became synonomous with the Sun's disc between two horns, symbolising the Sun as the source of the body and the soul.

Hathor, Mother goddess

magnetic structure of the Sun—facts only recently revealed to modern man, in 1962, by data received from the Mariner II spacecraft.

The swastika from ancient times evolved as a stylised squared-off version of the solar wind radiation pattern, rather than a facsimile of itself, because the 'square' was the mark of the educated and virtuous man. *The Book of Great Learning,* one of the great Chinese Classics from the school of the philosopher Confucius [d. 479 BC], explains the golden rule (referred to as the measuring square): 'a ruler should treat others as he would have others treat himself'. This sets out the ground rules for a relationship between two parties, as a measuring square sets into stone the relationship between two sides, bearing a close relationship to the Christian ethos that appeared much later.

The astute reader may have noticed that the swastikas in the Hallstatt scabbard carving borders are in fact reversed swastikas, rotating clockwise instead of, more correctly, counterclockwise, like the solar wind water-sprinkler pattern detected by Mariner II (figure 7b). Which means, surely (to the sceptic), that the Celts who carved the picture on the scabbard in fact knew nothing of the solar wind, nothing of the meaning of the square and nothing of astronomy. But these people were much cleverer than that—as were the Maya, Egyptians, Peruvians and Chinese.

The Mystery of the Hallstatt Swastikas

As the Sun spins on its axis every twenty-eight days, the showering positive and negative electrical particles collide with the Van Allen belts (figure 8b), the protective magnetic fields that encircle the Earth. Caught in the belts, the particles spiral between north pole and south pole every second, causing the Earth's magnetic field to vary at ground level.

In 1989, Dr. Ross Aidey, the White House chief medical advisor under the Reagan administration, discovered that the brains of rats, pigeons and guinea-pigs produce varying amounts of the timing hormone melatonin when bombarded by varying amounts of modulated magnetic fields. Melatonin stimulates the pituitary gland in the human brain, which in turn affects the production of the luteinizing hormone and the follicle-stimulating hormone. These in turn regulate

The Sun, the Solar Wind and the Swastika

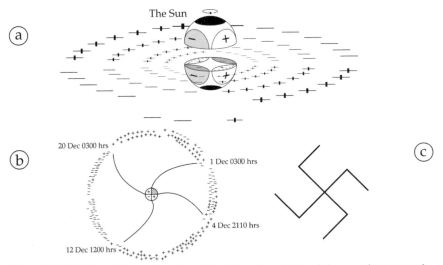

Figure 7. (a) The Sun radiates charged particles (the solar wind) and showers them towards Earth, like a water sprinkler. (b) The sectored structure of the solar wind was first detected by the Mariner II spacecraft in 1962 and plotted by IMP I (Interplanetary spacecraft I) in 1963. (c) The swastika represents a schematic of the solar wind pattern and was worshipped by many ancient sun-worshipping civilizations.

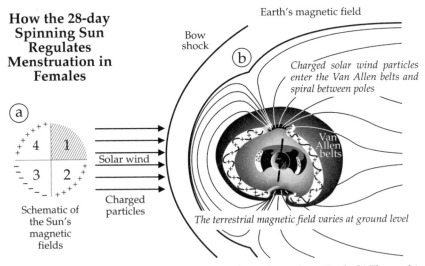

Figure 8. (a) The Sun spins on its axis and radiates charged particles to Earth. (b) The resulting varying magnetic field (at ground level) affects the manufacture of DNA in humans at conception, causing four types of genetic mutations, three times every year, resulting in twelve different types of personality (sun-sign Astrology). It later affects the human brain, causing variations in the production of the timing hormone melatonin every twenty-eight days causing variations in the production of the fertility hormones oestrogen and progesterone every twenty-eight days.

the production of the fertility hormones oestrogen and progesterone in females.[12] So as the Sun spins every twenty-eight days, it showers charged particles to the Earth which regulate the menstrual function in females every twenty-eight days, which explains why the ancient sun-worshipping civilizations worshipped the Sun as the god of fertility.

The spinning Sun also gives rise to magnetic cycles on the Sun's surface, causing the Sun's magnetic field to shift from a northeasterly direction to a southeasterly direction every few thousand years [the calculations are complex and non-periodic]. This magnetic twist has the effect of flipping the planets in our solar system upside down in their orbits. Clearly those nearest to the Sun will be affected most; the stronger the magnetic shift the stronger the effect will reach out into space and the more planets will be affected. Examination of historical solar magnetic activity reveals that a magnetic shift occurred in 3113 BC causing Venus to flip upside down on its axis.[13]

The 1950s writer, historian and scientist Immanuel Velikovsky believed that this 'birth of Venus' had been recorded the world over. In *Worlds in Collision* he wrote:

> In Greece, the goddess who suddenly appeared in the sky was Pallas Athene. She sprang from the head of Zeus-Jupiter. To the Chinese, Venus spanned the heavens, rivalling the Sun in brightness. 'The brilliant light of Venus', noted one ancient rabbinical record 'blazes from [one] end of the cosmos to the other'. (Immanuel Velikovsky, *Worlds in Collision*, Book Club Associates, 1973)

Clearly, the Earth, which is farther from the Sun than Venus, and less susceptible to topple on its axis for a given magnetic field strength, did not topple in 3113 BC.

Orthodox archaeologists have always been perplexed as to why Mayan calendrical inscriptions all refer back to a starting date in 3113 BC, because the Maya, civilisation did not appear in Mexico prior to the Teotihuacan period of around AD 100.

The Maya were master astronomers and knew—as we now know—that the Sun's radiation affects fertility on Earth, which is why they worshipped the Sun as the god of fertility. Because they knew just how important the Sun's radiation was to life on Earth, they monitored the Sun's radiation patterns, knowing that the Sun would fail their fertility needs 1,366,040 days after the solar magnetic flip that occurred on the 10th August 3113 BC. In AD 627, 1,366,040 days after the start of their calendar, the Maya began to die, just as they had predicted. For the next 187 years the Sun failed their fertility needs: fewer babies were born; at the same time an increase in solar X-rays, which affected equatorial regions more than other areas,[14] caused an increase in spontaneous foetal abortion and miscarriage throughout Mexico. These events coincided with a solar-inspired mini ice age. Less rain fell globally, but equatorial regions that were less able to cope suffered disproportionately to their neighbours in the north and south from drought, crop failure and famine. It was the end for the Maya.

The Maya encoded the important time interval of 1,366,040 days into one of their treasures, the sun shield of Monte Alban (plate 2a). They also, enigmatically, worshipped a number very close to this, the number 1,366,560, which they referred to as the 'Birth of Venus'. The *Dresden Codex*, one of the ancient Mayan bark books, records that the end of the world, for them, would come after 2,340 revolutions of Venus [2,340 x 584], 1,366,560 days after their calendar began in 3113 BC, meaning that they expected Venus to tilt upside down again in around AD 627.

This means that the swastikas on the Hallstatt scabbard are not drawn incorrectly. The carving is, more than anything, concerned with the planet Venus, which was flipped upside down in 3113 BC by a solar magnetic twist. So Venus now spins on its axis in the opposite direction to the axial rotation of all of the other planets in our solar system. From Venus, the Sun spins on its axis, clockwise, not anticlockwise. The stylised swastika on the Hallsatt scabbard explicitly recognises this by using a reversed (clockwise) swastika, rather than a regular one. Thus the Celts were not so careless after all. But why were the Celts, like the Maya, constantly drawing our attention to Venus?

The Spiritual Secrets of Venus

In 1989, while working at Cranfield University, I calculated the duration of magnetic reversals on the Sun. Using the university's massive computer I determined the figure of 1,366,040 days—the same as the number on the sun shield of Monte Alban, slightly less than the Mayan

Birth of Venus number of 1,366,560 days. So why did the Maya, who were aware of the true figure, go to such lengths to refer to the incorrect figure of 1,366,560 days as the Birth of Venus? Was it simply to enable them to track the cycle, knowing that Venus would flip again during the 2,340th Venus revolution as I had initially conjectured?

In 1997 (in *The Supergods*) I showed that many of the world's religious leaders shared much in common;[15] legend says that when Krishna (whose name means 'the anointed one' in Greek) was born, a bright star was seen in the sky.[16] When Buddha was born he was said to have been a 'bright star' in his mother's womb and when Jesus was born a bright star was seen in the sky.

When Lord Pacal died they say he went to Venus.[17] The last page of Revelation, in the Bible, says that when Jesus died he too became Venus: '. . . I Jesus . . . am the bright and morning star', meaning that the Bible explicitly states that Jesus was Venus.[18] In Peru, a statue of Viracocha appears alongside the 'two children' of Viracocha, the twins, suggesting that he likewise became Venus when he died. A picture in the tomb of Tutankhamun shows the dead king as twins, greeting Osiris, the god of resurrection in the constellation of Orion, meaning that Tutankhamun likewise became Venus when he died.

It becomes clear that Venus, as the brightest star (planet) in the heavens, is associated with spiritual leadership.

The sun shield of Monte Alban is also a Mayan transformer, a picture that transforms into many others when the decoding process is used.

Plate 2b shows a decoded picture of the Gateway of the Sun that today stands at Tiahuanaco in Bolivia on the shores of Lake Titicaca. The reflection (the mirror image) of the gateway can be seen clearly in the water. Closer inspection shows that the Star of David, the geometric symbol of Judaism, is also encoded into the design. When traced it becomes clear that the lower tip of the star ends in the mouth of a bas-relief carving of Viracocha on the lintel of the reflected gateway [appendix 1 explains the significance of the Viracocha bas-relief carving which also turns out to be another Mayan transformer].

Continued analysis of the sun shield reveals another picture showing another representation of Viracocha (plate 3a), similar to one found on the Viracocha vase of Tiahuanaco (plate 3b).

15

Further analysis reveals the picture of the distinctive head and face of Lord Pacal, the priest-king leader of the Maya in around AD 750, regurgitating a pearl from his mouth (plate 3c). The pearl is an ancient symbol used by many sun-worshipping civilizations to represent rebirth, or reincarnation. In the tomb of Lord Pacal at the Pyramid of Inscriptions, Palenque, a pearl was found in a seashell filled with cinnabar (the powdered form of liquid mercury) at the bottom of the stairs suggesting that Lord Pacal was reborn as the white planet Venus in Heaven [so inferred because the atomic number of the element cinnabar is 80. The pearl, in the cinnabar, thus becomes object number 81. 81 is composed of nine 9s, and 9 is the number of the soul, God or a Supergod].

The picture of Lord Pacal, in plate 3c, is contained within a vesica pisces, the geometric symbol of Christianity which is derived from two overlapping circles (plate 3d) representing the various manifestations of Venus. The series of decoded pictures (figure 9) suggests that Judaism (represented by the Star of David), Viracocha of Tiahuanco and Lord Pacal are all associated with Christianity (the vesica pisces). Plate 5 shows archaeological evidence from Central America to support the hypothesis. Moreover, the picture of Lord Pacal regurgitating a pearl (plate 3c) further suggests reincarnation and 'rebirth as Venus'.

We have already seen that Lord Pacal was Venus, Viracocha was Venus and Jesus was Venus. The inference must be that Jesus was born again as Viracocha and again as Lord Pacal. So here again we have 'the birth of Venus', just as we do with the Mayan number 1,366,560.

By using the two similar figures, the true scientific figure of 1,366,040 to describe magnetic reversals that cause infertility cycles and cause Venus to flip upside down on its axis [that is, cause Venus to be reborn]—and another very close figure of 1,366,560—referred to as the 'birth of Venus' (because it amounts to 2,340 revolutions of Venus)—they were attempting to convey the fact that 'Venus is reborn'. They were trying to tell us that Jesus, who was the Sun on Earth (light), was reborn as Lord Pacal, he was 'the rebirth of Venus', the rebirth of Jesus. Mayan transformers were just one of the living miracles that he left behind. Again, that this is the case is supported by more incredible composite pictures from the sun shield of Monte Alban, featured in plates 6–13, that show Lord Pacal as a stag, the birth of the baby Jesus,

The Secrets of the Sun Shield of Monte Alban

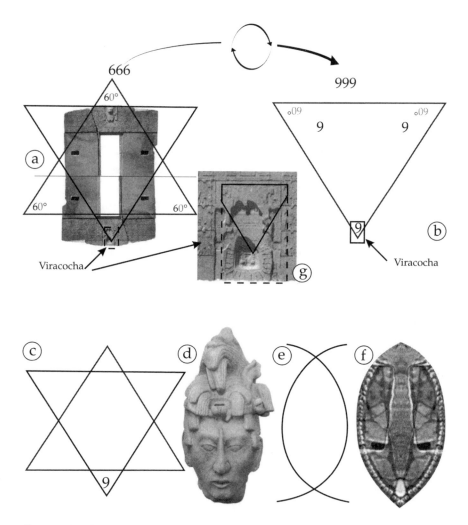

Figure 9. (a) Above and plate 2c show the decoded picture of a Star of David [the geometric symbol of Judaism] together with the Gateway of the Sun from Tiahuanaco, Bolivia. Note that the bas-relief carving of Viracocha on the gateway is positioned in the lower point of the star (b) corresponding to the number 9; meaning that Viracocha's number is 9, the number of a Supergod. (e) Plate 3c shows the decoded picture of a vesica pisces [the geometric symbol of Christianity] around the head and face of Lord Pacal. This reveals that Lord Pacal of Mexico (c. AD 750) and Viracocha (c. AD 500) were the same man as Jesus the Jew (c. AD 26)—different incarnations of Jesus on Earth. All three appear in decoded pictures from the sun shield, meaning that all three come from the Sun—all three were light, or God; proving that the sun shield of Monte Alban is a living miracle which shows the first pictures of Jesus. (f) In plate 3c Lord Pacal regurgitates a pearl. Regurgitation of a pearl (see main text) is a metaphor for the reincarnation of Venus (a Supergod) on Earth. Note the 66 pearls around the perimeter of Lord Pacal's head in (f). (g) The reason why the tip of the star forms the tongue of Viracocha is explained in appendix 1.

the adult life of Jesus, Jesus carrying the cross and Jesus dying on the cross. Plate 12 reveals the mechanism by which the Amazing Lid of Palenque can be decoded, and plate 13 suggests that those who live by the body find only death whereas those of the 144,000 find eternal life.

The ancients believed that the Son of God has visited Earth on many occasions, as Krishna in India c. 1700 BC, as Tutankhamun c. 1353 BC; as Buddha c. 450 BC; as Ch'in Shi Huangdi c. 220 BC; as Jesus, as the legendary white Gods Viracocha Pachacamac [God of the World] c. AD 300 and Viracocha [foam of the sea] c. AD 500, who walked the lands of Peru performing miracles; and as Lord Pacal of the Maya, c. AD 750.

As Krishna says, during his discourse with the prodigy soldier Arjuna, in the Bhagavad Gita, part of the epic Indian poem the Mahabarata:

> Whenever spirituality decays and materialism is rampant, then, O Arjuna! I reincarnate myself'. (*The Geeta*, Shri Purohit Swami, Faber and Faber, 1982)

The Hallstatt Celts not only understood the super-science of the Sun but by featuring Venus so prominently in their carvings declared a preoccupation with, and a knowledge of, each of the world's religions past and present and in so doing reveal that they understood the higher orders of spirituality.

The Tomb of the King of Hochdorf

Renate Liebfried, the deputy for Monument Preservation in Baden-Wuerttemberg, in Germany, was often called out to examine stones and timber ploughed up on the ancient earth-covered barrow at Hochdorf. Eventually it became clear that a circular ring of logs, spaced at around 3-metre intervals, had been buried vertically all around the 188-metre-(617-foot-) perimeter of the tumulus creating a henge along the lines of Stonehenge-I in England. In 1978, archaeologist Dr. Joel Biel decided to excavate before any more of the tumulus was damaged from agricultural activity. The 6-metre- (19-foot 8 inch-) high mound was surrounded by a wide trench.

About a year after excavations began a central rubble-filled shaft, measuring 4.7 metres (15 feet 5 inches) square, began to emerge, running down through the centre of the mound. Digging continued down to around ground level when they hit what appeared to be a timber platform. Unsure as to what they might find, they pressed on cautiously. Lifting the timbers, all they could see were fabrics draped on the walls and floor of a shallow chamber.

Entering the chamber they could only guess at what might lie below. Could this be the tomb of a 'Celtic Princess', like the one excavated in 1953 at the foot of the Celtic hill-fort at Mont Lassois, near Châtillon-sur-Seine in France, about 200 miles (322 km) west-southwest of where they were now digging? She was aged around thirty-five and estimated to be around 1.72 metres (5 feet 7 inches) tall. They found her laid out on a four-wheeled wooden wagon surrounded by all kinds of treasures, many of Greek origin including a massive 1.65-metre- (5-foot 5-inch-) high bronze urn that could hold 500 litres (132 gallons) of honey mead, three stone bracelets, a bronze bracelet with amber beads (on each wrist), two bronze anklets, amber and stone beads, bronze fibulae[19] decorated with coral and amber, and iron and gold fibulae together with a magnificent gold torc weighing 0.5 kg (1.1 lb.). The word *torc* derives from the Latin *torque*, referring to a twisted piece of flattened metal that the early decorative collars resembled. They became more popular throughout Europe after the Hallstatt period and developed from a simple twisted strip of gold wrapped around the neck like an open hoop to more ornate arrangements.

Their flashlights beamed into the dust-filled void below picking out a chamber 2.5 metres (8 feet 2 inches) deep and 7.4 metres (24 feet 3 inches) by 7.5 metres (23 feet 7 inches) wide, just below ground level. All they could see were woven and embroidered textiles and sheets draped around the walls and others, perhaps in bundles, on the floor.

Moments later the roof collapsed, crashing down into the space below, taking them with it. Soon it became clear, through the debris, that the chamber was constructed entirely of timbers (figure 10). The deck comprised sixteen short timbers and one longer end-timber, laid side by side. The walls were made of a stack of six longer-length timbers each carved with a mortise cavity to accommodate the tenon-like transverse interlocking beams. The arrangement of beams seemed over-elaborate. Why would anyone go to so much trouble to build such a sophisticated structure?

The Tomb of the King of Hochdorf

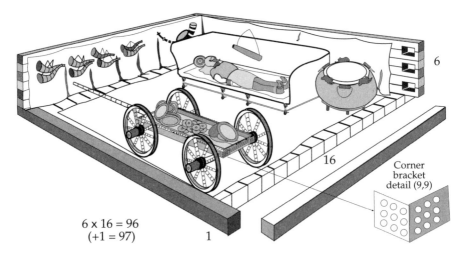

Figure 10. The Hochdorf tomb shares much in common with the tombs of other sun-worshipping kings. The Celts, like the Maya, Peruvians, Egyptians and the ancient Chinese, encoded the super-science of the Sun and the higher orders of spirituality into their treasures.

The enigma of the elaborate timbers concealed the true purpose of the tomb and its contents: the numbers and lengths of beams crucially convey the numbers 96 and 97. Appendix 2 explains how and why the ancients preferred to use numbers to encode esoteric information into their treasures. Figure 11 shows the numbers and explains why they chose them. Here again, this time at Hochdorf, we begin to see the emergence of an ancient practice that uses the same numbers used by other sun-worshipping civilisations in an attempt to convey the long lost knowledge of the Sun and the higher orders of spirituality.

The early Chinese were among the first to notice the periodic appearance of small black spots on the Sun's surface that manifest approximately every 11.5 years (figure 23b). Sixteen sunspot cycles subsist within every 187-year period. The same information was carved into a tablet by the Maya at their ceremonial site of Palenque, c. AD 750 (figure A12), encoded into the tomb design of Tutankhamun, c. AD 1353 (figure A13), and encoded into the tomb timbers of Viracocha Pachacamac in Peru, c. AD 300 (figures 12 and A14). These revelations, together with

Encoding Information Using Numbers

1,1 2,2 3,3　Numerical matrix often found in ancient tomb treasures to draw attention to the
4,4 5,5 6,6　practice of encoding using numbers. Appendix 2 (figure A17) shows one example
7,7 8,8 9,9　from the Pyramid of Inscriptions, Mexico.

Numbers used to encode esoteric spiritual knowledge

666　The Earth is carbon based. The Carbon atom consists of 6 negative charges (electrons), 6 positive charges (protons) and 6 non-charged particles (neutrons). The number appears in the Bible; 'here is wisdom, let him that hath understanding count the number of the beast; for it is the number of a man; and his number is 666 . . .' (Revelation XIII, 18)

999　9 is the highest number that can be reached before becoming one with God (as in 10). 999 thus represents Heaven above, God, the soul or a Supergod—a spiritual teacher. 666 represents the Earth below, Hell or the Devil. The purpose of life is to convert the body, 666, into Godly energy, 999.

144,000　Biblical number, refers to those destined for Heaven . . . 'I saw four angels standing on the four corners of the Earth holding the four winds of the Earth, that the wind should not blow on the Earth, nor on the sea nor on any tree. And I saw another angel ascending from the east having the seal of the living God: And he cried with a loud voice to the four angels, to whom it was given to hurt the Earth, and the sea, saying "Hurt not the Earth, neither the sea, nor the trees, till we have sealed the servants of our god in their foreheads". And I heard the number of them which were sealed; and there were sealed an hundred and forty-four thousand [144,000] of all the tribes of the children of Israel'. (Revelation VII, 14)

Numbers used to encode scientific knowledge—the super-science of the Sun

26　The time it takes, in days, for the Sun's equator to spin once on its axis.

28　The time it takes, in days, for the Sun's equator to spin once on its axis, viewed from the moving Earth.

37　The time it takes, in days, for the Sun's magnetic polar cap to spin once on its axis.

41　The time it takes, in days, for the Sun's magnetic polar cap to spin once on its axis, viewed from the moving Earth.

96　The number of solar magnetic cycles that subsist on the Sun every 187 years (made up of 16 observable 11.5-year (approximately) sunspot cycles (figure A11).

97　The number of solar magnetic cycles that need to be recognised when calculating the longer magnetic cycle of 18,139 years (figure A11).

20　The number of 187-year magnetic cycles that occur during 1 solar neutral sheet magnetic reversal of 3,740 years (1,366,040 days as calculated by computer.)

1,366,040　The interval, in days, between solar magnetic reversals that cause Venus to *physically* flip on its axis [encoded into the sun shield of Monte Alban by the Maya (plate 2)].

1,366,560　The Maya tracked the 1,366,040 interval using Venus; 2,340 revolutions of Venus (2,340 x 584) take 1,366,560 days, measured from the start date of their calendar in 3113 BC. They called the number 'the birth of Venus' but, importantly, only as a metaphor to describe the *spiritual* rebirth of Venus—Lord Pacal was the 'rebirth of Venus' (Jesus).

Figure 11.

The Tomb Timbers of Viracocha Pachacamac

6 x 16 = 96
(+1 = 97)

Figure 12. 16 wooden beams supported the roof of Viracocha Pachacamac's tomb (figure A8). 5 Y-shaped wooden beams supported these. 5 x 16 is not astronomically significant; however we note that one Y-shaped beam was found on top of the roof (top centre, above). Why would tomb-builders place one of six supports on top of the roof? The message here is that 6 is important: 6 x 16 = 96, the number of magnetic cycles in one sunspot cycle (figures A11, A12 and A13). One more transverse beam (figure A14) was embedded in the bricks (making a total of 97) but this did not support the roof.

the fact that the central shaft running down through the tumulus was exactly square [4.7 metres (15 feet 5 inches)], announce that the tomb designer was both aware of the sunspot cycle (the super-science of the Sun) and was also 'on the square', a virtuous man who was aware of the higher orders of spirituality. This had to be the tomb of a long-lost Supergod.

Removal of the sheeting used to wrap much of the contents of the tomb revealed what archaeologists described as the remains of an ancient 'Celtic Prince'. His bones were those of a Caucasian 1.87 metres (6 feet 1 inch) tall who was aged about forty-five years old when he died in around 550 BC.

He was wrapped in several woven blankets that were decorated with reverse-swastika patterns, identifying him with the planet Venus. At one end of the chamber, eight organic drinking horns hung from the wall in pairs alongside another larger, more decorative nine-section iron horn. That one appears to have a mouthpiece, plugged by a detachable stopper, and could therefore have been used as a sounding-horn. The ornate stopper consists of a slim tapering tube. A solar-style convex disc sits on the end, like an open umbrella, and a tiny white bead, fastened to the centre of the disc, terminates the end of the horn. What appear to be two identical tiny cast characters kneel either side of the tube with their arms raised as though worshipping the sun disc at the end.

The King lay on his back on a 3-metre- (9-foot-) long bronze funerary couch, made of six riveted bronze sheets, supported by eight caryatids (figure 13) adopting the raised-arm stance of the two sun worshippers found on the end of the iron horn [and similar characters found in the tombs of Lord Pacal and the Viracochas (plates 5b and 5c)]. Whether the figures are truly [female] caryatids, or male, is not clear. In any event, the dead man, above, was the ninth (9th) occupant of the couch, just as Viracocha Pachacamac was the ninth occupant of his tomb (figure A14).

Each of the caryatids stands, astride, on the axle of a bronze wheel decorated with red coral disc incrustations, emulating sunspots, suggesting that the dead man was preoccupied with the spinning Sun on its axis. The chest of each caryatid is pierced with a square stud, meaning that the man they carried, above, had a square heart, a pure heart, just like Lord Pacal and Viracocha Pachacamac.

A longbow lay beside the body and a quiver for arrows containing bronze and iron arrowheads—all that was left of the arrows—hung from the backrest of the couch. This did not necessarily mean that he was a hunter but more likely referred to the fact that as a spiritual teacher, like Tutankhamun who is portrayed in his tomb paintings firing arrows and like the terracotta archers from the mausoleum of Ch'in Shi Huangdi, he 'aimed at the heart'; he came to purify the hearts of others. His birchbark conical cap rested on the end of the couch behind his head, making a halo fit for a king.

He was adorned with jewellery: a gold neckband, a gold bracelet and a 33-cm- (13-inch-) long, 8.5-cm (3-inch-) wide belt cover made from a band of sheet gold. A 42-cm (16-inch) bronze scabbard with a bronze cast wheel shape at the sharp end rested on the belt around his waist. The under-side of the scabbard was dulled with patina but the surface, covered in gold foil, shone brightly in the flashlights of the excavators. The scabbard sheath concealed an iron dagger topped

The Secrets of the Couch Caryatids

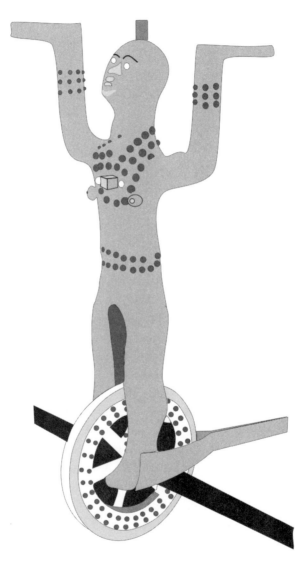

Figure 13. One of eight caryatids that support the bronze funeral couch of the King of Hochdorf. The raised arm stance resembles that of the small man who appears in the tombs of Lord Pacal, of Mexico, and the Viracochas of Peru (plates 5b and 5c). Like them, this one carries the mark of a pure heart on the chest, this time in the form of a square, a metaphor suggesting that the man being carried had a virtuous (pure) heart. He stands on the axle of the wheel that represents the Sun, that spins within him.

with a trident-shaped handle. [An iron dagger and a golden dagger were also found tucked into the waistband of Tutankhamun. There, the items explained that iron was more precious than gold because iron was magnetic and therefore enabled the owner to travel to far-off places and return again—using the magnetic compass—thus indicating spiritual leadership. The Tutankhamun iron dagger was the first appearance of iron known to man on Earth and thought to be of meteoric origin. The iron dagger in the gold-covered scabbard likely conveys the same principle.]

In the Hochdorf burial virtually every piece of gold, bronze, iron or fabric that could be decorated was adorned with solar circles, squares or reverse-swastika patterns.

What remained of his perished leather shoes was also embellished with gold foil, itself embossed with patterns of squares upon squares. It seemed that the foil pieces had been incorrectly fixed to the shoes, the right fixed in the position where the left should be and the left where the right should be, a metaphor suggesting that the next time the man would walk again would be in the spirit, as a soul (the mirror image of the body) in Heaven.

Next to the couch a sheet covered a large circular bronze cauldron trimmed with three bronze handles distributed around the rim. The three handles were interspersed with three cast bronze reclining lions or, more correctly, two reclining lions and one (seemingly poor) attempt at a lion casting. As though in error, it looks more like a sealion. The head and mane of the lion, from ancient times, referred to the face and rays of the Sun. Positioned around the rim of the cauldron it suggests that the spherical cauldron itself is also meant to represent the Sun. As though to emphasise the point a 13.4-cm- (5-inch-) diameter semi-spherical golden bowl embossed with patterns of circular sun-like discs was balanced between one defective lion, on the rim of the cauldron, and a good one. It is not clear why one lion was different from the other two or why the golden bowl was positioned as it was.

A magnificently ornate wooden four-wheeled carriage platform, decorated in iron sheeting, stood alongside the couch.[20] The corners of the carriage were held together by plates fixed with nine nails on either side (99, 99, 99, 99) like the coffin of Viracocha Pachacamac (figure A15). Onboard there were nine bronze plates, three bronze bowls, the remains of a wooden yoke, decorated with miniature bronze horse-shaped clips—to brace the horses—and a star-shaped bronze bridle arrangement made of six radiating chains (figure 14) held together by a central ring. Four of the chains consisted of seven circular rings (7, 7, 7, 7) whereas the other two contained only six circular rings (6, 6). Together these numerically refer to the rotation rates of the Sun's magnetic fields, 28 days and 41 days when measured from the moving Earth. The central larger ring carries a conical centre cap topped with a tiny sphere. The centre cone, capped with the Sun, clearly represents the polar magnetic cap of the Sun and with equal importance reveals that the conical birchbark hat worn by the dead man was a metaphor for the Sun confirming that he was, beneath the cap, the Sun itself and that his head was surrounded by light—a halo.

It took archaeologists two years to reconstruct the [approximately] 1,500 pieces of the carriage that was flattened under the weight of the crushing roof timbers. The engineering employed during its construction was of the highest order; two axles each carry two ten-spoked wooden wheels. The spokes of the wheels were mortised into oak hubs that turned on wooden roller bearings and each wheel is fitted with lath (wooden) tyres that are pinned to the individual wheels.

Many more golden discs, forming other parts of the equine headgear, were piled on top of the carriage platform.

The inside of the backrest of the couch is carved with scenes of a man standing on a four-wheeled carriage. He holds a longbow, and a whip to control the two carriage horses—giving an idea of what the burial party wanted to convey to grave robbers unfamiliar with how the ancients preserved and encoded their secrets.

Many other smaller items were found in the tomb including five circular carved amber rings, ranging in size from around 2.5 cm (1 inch) to 1.2 cm (0.5 inch) in diameter, all positioned beside the neck of the dead man.

Amber, found prolifically in the Baltic where it is often washed ashore by the sea, is the fossilised resin from coniferous trees from the middle tertiary [65–1.65 million years ago] period. It was treasured and used in jewellery from as early as 35,000 BC because of its special ability to generate static electricity—a negative electrical charge—when rubbed with a cloth; hence the name *elektron*, the Greek word for amber.

The Secrets of the Bridle

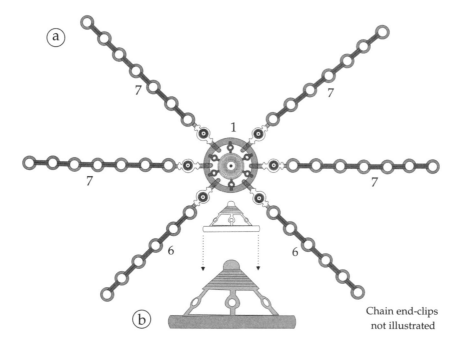

Chain end-clips
not illustrated

The Sun

Polar cap   41 days

Equator   28 days

Figure 14. (a) The bridle arrangement is made of six chains; four chains of seven circular rings and two chains of six, all retained by one central larger ring that carries a nine-tier cone (b) which is capped by a tiny sphere. 4 x 7 = 28, the number of days for the Sun's equator to rotate once with respect to the moving Earth. (c) The magnetic polar cap of the Sun rotates more slowly, every 41 days [(4 x 7) + (2 x 6) + 1] with respect to the moving Earth. The conical cap (b), illustrated here, is itself topped with a tiny sphere, suggesting that the cone represents the cap of the Sun. The conical cap shown here is the same shape as the birchbark hat (cap) worn by the man in the tomb, suggesting that the King of Hochdorf was the Sun (beneath the cap).

It is as though the five amber rings found next to the neck were placed out of position deliberately, rather than more appropriately alongside the bones of the five fingers—even though they are far too thick to have been used as ornamental finger rings. A similar conundrum was found in the tomb of Tutankhamun, where a cache of actual finger rings had been found out of position, on the floor of the tomb, as though discarded, threaded around a tubular piece of old cloth. There, the items amounted to an invitation to 'count' using the fingers. The anachronistic formation of amber rings next to the King of Hochdorf's neck might likewise be intended to convey the same information, an instruction to the observer to count the numerical attributes of the treasures in the tomb—the 6s, the 9s and so on—or, perhaps it amounted to a request to carefully *measure* the items in the tomb [a piece of thread wrapped around the base of the index finger five times stretches around the neck once].

Other small items recovered include gold snake-like fibulae around 6.5 cm (2.5 inches) long, some of which were used as hooks to hang fabrics from the walls together with three iron fishhooks, an iron fishing weight, a small quantity of fishing line and a small iron knife. Another iron knife was found in a wooden sheath. There was also a leather bag clasp with bronze pins and leather and bronze straps—that fitted to the horse yoke—sewing needles, bronze pins and nails, brooch parts and pendants, bone beads and slides, iron chains, an iron axe, a spear, a cleaver and horse bit (snaffle), a section of a deer antler and large quantities of woven fabrics.

This Hochdorf burial differed from other Celtic wagon tombs. The one at Mont Lassois containing the Celtic princess was less lavish and when analysed numerically contains none of the astronomical or spiritual numbers relating to esoteric tenets, unlike the tomb at Hochdorf or the tombs of other Supergods.

Moreover, the wheels of the funeral carriage at Hochdorf are the only four-wheeled ones that have been found attached to a wagon—as against others, like the wheels of the one at Mont Lassois that were found detached, resting against the tomb wall—and those of another wagon burial, at Mitterkirchen in upper Austria (northeast of Hallstatt) that likewise failed to yield any numerically significant information.

The evidence from the tomb at Hochdorf suggests that the occupant was, like Tutankhamun, Ch'in Shi Huangdi, the Viracochas and Lord Pacal, a Supergod leader of the Celts who lived in Hochdorf in around 550 BC.

Celtic Trade

In Europe, the Bronze Age subsisted from around 2000 to 800 BC.[21] Bronze is an alloy of copper (typically 75%) and tin (25%). The addition of tin makes the resulting alloy much harder than copper, corrosion resistant and ideal for casting. Thus it became the preferred metal for weapons, tools, vessels and artworks until the more plentiful iron was first smelted in Europe during the early Hallstatt period where swords, scabbards and daggers and other items made of iron were found in grave sites.

In around 600 BC the Greeks, who controlled the Mediterranean, enjoyed a plentiful supply of tin from mines in Cornwall, England, to facilitate the manufacture of bronze and bronze goods throughout the Greek Empire. Tin shipments crossed the Bay of Biscay southwards, through the Straits of Gibraltar and onwards to Greece.

Gaulish [French] Celts imported their own supplies from across the Channel up the River Seine into the Celtic heartland of Europe (figure 15) establishing hill-forts at Mont Lassois, at the end of the River Seine, and farther south at Camp de Chassey, to provide a safe and secure environment for the transfer of cargoes and to accommodate the movement of gold and goods bartered for payment. In turn, wealthy Celtic merchants used the gold to purchase goods from Greek markets in the south of France. As a result, a boom in trade occurred and as a consequence the Greeks developed the trading port of Massalia, modern-day Marseilles, in the south of France. Greek goods were shipped north from Massalia to the Celts in France and Germany and also to sites in Austria and Switzerland to compete with Etruscan goods arriving from established trade routes from Italy through the Alpine passes. They were also transhipped overland between hill-forts to the Seine and across the English Channel to Cornwall. The hill-forts became the crossroads of inter-European trade.

In turn the Greeks traded ivory from Africa; wine from the vineyards in the south; ceramics and dyes (used in fabrics) that the Celts

Euro-Celtic Hill Forts c. 580–480 BC

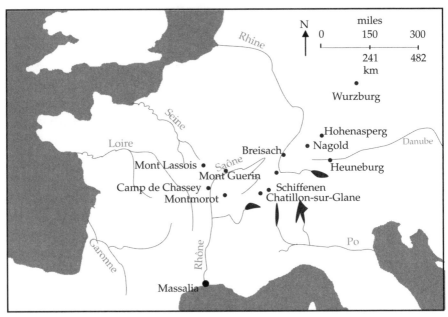

Figure 15. Map showing the principal Celtic trading sites that developed around the main rivers of Europe between c. 580 and 480 BC [not all rivers and sites are shown]. Heuneburg and Hohenasperg in Germany and Mont Lassois in France were the largest of the hill-forts that accommodated the transhipment of goods from Europe to the Mediterranean.

exchanged for woven textiles, gold, silver and iron. The large Greek bronze cauldron found in the tomb at Hochdorf and the massive Greek bronze cauldron and drinking vessels found in the tomb at Mont Lassois testify to the trade at the time.

Excavated hill-fort sites frequently contain workshops of bronze-, silver- and goldsmiths suggesting that they were indeed secure trading posts established to accommodate the safe transhipment of goods from the time they appeared in around 580 BC to the time they were simultaneously abandoned in around 480 BC.

Although the Euro-Celts began to drift westwards into Britain and Ireland as early as 800 BC, it is likely that the period between 580 and 480 BC, coinciding with the boom in Euro trade, witnessed the heaviest migrations. Copies of French Celtic hill-forts began to appear in Britain from around 580 BC; the remains of one, the Ivinghoe Beacon, excavated in 2002 in Buckinghamshire, England, is believed to have been constructed in a similar way to the one at Mont Lassois.

The reason for the collapse of the Celtic hill-forts on the European mainland in around 480 BC is not clear and remains a matter for speculation. It could be that the Celts eventually gained a monopoly in tin, forcing the price upwards, which in turn accelerated the introduction and use of iron. Or perhaps the appearance of iron reduced the demand for bronze and hence tin, not only by the Celts but also by the Greeks. Whatever the reason, it marked the end of the Hallstatt D period sites at: Mont Lassois, Camp de Chassey, Mont Guerin and Montmorot in France; Breisach, Nagold and Hohenasperg in Germany; and Schiffenen and Chatillon-sur-Glane in Switzerland, and the beginning of the La Tène period of Celtic archaeology.

Glauberg

Of all of the Euro-Celtic archaeological sites, one located just south of Hochdorf dating to around the same period (c. 500 BC) deserves a mention here. The Glauberg site, 32 km (19.9 miles) northeast of Frankfurt, was located from the air in 1987. Excavation of the 50-metre- (164-foot-) diameter tumulus (figure 16a) surrounded by a 70-metre- (230-foot-) diameter trench began in 1996. A chamber located in the centre of the mound was found empty. Two burials excavated between 1998 and 2001 were found either side of the central chamber. Grave number 1 revealed a 2.25 m x 1.07 m x 1-metre-high (7 feet 5 inches x 3 feet 6 inches x 3 feet 3 inches) timber coffin containing cremated human remains together with burial goods typical of the period, including a bronze jar-like flagon, two groups of bronze buttons, a bronze brooch, a belt (with a bronze belt hook, fastening clasp, hole rings, small chain and ornamental rivets), an iron sword with a bronze and iron sheath, iron spearheads and iron arrowheads.

Grave 2 contained the remains of human bones, three wooden spears with iron spearheads, a leather quiver with three iron-headed arrows, a longbow, a wooden shield—with an iron frame—two gold earrings, a 21.5-cm- (8-inch-) long gold necklace, a belt (with a bronze belt hook, small chain, hole rings and ornamental rivets), two bronze rings, one golden bracelet, one gold finger ring, an iron sword with

The Glauberg Tumulus

Figure 16. (a) The tumulus at Glauberg was discovered in 1987 and has been under excavation since 1996. Two graves were found together with burial treasures and a magnificent sandstone statue that was given the name 'the Celtic Prince' (b).

0   20 m

(a)

Statue

Grave 1

Central Chamber

Grave 2

The Bat God

(c)

(b)

(b) Sketch of 1.82-metre (6-foot), 227-kg (500-lb) statue c. 500 BC, excavated at Glauberg in 1996. Appendage markings on the forehead, triple neck pendants and massive ears suggest that the statue represents the Bat God. (c) The bat god represented death in many cultures from the Olmec, in Central America, onwards. This twenty-five-piece jade figure, found in a tomb at Monte Alban, Mexico, dates from around AD 700.

a bronze scabbard, six small wooden rods with iron spouts, a bronze brooch, fragments of bronze rings, three small iron rivets, two bronze bird-headed brooches and a 52.2-cm- (20-inch-) tall highly decorated bronze flagon.

These followed on from the 1996 discovery of a 1.86-metre- (6-foot 1-inch-) tall sandstone statue found in a wide trench west of the tomb (figure 16b). The excavators, unsure how to describe the highly unusual sculpture, labelled it 'a Celtic Prince'. But such an unusual-looking prince would be hard to find; his unique appearance with his massive ears, forehead appendage and triple neck-drops identify him more closely as a representation of the Bat God, worshipped through-out Central America as the god of death. This is not the first time the Bat God has been found in Hallstatt period excavations; the head of another so-called Celtic Prince, identical to this one, was found in Heidelberg, which is an interesting and unusual discovery, because it means that the sun-worshipping Celts shared the same mythological beliefs of the Maya. That this is the case is further supported by the appearance of stag and snake carvings found prolifically on the swords, scabbards, flagons and jewellery in the two graves at Glauberg.

The stag is a solar symbol known to have been worshipped by other sun-worshipping civilizations; it sheds its antlers at yearly intervals—and the Earth orbits the Sun at yearly intervals. It is also closely associated with fertility—because the Sun's radiation regulates fertility on Earth. And because grass contains high amounts of cellulose, making it difficult to digest, it is a ruminator (it regurgitates food already swallowed, to chew again [up to four times]), associating the stag with the notion of regurgitation [as in the case of regurgitation of a pearl in plate 3c] and reincarnation of the human soul on Earth.

And, stag-like associations do not end there:

- God is light, therefore God is the Sun and Jesus (as the Son of God) is therefore the Sun incarnate on Earth. This is to say that Jesus is the Sun and the stag is the Sun, so Jesus is the stag (figures 17 and 18).
- Jesus is also known to have healed the sick with his bare hands, which is why pharmacies in France and Germany often carry the picture of a stag above the door. One example is the Pharmacy

The Stag, the Sun and the Cross

Figure 17. A label from a bottle of herbal liqueur made in Germany and sold internationally today, showing that the stag is still associated with the Sun, the cross of Christ and the medicinal healing qualities of herbs.

The Stag, the Antlers and the Crown of Thorns

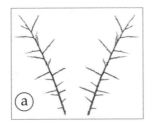

Figure 18. (a) Thorn sprigs. (b) Roman soldiers preparing Jesus with a crown of thorns in readiness for execution.

of the Stag, built in 1268, which survives today on the plaza of Strasbourg cathedral in France.

- Stag antlers can be used to represent thorn sprigs (figure 18a), emulating the crown of thorns worn by Christ at the crucifixion.

The snake was used by sun worshippers to describe the solar neutral sheet that twists and turns, snake-like, as it wraps itself around the Sun (appendix 3).

The stag was also one of the favoured eponyms of Lord Pacal, who often appears in Mayan transformers as the stag Xipe Totec (pron. *Shypee toe-tek*), the so-called Lord of the Stags and the Lord of Sacrifice in Mexico during the Mayan period. The Mural of Bonampak, a Mayan transformer, shows pictures of Xipe Totec being born in a stable and performing miracles, before going on to show him in another emanation as a man with a beard carrying a cross made of two pieces of wood.[22] Finally, he appears bowing to an audience of two stags (plate 4) who applaud the end of the performance.

La Tène

In 1867, during a heat wave, the waters of Lake Neuchâtel in northwest Switzerland fell to their lowest level in living memory. It was then that an amateur archaeologist, Friedrich Schwab, noticed the ends of timbers sticking out from the bed of the lake. It was clear that the timber piles must have been driven in long ago and he eventually persuaded the authorities to allow him to excavate the area to determine what they might be. His digs in the lake sediment uncovered around forty iron swords and spears. In 1868 the lake was drained completely during civil engineering works intended to regulate inflows. More Celtic pieces were pulled from the mud including another 160 iron swords—slimmer than those found at Hallstatt—iron spearheads, shields, armour, tools and fibulae showing a style and decoration unfamiliar to archaeologists. Since then more than 3,000 pieces have been pulled from the lake, showing that La Tène was an important Celtic centre that flourished from c. 480 to 50 BC. The style and design of the pieces is livelier than the earlier Celtic period drawing upon the influence of classical Greece—with the appearance of swirling acanthus-leaf patterns, loops, and anthropomorphic representations of stags, snakes, birds and unfamiliar creatures [perhaps mythical] all fused together with oriental and Hallstatt influence.

The La Tène period is divided into four phases: La Tène A (c. 480–400 BC); B (c. 400–250 BC); C (c. 250–120 BC) and D (c. 120–50 BC) corresponding with the appearance, design and style of four identifiable styles of weaponry—the appearance, design and length of swords, scabbards and spears; battle dress—shields and helmets; jewellery—brooches, necklets and torcs, bracelets, anklets and fibulae; pottery—vases, jugs, urns, cauldrons, buckets, jars, plates, drinking vessels and, most importantly in the colloquial sense, decorative Celtic art.

The early style of La Tène A was first observed in grave finds at the sites of Reinheim (figure 3) and Kleinaspergle in Germany and Basse Yutz in France. The Katzenbuckel group of tumuli, near Reinheim, just north of the German/French border on the River Blies, were completely flattened in antiquity and only rediscovered when quarrying activities in the area exposed the remains of a tomb, part of which was destroyed in the process. In 1954 excavations showed the burial to be that of another Celtic 'princess' from the early La Tène period, although the tomb was not as lavishly furnished as the earlier ones found at Hochdorf or Mont Lassois. Indeed, it is uncertain whether or not the tomb contained the remains of a male or female, the bones having long since perished in the acidic soil.

The treasures included a large twisted gold torc, two lignite bracelets, gold finger rings, bronze and gold fibulae, one resembling a rooster and inlaid with coral—used to tie clothing, almost none of which remained—a large quantity of amber and glass beads, a large bronze mirror with an anthropomorphic handle—found smashed despite being wrapped in fabric for protection—two bronze basins and a bronze flagon over 1 metre (3 feet 4 inches) in height. Two cylindrical gold bands were all that remained of an organic drinking horn. These last three items are together described as a 'banqueting set'. The absence of weapons and the quantity of jewellery are the only reasons to suggest that the occupant of the tomb was female.

In 1879 another tumulus was excavated, at Kleinaspergle, just 1,000 metres (3,280 feet) south of the Hohenasperg (figure 15) hill-fort in

Germany. This one stood at around 7.6 metres (25 feet) high and measured 60 metres (197 feet) in diameter. The central timber-clad chamber was empty and thought to have been robbed but a second chamber 2 metres (6 feet 6 inches) by 3 metres (9 feet 9 inches), to the west, was found intact. Only a few items were retrieved: a gold brooch and bracelet, three bronze plates, a large bronze bowl, a bronze Etruscan *stamnos* (a kind of cauldron), two gold drinking horn ends and four other drinking horn bands and discs. Two shallow drinking cups *(kylikes)* of a type made in Athens in around 450 BC had been embellished locally with gold foil without regard for the underlying Greek decoration. A large bronze flagon was found, typical of the period in style but not in decoration; the handle at the base end was attached to the body with the cast of a tiny human head and at the rim with an anthropomorphic face. Again, the absence of weapons persuaded archaeologists that the remains must be those of a female.

In 1927 at Basse Yutz, in France, a pair of bronze flagons of a similar style (plate 14) was found, during construction of a new road, together with two stamnoi. In 1929 the British Museum raised £5,000 to purchase the flagons which are now kept in its collection in London.

The 39.6-cm- (15.6-inch-) and 40.6-cm- (16-inch-) high flagons date from c. 400 BC and are particularly beautiful and of the highest quality craftsmanship. Each has a lid that can be removed and stored on a safety chain that is gripped in the mouth of a dog-like bronze head, on the handle, and the rim and the base are circumscribed with coral inlay. The lid contains a beautiful semi-spherical bronze stud patterned with tracery of bronze wire in-filled with coloured enamel (molten glass), the earliest known appearance of the *champlevé* technique.[23] The second of the La Tène phases is characterised with finds of a burial at Waldalgesheim on the junction of the Rivers Rhein and Nahe at Bingen near Mainz in Germany. In 1868 a farmer ploughing his land crashed into what was left of a tomb now described as that of another Celtic 'princess'. Only the metal fittings from what was once the yoke of a team of horses and parts of iron wagon wheels remain to suggest that the burial may indeed have been a wagon burial. No skeletal remains or clothing were found. The occupant wore a large ornately cast gold torc, three gold bracelets and two gold anklets. A large bronze flagon, found with a bronze jar, was incised with delicate compass-rendered floral geometric carving in the form of winding tendrils and leaves, representing the first appearance of the style which more than anything typifies the art style of the Celts as we know it today. The same style is found on a gold helmet from the same period at Amfreville-sous-les-Monts.

Metalsmiths of the day covered surfaces of pots, swords, scabbards, helmets and jewellery with patterns interspersed with animal and human heads. It is still not known how the gold filigree work, with its arabesques, arches and curves that twist and turn, encompassing human faces with goggle-eyes, full-blown cheeks, bulbous noses and twisting mouths, could have been carried out on such a seemingly microscopic scale so successfully and all, ostensibly, without magnification to aid the production process.

The La Tène A period is thus characterised by the presence of tumulus tombs—some of which contained bodily remains and others cremated remains; Hallstatt-style swords—where the longer and slimmer blade is counterbalanced by either a trident head or an antenna-like handle termination; and developments in the Hallstatt style of fibulae—but with turned-up ends.

The La Tène B period is characterised by tumulus burials and surface graves, swords, some with a curved scabbard mouth and miniature circular openwork (for example, a Celtic cross with open [see-through] segments) termination at the sharp end. The phase began with the appearance of decorative coral incrustation and enamelled glasswork beading set in mounts, as with the Basse Yutz flagons.

During the third period of La Tène the beautiful rococo decorative artwork developed further and even more delicately. Coral incrustation became more prolific. Enamel glasswork became more commonplace and swords became even longer, without the openwork on the scabbard.

During the final La Tène phase the tips of swords became blunt and rounded, scabbards straight-mouthed, fibulae cast and enamelled beads more sophisticated and ambitious with the introduction of different colours to the glass enamel inlay. But the closing of the third phase of the La Tène period had one last thing to reveal, probably the most famous Celtic treasure of all: a curious silver bowl.

The Gundestrup Cauldron

In 1891 a 35-cm- (14 inch-) high, 71-cm- (28 inch-) diameter highly decorated blackened and battered silver cauldron (figure 19a) weighing 9.1
kg (20 lbs) was discovered in a peat bog at Raevemose, Gundestrup,
North Jutland, Denmark. It shows, say archaeologists, scenes of Celtic
life on each of thirteen tiny embossed gold plated silver panels, or
platelets, clipped to the main silver bowl. One of five platelets, hanging from the inside wall, features the Celtic so-called god of hunting
Cernunnos (figure 20) who sits semi-cross-legged surrounded by nine
creatures. In his right hand he holds high a torc and wears another
around his neck.

Those aware of the true nature and purpose of Celtic mythology
will see more in this scene. On his forehead Cernunnos wears the horns
of a stag, associating the wearer with the Sun, light, God, and healing.
As we noted earlier, the stag is also associated with Jesus. The ellipse-
shaped torc in the right hand of Cernunnos depicts the path of the
Sun, proclaiming reverence for the Sun. The ends of the torc terminate
with two spheres, representing the various manifestations of Venus
as the morning star and the evening star. His body, within a second
torc [around his neck], thus becomes the body between the morning
star and the evening star—the Sun, light, or God. Cernunnos is hence
explicitly portrayed as Jesus on the Gundestrup Cauldron, as he is in
the Bible, which surely means that the Gundestrup Cauldron tells, at
least in part, the story of Jesus. But in c. 100 BC, the time the cauldron
was manufactured, Jesus had not yet appeared on Earth, which can
only mean that the appearance of the Celtic God Cernunnos refers, like
the Old Testament of the Bible, to the future coming of Christ (if the
dating of the cauldron is correct).

This interpretation is also supported by the appearance of another
character nearby Cernunnos, a small child riding on the back of a
dolphin. The Greek and Roman sun god was Apollo, the twin child
(together with his sister Artemis) of the creator god Zeus. Legend says
that Apollo was carried on the back of a dolphin from his birthplace,
the island of Delos, to Mount Parnassus, where he seized control of the
oracle from the Earth Mother. His chief oracular shrine was in Delphi
which he won by killing the oracle's serpent protector, Python. We

The Gundestrup Cauldron

Figure 19. (a) The Gundestrup Cauldron, c. 100 BC, found at the Raevemose peat bog in Jutland, Denmark, in 1891. (b) Slaughtered bull (inside base).

Cernunnos

Figure 20. Detail showing Cernunnos, the Celtic God. In his right hand he holds the elipse-shaped Celtic torc that depicts the path of (and hence) the Sun. The ends of the torc terminate with spheres, representing the various manifestations of the twin-star (planet) Venus as the morning star and the evening star. His body, within a second torc [around his neck], thus becomes the body between the morning star and the evening star—the Sun, light, God. Cernunnos is hence associated with the Sun. On his head he wears the horns of the stag that sheds its antlers annually associating the stag with the Sun, light and God. The stag is the eponym of Jesus. The antlers also resemble sprigs of thorns and close examination shows Cernunnos wearing a twisted band around his forehead—representing the crown of thorns worn by Jesus at the Crucifixion. The Gundestrup Cauldron, like the Old Testament of the Bible, tells of the coming of Christ [for the Celts].

noted earlier (endnote 15) that Chi Zeus was the name given to Christ in the Bible. On the cauldron Cernunnos is likewise associated with the son of Zeus and he holds what appears to be a serpent, safely behind the jaw (as though in conquest) in his left hand. It is worth mentioning here that Apollo was also known as the archer, who, like Jesus, aimed at the heart.

Other scenes on the inside platelets show what can only be described as scenes of hell, with individuals hanging upside down, being submerged into vats of boiling liquid, and soldiers carrying spears, marching alongside cavalry, wearing boot spurs—dating the object to no earlier than c. 100 BC, when spurs were first identified as part of Celtic armoury.

The centre circle on the base inside the cauldron features a remarkable scene of what has been described as 'a dying bull pursued by a hunter and two dogs' (figure 19b). Between 1400 BC and AD 400 Persians, Indians and Greeks worshipped the sky god Mithras, who was also popular with the Romans in the first century BC. Legend says that the Sun god sent his messenger the raven to command Mithras to sacrifice a great bull. Mithras reluctantly obeyed and when the bull died a great miracle occurred—the world began. The cloak of Mithras was turned into a celestial globe on which the planets and stars were shining.[24] Sacrifice of the bull was the central theme of Mithraism. Another account says that seeing the afflictions suffered by mankind, Mithras came down to Earth, where his birth was witnessed on December 25th by shepherds.[25]

In Ireland the Celtic bull-sacrifice (tarb-feis) was an integral feature of the inauguration of a new king, a ceremony of deep religious significance in Celtic Irish society.

Seven platelets clipped to the outside wall of the cauldron feature a man with raised arms, contemporaneously described as one of the barbarian Teutons that roamed Germany during those times.

The so-called Teutons with raised arms (figure 21a) have more to say: figure 21b shows the man with raised arms that covers the face of Lord Pacal from one of the decoded pictures from the Amazing Lid of Palenque (plate 5b). Figure 21c shows another representation of the same character with raised arms from the tomb of Viracocha in Peru. Both appearances of the small man are characterised and distinguished

The Mystery of the Man with Raised Arms

Figure 21. (a) Scene of a man with raised arms, from the Gundestrup Cauldron, shown with two stags, like Lord Pacal in the Mural of Bonampak (plates 4 and 6). (b) Decoded picture of a man, also with raised arms, from Lord Pacal's Amazing Lid of Palenque (plate 5b). (c) Figure of a man with raised arms from the tomb of Viracocha Pachacamac, Peru.

by the fact that each wears a hat with corks dangling from the rim—in Lord Pacal's case his upper front set of teeth in the decoded picture represent the corks. This ostensibly innocuous point is revealing, because it depicts Lord Pacal and Viracocha in the place of flies, on Earth, the place of filth, which is opposite to the place of purity, Heaven. In so doing it depicts each as the Son of God on Earth. How else could this subtle point be conveyed?

Figure 21a shows one of the Teutons adopting the same raised arm stance. And the Teuton carries a stag in each hand, Jesus to the left, Jesus to the right, and Jesus in the middle.

As we have seen, decoded scenes from the sun shield of Monte Alban reveal that Lord Pacal and Viracocha and Christ were all different incarnations of the Son of God on Earth and analysis of the scenes from the Gundestrup Cauldron appear to be telling the same story about Cernunnos.

The scene showing seated Cernunnos contains even more esoteric information; ['here is wisdom, let him that hath understanding count the number of the beast; for it is the number of a man', Revelation XIII, 18]. The number of horns on the antlers that Cernunnos wears on his forehead amounts to 7 on each antler, 7, 7 (figure 22a), and we note that the number 144,000 [the number of the pure]—that appears on the forehead of Lord Pacal in the decoded picture of Lord Pacal (plate 5b and detailed in figure A10)—does so only when the transparencies are each positioned at 7° each from the vertical (7° and 7°). That this information was deliberately intended to be conveyed is confirmed by further numerical analysis of the scene: the real stag, standing next to Cernunnos (figure 22a), does not have 7 horns on each antler; he carries 8 on each (8, 8). The grouping of horns can be further analysed as in figure 22b which shows the numbers 3, 3, 3, 3, 4, 4, and 5, 5 (in addition to the sequences of 7, 7, and 8, 8, from above). The numbers 6, 6, 6 [the number of the beast] are missing from the sequence, as they are in the numerical matrix from the tomb of Lord Pacal (figure A17). The snake that Cernunnos carries in his left hand curiously carries what appears to be the beak of a bird, a duck's bill, extending from the head, or else the creature may be meant to represent a dragon, a mythological composite of a bird, a snake and a stag. Either way, Cernunnos is here associated with the feathered snake (the bird and the snake) of Lord

Figure 22. (a) Each of the antlers on the forehead of Cernunnos carries 7 angular horns (7, 7). Figure A10 shows that the number 144,000 [the mark of the pure] only appears on Lord Pacal's forehead when the transparencies are juxtaposed by 7°and 7° (7, 7). Cernunnos hence likewise carries the number 144,000 on his forehead. That this is so is confirmed by further numerical analysis of the numbers in the scene; the real stag, standing next to Cernunnos, does not have 7 horns on each antler, he carries 8 on each (8, 8). The grouping of horns can be further analysed as in (b) which shows the numbers 3, 3, 3, 3, 4, 4 and 5, 5. The numbers 6 6 6 [the number of the beast] are missing from the sequence, just as they are in the numerical matrix from the tomb of Lord Pacal (figure A17).

Pacal, Tutankhamun, the Viracochas and Ch'in Shi Huangdi. Hence, on the one hand Cernunnos is the feathered snake (appendix 3) and on the other hand the Sun.

The feathered snake shown in figure A27 appears only when the transparencies of the mosaic jade mask of Lord Pacal, which was found covering his face in his tomb at Palenque, are each rotated by 66.6° and then overlaid. In the same way, Lord Pacal appears as Lord of the Stags in the Mural of Bonampak (plate 4) only when each transparency is rotated by 33.3° each, when they are juxtaposed by 66.6° (in relation to each other) and then overlaid. All of these go to illustrate the importance of the number 666 when encoding information by the ancients into their treasures and the cauldron is no exception.

The March of the Romans

In 486 BC, following the collapse of the hill-forts, the Celtic population spread out from central Europe. As many as 200,000–300,000 crossed the Alps into northern Italy. In 391 BC a group of 30,000 Celts attacked the Etruscan stronghold of Clusium (modern-day Chiusi).

The Etruscan army called upon the support of Rome who responded by sending ambassadors in an effort to mediate. But the ambassadors took sides with the Etruscans forcing Rome to send troops. The coalition fought bravely but were no match for the Celtic 'barbarians' from the north who took the city for themselves and then, gaining in strength and confidence, continued their push southwards into Italy.

In 387 BC the Celts attacked the Roman army on the banks of the River Allia, a tributary of the Tiber, around 16 km (10 miles) north of Rome and, victorious, marched on to sack Rome itself. But this time fate was on the side of Rome; weakened by disease and epidemic, the Celts were persuaded to return north in return for gold. The military defeat shook the Romans who, in response, fortified the capital with a protective wall. The experience, at least for a while, encouraged them to adopt a more conciliatory approach with their neighbours. But it was not to last. Within fifty years the Romans recommenced their aggressive campaigns in pursuit of empire.

By 295 BC they turned the tables on a coalition of Samnite, Etruscan and Italian Celts who they crushed at the battle of Sentenium. The

Celts fled north to consolidate their position. Some shifted southeast-wards, into Greece, where they ravaged Delphi in 279 BC and paused to enjoy the spoils of war. But the Greeks, as though in the lap of the gods, helped by earthquakes, thunderstorms and avalanches regained control killing 30,000 Celts. Those that were left dispersed and fled to Turkey. In 225 BC bands of mainland Italian Celts supported by Alpine Celts attacked Rome. But they were no match for the Roman legions who cornered and destroyed them at the battle of Telamon.

The disciplined and organised Roman army grew in strength. By 125 BC it assumed control of Massalia, long since lost to Greek control, giving them a foothold from which they would later advance north-wards into France. In 57 BC, under the command of Julius Caesar, the Roman army attacked and slaughtered Celts at Sambre in northeast France, capturing more than 50,000 who were interned into slavery.

In 55 BC Caesar, together with two legions of troops, crossed the English Channel on a mission to ascertain the extent of defences that might oppose a future full-scale invasion. Their presence was quickly detected resulting in skirmishes with local Celts who, subdued with bribes, accepted assurances that the Romans would leave within days, and they did. Two years later Caesar returned, this time with 600 ships carrying 25,000 men. But the Celts, in the meantime, alerted by the first appearance of the Romans, had organised themselves under the leader Cassivellaunus whose troops repelled the Roman invasion and pushed them back to France.

By 52 BC, in response to Roman defeats and subjugation, French Celts had organised themselves into a cohesive fighting force under the Celtic warrior Vercingetorix (d. 46 BC) who launched raids on the Romans in the south. Caesar intercepted, forcing the Celts to retreat to the hill-fort at Alesia (today's Alise-Sainte-Reine in eastern France). There, Caesar's 50,000-strong force besieged the garrison who, half-starved, were unable to breach the Roman lines, even with the help of reinforcements from forty other Celtic tribes that swelled their num-bers to over 200,000. Suffering massive casualties, the relief forces withdrew and Vercingetorix surrendered to Caesar. The whole of Gaul was now under the control of Rome. One million Celts were dead and another million were sold as slaves.

The Druids

The Roman conquest of Britain began in AD 43 during the reign of Emperor Claudius and lasted for more than forty years. In the latter years (during the reign of Emperor Domitian), the Governor Agricola took the campaign north to Scotland but after several unsuccessful attempts to conquer the country fixed the frontier with a boundary that spanned England between the Rivers Solway and Tyne.[26] Roman colonies established themselves at London, York, Chester, St. Albans, Lincoln, Gloucester, Bath, Chester, Manchester and Colchester. It was at Colchester in AD 60 that Celtic troops led by Boudicca (d. AD 61) rallied and revolted against Roman imperialistic rule without success. Eighty thousand Celts were killed. It put paid to Celtic resistance against the Romans throughout Britain, except for die-hard stoical Druids who defended their religious centre at Ynys Môn on the island of Anglesey in Wales until that too was destroyed by the Romans in around AD 70.

Druidism (from the Greek, *drus*, 'oak' tree) was the outlawed religion of the Celts in Roman Gaul, and in Britain where it originated. The oak was so revered because it sustained the parasitic plant mistletoe that bears translucent white berries that epitomise fertility, the soul [the seed within] and Venus—the white planet of love.[27]

The Druids, like the Maya, Egyptians, Peruvians and Chinese, were sun-worshipping astronomer-priests who believed in the immortality of the soul, reincarnation (transmigration of the soul) and astrology. The Druidic year of only 354 days (twelve lunar months of 29.5 days) referred to auspicious and inauspicious days and could be used to predict the best times for planting and harvesting. In 1897 a bronze example of a Druidic calendar used during the reign of the first Roman emperor, Augustus (63 BC–AD 14), was found at Coligny, near Bourg-en-Bresse, France, demonstrating that Druidism was practised at that time. The calendar lists sixty-two months over a five-year period and concerns itself with movements of the Sun and Moon. Good days were described as 'mat' and bad days as 'anm'.

Many Classical writers wrote about Druidic ritual and practice. Strabo (63 BC–AD 21), Athenaeus (c. AD 200), Diodorus (AD 60–30) and Caesar (100–44 BC) base their evidence on the earlier works of Posidonius. Much is learned from Pliny the Elder and in his *Historia Naturalis (Natural History)* of AD 77 he suggests that Druidism originated from the Magi, the wise men of Persia who as priests were aware of the higher orders of magic. Strabo associates them with the shamans of antiquity who appear in cave paintings made during the hunting period of c. 30,000 BC. Shamans, some of whom survive today, believe that every living thing has 'spirit', in the same way that modern science acknowledges that all tangible things are comprised of atoms that are held together by the *strong nuclear force* (that binds the nucleus of the atom together) and the *weak nuclear force* (that holds the outer negative electrons in orbit around the nucleus).

In those days the shaman was able to locate quarry through sense and to leave his body at will, to have an out-of-body experience and visit the soul world—a gift useful to pacify and bless the departing souls of animals and so avoid karmic retribution.[28]

We can be sure that whenever human sacrifice is mentioned in the context of sun-worshipping civilizations, the reporters are unfamiliar with the real reason for the killing which undoubtedly took place. In Mexico, the Maya believed that this Earth is Hell (figures A18, A19 and A20) and that the only way to escape from Hell was to die either in sacrifice or in duty-inspired death—through battle. The strongest and finest of athletes, invariably soldiers, could compete in the national ball game, which involved hitting a small ball through hoops located high up on either side of the stadium. The hoops represented the twin manifestations of Venus in the sky. As a reward the winners were killed, escaped from Hell (the Earth) and travelled to Paradise. Thus they were made sacred, sacrificed. Others simply died naturally, without purpose, to reincarnate over and over again. In this way sacrifice was rationalised as a sign of love, a means of escape from Hell, and compassion. (Appendix 2 describes what the soul is and how it gets to Heaven).

The Maya were also preoccupied with the fertility-inspiring effects of the Sun, which at that time was failing the fertility needs of the people. They left behind stone carvings showing ostensible bloodletting practices. But there is more to the carvings than a senseless portrayal of masochism; they were attempting to convey the message that the Sun was failing their fertility needs, failing the production of oestrogen and progesterone, failing menstruation (blood). The Aztecs, who came later, misunderstood the message, lost the plot and slaughtered millions needlessly. Accounts from Classical writers and from archaeo-logical remains indeed suggest that human sacrifice took place among the Druids but no evidence remains that might explain why. The real reason no doubt lies somewhere between the accounts of the Maya and Aztecs. It was this belief in transmigration of the soul (reincarnation), a promise of a place in Paradise, that made the Celts such fearless fight-ers, eager to die in battle, as noted by Julius Casesar who questioned the source of their courage:

> They wish to inculcate this as one of their leading tenets; that souls do not become extinct, but pass after death from one body to another, and they think that men by this tenet are in a great degree excited to valour, the fear of death being disregarded. (*Gallic War*, Wm. A. McDevitt [trans.], Book VI, p. 14)

Lucanus adds:

> From you [the Druids] we learn that the destination of man's spirit is not the grave nor the Kingdom of the Shades. The same spirit in another world animates a body and if your teaching be true, death is the centre, not the finish of a long life. (*Pharsalia* [c. 48 BC], Loeb, 1962)

The word Maya derives from the ancient Indian Sanskrit word Maya, meaning illusion. The Maya of Central America adopted it because they believed that this physical world could only adequately be described as illusion. These master astronomers and timekeepers believed that time was the key to understanding all physical existence. A beautiful flower, for example, gently cupped between the fingers of the hand, appears to be a flower. It smells like a flower, it feels like a flower, it looks like a flower, and it tastes like a flower, therefore it must be a flower. But therein lies the illusion. In reality the flower is actually a combination of physical elements: atoms, molecules and DNA, bound together with electrical energy. In common with the human body, the flower, as it grows, develops physical systems that in turn generate electrical activity. That electrical energy then attracts electrical energy (with a charge equal and opposite to itself) from outside of itself, mean-ing that plants, in common with people and all living things, contain an electrical charge acquired from outside of itself, a soul. So the Godly energy inside the flower is at one moment in time only inside the flower. At another moment in time, perhaps four weeks later, the DNA in the flower will have begun to decompose. The electrical charge will be released and will transmigrate to another collection of DNA which is beginning to live (beginning to attract a soul from outside of itself), perhaps to the DNA of a developing butterfly or worm or dog. The soul therefore is only in disguise at any one moment in time, which means that everything around us is illusion. This is to say that everything around us is a manifestation of God, in either a physical form or an energy form. The flower is not a flower, it only appears to be a flower; it is actually God in disguise.

This way of looking at the world explains away life's imponderables, why we live, why we die and why this has to be. Soul energy that has increased in voltage (figure A20) during its time in the physical world rises up the energy chain, each time transmigrating into a higher-voltage collection of physical cells: from plant, to insect, to animal to man. High-voltage souls return to God when the body dies. In this way God grows, which is seen as good, because 'God is good'. The Universe grows. In this scheme low-voltage souls return to lower-voltage collections of developing physical cells.

The Druids must have acquired the super-science of the Sun and the higher orders of spirituality from a Supergod teacher who lived during the earliest of times, perhaps the King of Hochdorf of c. 550 BC.

But the teachings go back further in time; the timber piles that depict the radiating solar wind, near the tombs in the Taklamakan Desert, and the adoption of the solar cross by the Celts means that the Celts must have been aware of the super-science of the Sun as early as 2000 BC. In Europe the earliest artefacts to surface appeared in around 800 BC, in Ireland. Figure 23a shows a pair of Irish copper plates, from around 800 BC,[29] that depict the cross-sectional nature of the Sun's magnetic fields and figure 23b shows in some detail that sunspots, and the effect they have on life on Earth, must have been important to the people of the time. Figure 24 shows a golden Celtic 'necklet', one of more than eighty discovered so far. The necklet takes the shape of a modern-day lunula astronomical calculator. Whether the golden lunulae were actually used as part of a pre-historic navigation regime or purely decorative is not known.

Celtic Astronomy (I)
The Sectored Structure of the Solar Wind
and Sunspots

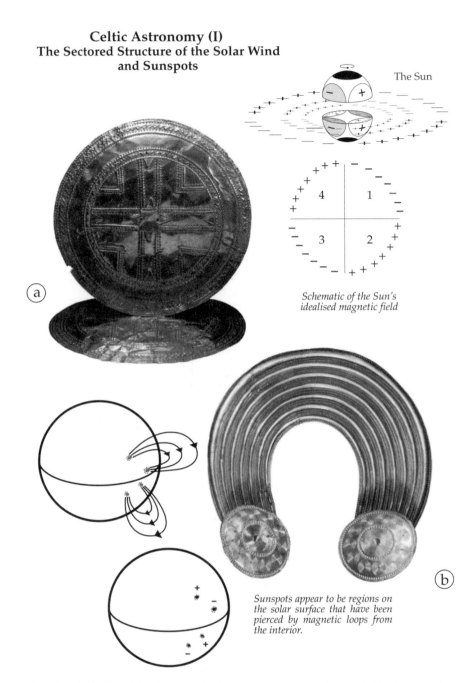

The Sun

Schematic of the Sun's
idealised magnetic field

(a)

(b)

Sunspots appear to be regions on
the solar surface that have been
pierced by magnetic loops from
the interior.

Figure 23. (a) Celtic golden Sun discs depicting the sectored structure of the Sun's magnetic fields (Ireland, west coast, c. 800 BC). (b) The Gleninsheen gorget (Ireland, west coast, c. 800 BC). A Celtic so-called golden neck-collar showing magnetic bursts from sunspots on the Sun's surface. The Celts understood the super-science of the Sun and the higher orders of spirituality.

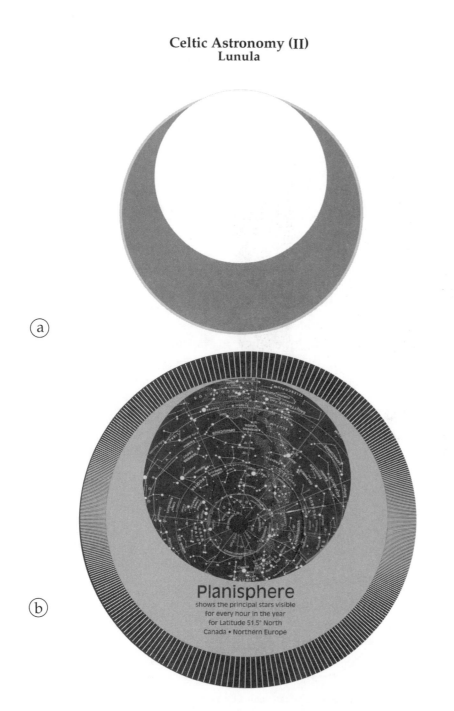

Figure 24. (a) Sketch of Celtic golden 'Ross' Lunula (Ireland, west coast, c. 800 BC, one of more than eighty found in Ireland to date. The piece is so named after the night-time lunar rise and set astronomical calculator (b) used in navigation.

CHAPTER TWO

Who Wrote the Bible?

The Old Testament

As the early Celts migrated westwards from the Taklamakan Desert, tribal settlements were developing in the fertile valleys of the Nile and on the Sumerian plains between the rivers Tigris and Euphrates between today's Iraq and Iran, and in Canaan [today's Israel].

Abraham, the founding father in Jewish history, was born in around 1900 BC in Ur, Sumeria (figure 25). The Bible says that God told Abraham to lead the Hebrew tribes out of Sumer to escape the famine of the times. Together they followed the Euphrates upstream and crossed the desert to Egypt. At first the Egyptians tolerated their presence but in the years that followed they succumbed to slavery in a land where the natives worshipped a variety of gods.

Beliefs competed for supremacy in regard to which system best explained how the world was created, what forces controlled nature, which prayers and practises offered the best protection against malevolent forces and what might be the best ways to maximise prosperity. In time, tribes grouped together for protection as well as for economies of scale that accommodated efficient planting and harvesting of crops, food storage and transportation.

Unification of Egypt began under the reign of King Narmer in around 3000 BC[30]—the first of a line of pharaohs that continued through thirty dynasties until 525 BC. With unification the diversity of gods became structured leading to a hierarchy in polytheistic belief. The many gods, though, now reported to a principal god Atum, or Ra,

Sumerian Civilisation

Figure 25. Mesopotamia lies between the rivers Tigris and Euphrates in present-day Iraq. The civilizations of Sumer, c. 3500 BC, and Babylon, c. 609 BC, flourished here.

the Sun God who created the Earth and the heavens. He controlled the lesser gods who in turn managed the elements on Earth, the air, earth and water. He also controlled the sky god Osiris, the god of resurrection and afterlife who lived in the constellation of Orion. It was from here that the notion of body and soul emerged with the belief that this earthly existence merely sustained the body for a short time and could be followed by a heavenly extension that sustained the soul—for millions and millions of years; pure souls would be reborn in the stars and impure ones returned to Earth for another attempt at spiritual purification. This new concept of 'reincarnation' called for a disciplined heart, mind and body. At the same time the polytheistic pantheon of gods, under the control (for the first time) of a single supreme creator God (Ra), meant that monotheism—one-god worship—had in effect established itself without even a single shot being fired.

As sun worship blossomed Egyptian civilization rose to new heights with a miraculous flowering in intellectual ability. Mighty pyramids, emulating the rays of the Sun from the sky to the Earth, arose as though by magic from master masons with a knowledge that could only have been acquired from the gods—or a Supergod—who must have walked among them. The timely appearance of hieroglyphic writing enabled the expression of the new beliefs in praise of God the great architect of the Universe. The new holy pyramids became the place for prayer and for the texts of prayer of which more than 800 have been found carved in columns inside pyramids between 2375 and 2055 BC. Those in the pyramid of Pepi I, just south of Unas at Saqqara, were the first to be discovered, although those of Unas themselves date from the earliest written (2375–2345 BC). Nine pyramids belonging to six kings buried at Saqqara (who reigned between the sixth and eighth dynasties) and three pyramids of Pepi II together contain the entire collection of pyramid texts. Some were intended to protect the deceased from harm in the afterlife; others made offerings and appealed to Osiris on behalf of the deceased to propitiate resurrection. Some were read to the deceased to ease the way into the underworld or to Ra in the afterlife.

More than 1,000 'spells' have been found inscribed on coffins made between 2055 and 1795 BC. It was essential to set down the hopes and desires of the deceased along with prayers, chants and incantations inside the coffin, to preclude any misunderstanding with the gods in regard to the final resting place of the soul. Inscriptions in the pyramid of Unas document the myth of Osiris and take the story one stage further: ' . . . Oh King, you are the companion of Orion . . . may you traverse the nearby Milky Way . . . and may you go to the place where Osiris is'. This was intended to escort the dead king to the constellation of Orion to become a star. The pyramid at Unas near Giza contains some of the most remarkable inscriptions, including the wisdom of Ptah-Hotep text. The circular zodiac on the ceiling of the temple at Dendera shows the constellations of the stars depicted by animals, exemplifying a sophisticated knowledge of astronomy and astrology. But the peace, prosperity and tranquillity were not to last.

As Egypt grew larger it beseeched and sustained an administrative bureaucracy to control and delegate power and authority. Civil servants who at first served the interests of the Pharaoh increasingly began to serve their own—levying their own taxes, proclaiming their offices to be hereditary and ultimately styling themselves as princes to succeed the throne, which they did during the eleventh and twelfth dynasties.

Around 1680 BC central authority broke down and control was lost. Egypt was invaded by the Hyksos ('rulers of foreign land'), the bold, swift and agile invaders from the East who swept through the country with horses and chariots to seize the throne of Egypt and the land of Canaan—to Mesopotamia—inspiring trade and culture with people on the Tigris and Euphrates. But their tenure was short-lived; within 100 years the Hyksos were in turn displaced by Kanes, a local dynast from Upper Egypt, who drove them out, restoring power to the pharaohs. Thus began the 'New Kingdom' of Egypt.

By 1323 BC the Supergod sun king Tutankhamun *'the living image of God'* had been and gone. His brief reign was over by the age of nineteen. Treasures in his tomb, discovered in 1922 in the Valley of the Kings by the archaeologist Howard Carter, reveal that he was known to his people as the feathered snake, which he carried on his forehead, meaning that he, like Lord Pacal, understood and taught the superscience of the Sun and the higher orders of spirituality.

A name carved on the wall of his tomb says that the architect of his tomb was called Maya. Like Lord Pacal he took to the throne at the age of 9. His tomb was marked by door seals containing groups of 9 socalled prisoners (figure A16) bound by ropes that terminate with the lotus blossom, the symbol of sun worship—because it opens its petals in the morning, follows the Sun across the sky and closes them again at sunset. The scene in the cartouche was a complex metaphor used to convey three messages: firstly, that this earthly existence amounts to divine bondage—the place where individuals are imprisoned and controlled by the effects of the Sun. By referring to *captive* prisoners the scene, at the same time, denounced the *killing* of prisoners, effectively espousing the notion of 'thou shall not kill'. And, finally, the collection of seals endowed the door of Tutankhamun's tomb with the number of a Supergod, 99999. To ensure that the numerological significance of this did not go unnoticed, he was entombed in 9 levels of coffin.

The number of those destined for Heaven was cleverly concealed within the bandages of his mummy which contained 143 treasures, making his body the 144th treasure in the bundle. The super-science of the Sun was well represented by all of the solar astronomical constants which appear over and over again, in his jewellery and in the architecture of his tomb—proving beyond doubt that he taught the super-science of the Sun. And, as we have already heard, a painting on the wall of his tomb shows him as twins, aged around nineteen, embracing Osiris in the sky, implying that, like Lord Pacal and Jesus, Tutankhamun when he died became Venus.

His mother and father are thought to have been Queen Nefertiti and Akhenaten, the son of Amenophis III (who reigned from 1391 to 1351 BC)—but decoded treasures from Tutankhamun's tomb also reveal that Akhenaten could not have been his biological father because his treasures reveal that Tutankhamun was conceived, like Jesus, through an Immaculate Conception.[31]

No one knows what happened to Nefertiti, who was almost always portrayed wearing clothes adorned with the Sun and its rays. But a passage in Revelation may have something to say:

> And there appeared a great wonder in Heaven; a woman clothed in the Sun and the moon under her feet . . . and she brought forth a man child who was to rule all nations with a rod of iron, and her child was caught up unto God and to his throne. And the woman fled into the wilderness, where she has a place prepared of God. (*Revelation* XII, 1–6)

Howard Carter believed that tomb robbers had stolen a heavy iron measuring rod from Tutankhamun's tomb. But analysis of the treasures suggests that the rod had been deliberately omitted to convey the message that 'Tutankhamun ruled with a rod of iron'—a divine rod that could be magnetised and used as a compass, allowing him to lead his people to the 'Promised Land'. This explains why he carried the crook and flail; the crook carried by the shepherd is associated with spiritual leadership—to provide spiritual nourishment, food for the soul. The flail, used to thresh corn, provides food for the body.

His mother Nefertiti is portrayed in a famous sculpture by the potter Thutmose with her left eye [the symbol of the moon] missing, associating her with the moon (perhaps under her feet). And the painting in Tutankhamun's tomb shows him being raised up to Heaven.

Those unfamiliar with *The Tutankhamun Prophecies* will be unaware of the true life and times of the great king. The discovery of his tomb in 1922 gave way to a frenzied media circus that swept the Western world. The breathtaking beauty, style and sophistication of his treasures at first inspired awe in all who beheld them but then raced on to fuel a new art form—*Art Deco*—that struggled and hopelessly failed to live up to the quality and genius of the Tutankhamun prototypes that were made by a miracle.

Akhenaten's unfinished tomb, to the east of Amarna, never received his body. The psychoanalyst Dr. Karl Abraham, a precursor to Sigmund Freud, proposed that Akhenaten, who reigned from 1353 to 1335 BC, was actually Moses of the Jewish faith (*Imago*, I, 1912, pp. 346–7). Freud, for his part, believed that Akhenaten's reign in Amarna came to an end when he was deposed and exiled to Sinai but later returned in an attempt to seize power from Rameses I. Failing in this he persuaded a band of Hebrew slaves to follow him into the desert to start a new religion based solely on monotheistic sun worship, without any regard for subordinate gods.

The official account says that Moses was a Hebrew judge and a lawgiver who led the Israelites out of Egypt to the promised land of Canaan.

After wandering in the desert for forty years, he led them south along the coast of the Gulf of Suez (plate 15) to Mount Sinai where he received the oral and written law, including the Ten Commandments engraved on two stone tablets from Jehovah [God]. He then went on to compile the first five books of the Jewish holy book, the Torah. The commandments from God were these: have no other God but Jehovah; make no idols; do not take the Lord's name in vain; remember the Sabbath and keep it holy; honour thy mother and father; do not kill; do not commit adultery; do not steal; do not bear false witness [do not lie], and do not covet the possessions of others. Thus was laid the foundation for Jewish history upon which all else followed and from which all Jewish law and custom is based.

Moses then built the most sacred treasure of the Israelites, a throne for God, the Ark of the Covenant, and carried it with him on his travels north along the Gulf of Aqaba into the wilderness where once again his tribes experienced hunger, thirst and hardship for several more years.

Moses at last gazed upon the Promised Land but died before settling there. His successor Joshua took up the mantle leading the Israelites into Canaan in around 1200 BC.

Saul, the first king of Israel, was wounded in a battle with the Philistines from the north and later committed suicide. He was succeeded by King David (1060–970 BC) who took the Ark to Jerusalem and made it the capital. In both Jewish and Christian belief the Messiah would be a direct descendant of David.

Although 'the five books of Moses' date back to his era, scholars agree that he could not have written them all, given that his own death is described in the last chapter. They more likely developed as the works of many scholars based on ancient traditions and stories told during their exodus in the wilderness:

> And the Lord Said unto Moses; write this for a memorial in a book,
> and rehearse it in the ears of Joshua. (*Exodus* XVII, 14)

Comprehensive accounts of wars were written during the reign of King David together with the names and deeds of his followers. The story of the Ark and the life of Saul fill the two books of Samuel. He also probably compiled the Psalms of David.

Once a year the twelve tribes of Israel met before the Ark at its resting place on Mount Zion in the centre of Jerusalem to confirm their allegiance to God and to follow the divine edicts.[32] The Judge—the president, priest and lawmaker of the day—who administered the Mosaic Law and interpreted the Holy Scriptures as they developed, maintained social order. The first biblical scriptures were thus in existence during the 'time of the Judges'; the seventh book of the Bible, Judges, sets down their genealogies (*Judges* X, 1–5; XII, 7–15), their achievements and the legal code. The Ten Commandments found their way into Exodus (XX, 1–17).

During David's reign Israel was at its peak, socially, politically and militaristically, until his son Absalom organised a rebellion and marched on the capital. David crushed him and his supporters but fearful of future rebellions was slow to relinquish the throne to another son, until 963 BC when he chose Solomon to succeed him.

Solomon, who was known for his wisdom, wrote more than 3,000 proverbs that together form the body of the book of Proverbs, the twentieth book of the Bible. His scribes chronicled his times, in the books of Samuel I and II, and a version of Creation that was set down on record to compete with one from the times of David.

Solomon, like his father, was a Freemason. David's emblem, the six-pointed Star of David, the symbol of Judaism, consists of two equilateral triangles. The upright pyramid-shaped triangle contains the angles of 60°, 60°, 60° (666) (figure 9). These numbers in the inverted triangle of the star become 999. Meaning that David and Solomon understood the higher orders of spirituality; they understood that the purpose of this earthly existence was to purify the soul inside the body [666] and thereby convert it into a higher-voltage soul [999] fit for Heaven.

The black and white chequered pattern on the floor of the temple was adopted by the board game of checkers (or 'draughts') to likewise carry the knowledge forward. The black and white represent the opposing forces of good and evil, and the nights and days of reincarnation; the squares, virtue and knowledge. Each player was given twelve discs, representing the twelve haloes of the Disciples, to help journey across the board where they must negotiate, in turn, each night and day [each incarnation], snake-like, across the board of sixty-four squares (2^6) [good and bad raised to the power of 6]. The player who reaches the far side of the board wins the earthly battle after snaking the least and taking most prisoners (killing the least) to become a double-decker disc, the twin star (planet) Venus in the heavens, which now, unconstrained and unfettered in the physical world, has the power to move both forwards and backwards on the board, ghost-like.

The book of Ecclesiastes in the Bible is attributed to Solomon because it begins with: 'The words of the preacher, the son of David, King in Jerusalem'. It is also the book most revered by esoteric orders containing much wisdom and mystery, lamenting in great detail on how all of man's activities in the physical world are a complete waste of time: 'Vanity of vanities, all is vanity' (*Ecclesiastes* XII, 8). Other observations include:

- That which is crooked cannot be made straight and that which is wanting cannot be numbered.
- In much wisdom there is much grief.
- He that increases knowledge increases sorrow.

- To every thing there is a season and a time to every purpose under Heaven.
- He that loves silver shall not be satisfied with silver.
- For as the crackling of thorns under the pot, so is the laughter of the fool.
- Anger rests in the bosom of fools.
- He that digs a pit shall fall into it and whoso breaks a hedge a serpent will bite him.
- He that watches the wind will never sow, and he that watches the clouds will never harvest.

Solomon died in 929 BC by which time the land of Israel, drained of funds, was in decline. The country was split into two nations, Israel and Judah, that squabbled for 200 years, allowing the Assyrians to seize the throne of Israel in 745 BC. Judah's demise followed quickly when it fell firstly in 609 BC to the Egyptians and then to the Babylonians. The 200-year period that hosted eighteen kings, the land of the Hebrew, was gone. But all was not lost.

During the troubled times the stories of the Patriarchs, from the time of the Exodus had been committed to parchment. The Song of Lamech (*Genesis* IV, 23–24), the Songs of Miriam (*Exodus* 15, 21), the Well (*Numbers* XXI, 17–18) and Heshbon (*Numbers* XXI, 27–29) had all found their way on to papyrus. The histories of Ahab, Jehu, and Micah (Kings I and Kings II) had been chronicled. The stories about Elijah and Elisha had been collated and the Law containing the Ten Commandments had been edited.

The age of the Kings had produced a school of divinely inspired prophets who preached to anyone willing to listen. As Israel spiralled into decline they were succeeded by another group known as the Classic prophets, the '*nevyim*', who also preached by word of mouth, whose teachings appeared in books after their death.

The first of the *prophetic books* to appear was that of Amos who preached goodwill, justice and social responsibility and that monotheism extends to all men in all places. Hosea preached the love of God and that all sins could be forgiven through God's mercy, believing that God was not only wrathful and vengeful but also all loving and forgiving. Lesser prophets like Habakkuk, Zephaniah, Jonah, Obadiah and

Micah had their say but failed to inspire intellectual change along the lines of the three great prophets Isaiah, Ezekiel and Jeremiah.

Isaiah, born in Jerusalem in 775 BC, was a doctor and a learned scribe known for his wisdom who preached that divine retribution would snare unrepentant sinners.

Ezekiel preached in Jerusalem during Israeli occupation of the city and warned of the future fall of the nation; when the inevitable happened he could only promise that one day they would have a new home, a new heart and a new spirit.

Jeremiah had foreseen the destruction of Jerusalem and the desecration of Solomon's temple, which actually occurred in 587 BC when Zedekiah—successor to the Babylonian king Nebuchadnezzar—defeated Israel, resulting in the exile of Israel and the captivity of the country by the Babylonians.

In 539 BC the Persian king Cyrus defeated the Babylonians putting an end to Babylonian rule. Jerusalem was in ruins. The prophet Haggai compiled an account of the reconstruction of the temple on Mount Zion. The prophets Zechariah and Malachi chronicled their lives and events of the time.

In 445 BC the prophet Nehemiah was appointed governor of Judah by Cyrus and the smaller neighbouring province of Israel was given the title of Samaria. But, as before, the people of the divided land squabbled.

Nehemiah supervised the physical reconstruction of Jerusalem and kept a detailed account of his own activities. His book, which only appeared 100 years after his death, become the most complete and reliable historical account of the Jews after their captivity.

Under Cyrus the Persians were true liberators of the troubled lands of the Hebrew. Canaan began to be called Palestine 'the land of the Philistines' referring to the lands that 'the Philistines had once tried unsuccessfully to conquer and control' and the Hebrews, previously 'the children of Judah and Israel' came to be known as 'the Jews'.

A new book of Nehemiah was written. More Psalms were added to those that existed and two poems—the Book of Job and the Song of Solomon—were composed. The history of David's reign was set down in Chronicles and the first five books of Moses; Genesis, Exodus, Leviticus, Numbers and Deuteronomy were edited.

Ezra, prophet and chief priest at the time, revised and reviewed religious thought and codified Jewish law into the system used today. This enabled non-Hebrew aspirants to understand the spiritual teachings and adopt and convert to the belief if they so chose. The name 'Jew' thus described the people who subscribed to the monotheistic laws of God handed to Moses as set down, clarified and codified by Ezra, rather than to the genetic national bloodline of the Hebrews. Conformance with the Law entitled the adherent to a place in Paradise in the afterlife and was therefore of the utmost importance in the life of the holy. Ezra's codification, set to papyrus scroll, meant that Jews could refer to undisputed holy texts whenever they travelled. By around 330 BC the canon of the Pentateuch was completed and every synagogue now possessed its own copy of the Law, the Jewish Torah.[33]

In 338 BC the victory of Philip II over the rest of Greece at Chaeronea (figure 26) was to have repercussions. His son, Alexander the Great, went on to conquer the eastern Mediterranean and in 333 BC defeated the Persian king Darius in Asia Minor, giving the Hebrews new overlords. Alexander marched on to Egypt and in 331 BC established the city of Alexandria. His death, in 323 BC, led to struggles by would-be successors; Seleucids won the area from Antioch, in Syria, and the Greek Ptolemies secured the lands of Egypt for themselves.

Between 283 and 246 BC Alexandria (under the Macedonian king Ptolemy II) sustained a population of around 150,000 Greeks and quickly become the centre of Greek learning and culture throughout the Mediterranean. Learned philosophers, writers, mathematicians and scientists filled the great library where the first translation of the Pentateuch [from Hebrew to Greek] the Septuagint (Latin for 'the seventy') was written—by seventy-two Jewish scholars imprisoned in a monastery under the instructions of the king. The Septuagint now refers to the first Greek translation of the Old Testament that appeared slightly later. Around the same time Esther's history and Daniel's account of the Exodus appeared in Palestine in Hebrew.

In 168 BC the Seleucids swept down from Antioch seizing Palestine from the Ptolemies—declaring that the only God to be worshipped would be the Greek creator god Zeus, to whom they raised an altar at the Temple. In 166 BC the Jews, enraged, rose against the Seleucids and

Route of Alexander the Great

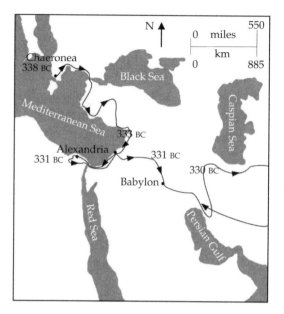

Figure 26. Route of Alexander the Great through Asia Minor to Alexandria in Egypt and beyond to the eastern boundaries of present-day Afghanistan and Pakistan.

within two years ousted Zeus to re-establish their faith. The leader of the rebellion, Judas Maccabaeus, died in 160 BC but fighting continued led by the Maccabaean family, or Hasmonaeans (in Hebrew), until the Romans arrived in 63 BC.

The book of Daniel describes the Maccabean revolt, along with two books of Maccabees. The story of *Susanna, Bel and the Dragon, The Prayer of Manasses* and *The Song of the Three Children* were never included in the Protestant version of the Bible but appeared in a second version called the Apocrypha *(secret teachings)*, some of which are included in the Roman Catholic version. The Old Testament as we know it today was completed in around AD 90. The two books of the Maccabees, The Wisdom of Solomon and Ecclisasticus, were included at the time but have since been relegated to the Apocrypha.

The Old Testament was now complete with its seventeen historical books: Genesis, Exodus, Leviticus, Numbers, Deuteronomy, Joshua, Judges, Ruth, the First Book of Samuel, the Second Book of Samuel, the First book of Kings, the Second Book of Kings, the First Book of Chronicles, the Second Book of Chronicles, Nehemiah and Esther; the five teaching books: Job, Psalms, Proverbs, Ecclesiastes and the Song of Solomon; and the seventeen prophetic books: Isaiah, Jeremiah, The Lamentations of Jeremiah, The Book of the Prophet Ezekiel, The Book of Daniel, Hosea, Joel, Amos, Obadiah, Jonah, Micah, Nahum, Habakkuk, Zephaniah, Haggai, Zechariah and Malachi.

The New Testament

Most of what we know about Jesus comes from the Gospels (Greek for 'proclamations') which his followers Matthew, Mark, Luke and John set down after his death and these appear in the New Testament of the Bible. There are other texts, not quite so celebrated, including thirteen Coptic [early Egyptian Christian] papyrus codices found in a sealed ceramic jar in the desert in 1945 at Nag Hammadi, in Egypt, that include the Gospel of Philip, The Gospel of Thomas, The Acts of Peter, The Gospel of Truth (dating from around AD 150) and The Gospel of Mary Magdalene (c. AD 135).

By AD 63 the Roman Empire extended as far as Palestine, a region of more than 8,000 square miles supporting a population of around a million Jews. They were reluctant bedfellows of the Roman army, who squeezed them to fund their massive projects of roads, bridges, aqueducts and buildings.

About fifty-seven years later, in pursuit of taxes, ruler Caesar Augustus decreed a census be taken of the population to quantify the taxation possibilities, and it was this census that sent the would-be parents of Jesus on a 145-km (90-mile) journey to the town of Bethlehem. His mother Mary was unmarried but engaged to Joseph when she became pregnant through an Immaculate Conception. Visions and dreams persuaded the couple that the child should be born and raised within marriage. The couple agreed to continue into marriage, thereby fulfilling the divine orders of the New Testament and of the Old:

> And the angel said unto her, 'fear not Mary, for thou hast found favour with God . . . thou shalt . . . bring forth a son and shall call his name Jesus . . . and the Lord God shall give unto him the throne of his father David'. (*Luke I*, 30–32)

During the journey Joseph and Mary follow a bright star that leads them to a stable in Bethlehem where Jesus is born (figure 27). Because stepfather Joseph was descended from the line of David, the birth of Jesus, as far as Christians are concerned, fulfils the Old Testament prophecy of Psalms:

> The Lord hath sworn in truth unto David; he will not turn from it; of the fruit of thy body will I set upon thy throne. (*Psalms* CXXXII, 11)

Jesus grew up the son of a carpenter, spending the first few months of his life exiled in Egypt, removed from the despot king, Herod. When Herod died the family moved back to Nazareth where Jesus spent his early years. By all accounts he was a remarkable child with a liking for the Jewish scriptures, from the oral traditions that had sustained the Hebrews in the desert to the Laws of Moses and the stories of the patriarchs in the Pentateuch.

His exact movements between the ages of twelve and thirty are little known. Some say he travelled extensively through Tibet, India and Greece. Others say that he visited England with Joseph of Arimathea, a wealthy Pharisee merchant, one of the seventy-one-member Sanhedrin council of Church ministers and possibly a close relative of Jesus. It is Joseph's merchant background that leads some observers to believe that he was a metal merchant who travelled to Cornwall by ship seeking cargoes of tin, lead and copper.

The Englishman William Blake (1757–1827) believed that Jesus did indeed visit Cornwall. The poet, artist and engraver claimed to have had many spiritual experiences including witnessing the appearance of angels and visions of Heaven and Hell. He wrote several prophetic books, among them: *The Marriage of Heaven and Hell*, 1790; *America*, 1793; and *Milton*, 1804. He illustrated editions of the Bible and works of Shakespeare with his own artistic style based on that of Michelangelo and Raphael and he wrote the poem *Jerusalem* in around 1800, speculating that Jesus once walked the land of Cornwall:

> *And did those feet in ancient times*
> *Walk upon England's mountains green?*
> *And was the Holy Lamb of God,*
> *On England's pleasant pastures seen?*

Jesus, as the Twin-star Venus

Figure 27. Shrine, from the cathedral at Guadalajara, Mexico, showing the newborn baby Jesus beneath a twin-star, together with Mary and Joseph. Silver spheres, mounted on urns, either side of Jesus represent the various manifestations of the planet Venus as the morning star and the evening star. Joseph and Mary hence introduce Jesus as the twin-star Venus.

And did the Countenance Divine
Shine forth upon our clouded hills?
And was Jerusalem builded here,
Among those dark Satanic mills?

Bring me my bow of burning Gold!
Bring me my arrows of desire!
Bring me my spear! O clouds unfold!
Bring me my Chariot of Fire!

I will not cease from mental fight;
Nor shall my sword sleep in my hand
'Till we have built Jerusalem
In England's green and pleasant land.

Some say that Blake's rendition, put to music in 1916 by Sir Hubert Parry, is, simply, fanciful thinking. After all, verse two questions whether Jerusalem could have been built among the dark satanic mills of England—that did not appear until the age of water-power during the Industrial Revolution, in around the 1830s—a long time after the age of Jesus.

Others maintain that although Blake's account may be romanticised, evidence does exist to substantiate the story. Researcher Sean Thomas, a Cornishman, cites the popularity of 'safron cakes' in Cornwall, pointing out that the spice saffron is a native of Southeast Asia and plentiful in the Middle East.[34] Another ancient Cornish dish, 'date and lemon' pie, must have likewise been made from imported ingredients from the Middle East where the dates grow. He also notes similarities in Cornish place-names with those in the Middle East: the village of Joppa might be named after the Phoenician port of Joppa; the ancient town opposite St. Michael's Mount known as Marazion could be derived from Mara Zion or 'Zion across the sea', suggesting an early Zionist connection, as could the Cornish-named towns of Jericho and Bojewyan and places named Market Jew Street and Joseph's Lane in the tin-mining village of Redruth. Smelting houses in those days were known as 'Jews Houses' and the word *sarazin* (perhaps from Saracen) was used to describe tin slag. There is even a Cornish hymn that begins with the line 'Joseph was a tinner'.

In the port of Padstow, in North Cornwall, there is a well called

'Jesus's Well', from where Joseph and Jesus could have sailed north to Somerset and onwards up the River Brue to the silver- and lead-bearing Mendip Hills near Glastonbury. Silver mines at Charterhouse above the Roman settlement of Aquae Sulis (Bath) are known to have been in operation by at least AD 49.

Jesus's life as a teacher, as opposed to that of a novice, seems to have begun after meeting with his forerunner John the Baptist at the age of thirty. He had twelve Disciples, followers who with discipline absorbed the holy teachings and who would later go forward to spread the word as Apostles (teachers).

The names of the Apostles listed in the New Testament Gospels of Mark (III, 14–19), Luke (VI, 12–16) and Matthew (X, 2–4) are these:

The Original Twelve Apostles—according to Mark (III, 13–19):
- Simon [he surnamed Peter]
- James the son of Zebedee
- John the brother of James
- Andrew
- Philip
- Bartholomew
- Matthew
- Thomas
- James the son of Alphaeus
- Thaddaeus
- Simon the Canaanite
- Judas Iscariot

According to *Luke* (VI, 13–16):
- Simon (whom he also named Peter)
- Andrew (Simon's brother)
- James
- John
- Philip
- Bartholomew
- Matthew
- Thomas
- James the son of Alphaeus
- Simon called Zelotes

- Judas the brother of James
- Judas Iscariot

According to Matthew (X, 2–4):
- Simon, who is called Peter
- James the son of Zebedee
- John [James's brother]
- Andrew [Simon Peter's brother]
- Philip
- Bartholomew
- Thomas
- Matthew the publican (a tax collector called 'Levi' by Mark)
- James the son of Alphaeus
- Lebaeus whose surname was Thaddaeus [Jude Thaddeus]
- Simon the Canaanite
- Judas Iscariot

According to Luke he began his ministry around the age of thirty. Quickly acquiring his group of Disciples, he set off for Galilee, establishing a new ministry at Capernaum, a small Jewish lakeside town with a population of some 5,000 located between Damascus and Alexandria. He taught the Laws of Moses and the Ten Commandments and began to make his mark as an unusual teacher. The people were astonished at his teaching because he taught them as one who had authority and not in the manner of scribes.

> Jesus added another commandment to those handed down to Moses; 'Love thy neighbour as I have loved you'. (*John* XIII, 34)

This 'love' Jesus spoke of was not the sentimental love of *affectionados* drawn together by desire. Yes, he was aware of how the physical senses stimulate hormonal production in the mind and body and how those chemicals can drag the mind, heart and soul into the world of illusion and 'hormone induced insanity' that many people call 'love'. But he was also mindful of the General Theory of Existence and the Theories of Divine Reconciliation and Iterative Spiritual Development (figures A18, A19 and A20) that demand a continuous supply of babies that only insanity can accommodate. Nor was it the love between two brothers willing to die for each other. It was more than both of these.

The love of which he spoke referred to an unconditional *sincere and genuine wish for the spiritual, physical, intellectual and emotional well-being of another living thing*. A love that could survive ingratitude, evil conduct and repudiation of God. A love spontaneously tendered to those who had done nothing to deserve it, to all those who had any spark of goodness. 'And who has not?' asked Jesus, saying that his Father wanted no one to perish.

His perception envisaged one God, the Father unseen but all seeing, ever watchful over the actions of his children, mindful of both thought and deed. No other religion had brought the Father so intimately close to his children with equanimity for all, the good the bad and the thankless.

The belief that a final day of judgement would take place, at which the condition of the departing soul would be determined according to past actions in this life, is perhaps the most salutary for Christians. The path to salvation was a spiritual one requiring little ceremony, no payments and no daily orders. Sins would be forgiven and forgiveness would alleviate the soul from the burden of guilt, allowing purification through inward truth. Sincerity in thought was more important than acts of charity.

Jesus taught in parables, stories that had meaning on two levels, literal and figurative. Generally they formed allegories which impressed a picture in the mind, which as we have seen was also the preferred method of teaching by Lord Pacal.

The purpose of the parable was to persuade the listener to consider deeply the underlying issues and so inspire change. In Matthew XIII, 3–23, Jesus points out how different people react to hearing the word of God: 'Some of the sower's seed fell on the footpath and were eaten by birds. Some fell on rocky ground and perished on the hot earth. Some fell on good ground and thrived to produce gain of a hundred fold', the message being that those who hear and understand the word of God yield astounding results. Twenty-nine parables of Jesus appear in the Gospels of Matthew, Mark, Luke and John.

Rabbi Moses Maimonides, the great Jewish theologian, comments:

Every time you find in our book a tale, the reality of which is repugnant to both reason and common sense, then be sure that the tale contains a profound allegory veiling a deeply mysterious truth; and the greater the absurdity of the letter, the deeper the wisdom of spirit. (*Hidden Wisdom in the Holy Bible*, vol. 1, G. Hodson, Wheaton, Ill., Theosophical Publishing House)

The Parable of the Sower has more to say. It implies that God's teachings inculcate knowledge and wisdom in the individual and in so doing engender talent that produces good works. The inference here is that no man is cleverer than the next. And yet, paradoxically, it is clear that some men do have better ideas than others.

God is light and light enters the mind through the eye. Every eye is a different combination of colours, which means that every eye is tuned to receive light of a different frequency. The eye converts light into electrical signals that travel along the optic nerves to the brain that detects the light signals. Eyes tuned to the God frequency thus receive and process ideas from God.

This is to say that voltage alone, brought forward from a previous incarnation, is insufficient to boost intellectual processing and the acquisition of wisdom and virtuous growth in soul voltage during the current incarnation; to hear the message of God, individuals need to have a pure heart and be tuned in to the God frequency. Good ideas come from God. Bad ideas come from the body.

Christ openly states that some knowledge is purposely concealed: 'he that has ears to hear let him hear'. (*Revelation* II, 7, 11, 29, III, 6, 13, 22, XIII, 9) To his Disciples he says:

Unto you it is given to know the mysteries of God: but to others in parables; that seeing they might not see, and hearing they might not understand. (*Luke* VIII, 8–10)

The reasons for the secrecy become apparent with the discourse:

Give not that which is holy unto the dogs, neither cast ye your pearls before swine, lest they trample them under foot and turn again to rend you. (*Matthew* IX, 6)

Author Roland Peterson says:

Certain knowledge can be destructive in the hands of those who are morally unprepared—destructive to self and others. (*Everyone Is Right*, Roland Peterson, De Vorss & Co., 1986)

The Popol Vuh, the holy book of the Maya, begins with the words:

> The Popol Vuh cannot be seen any more . . . the original book written long ago existed, but its sight is hidden from the searcher and the thinker. (*The Popol Vuh*, Delia Goetz and Sylvanus G. Morley, University of Oklahoma Press, 1947, p. 79)

Another passage from the same book says:

> We are going away [to die], we have completed our mission here. Then Balam-Quitze left the symbol of his being. "This is a resemblance which I leave for you, this shall be your power" . . . He left the symbol whose form was invisible because it was *wrapped-up* and could not be unwrapped: the seam did not show because it was not seen when they wrapped it up. (*The Popol Vuh*, Delia Goetz and Sylvanus G. Morley, University of Oklahoma Press, 1947, p. 79) [author's italics]

Meaning that Lord Pacal chose to conceal his holy knowledge 'wrapped-up' in Mayan transformers. Hidden from the archaeologist and the grave robber. Hidden from the searcher and thinker.

But it was another gift from Jesus that caused his fame to spread; he could heal the sick with his bare hands, or simply with his will. Like the other Supergods, Jesus worked miracles; thirty-four ascribed to him are set down in the Gospels. He appeared to overcome physical laws to achieve super-human results for his efforts and, in addition, to have a deep insight into the foundations of physical nature and the influence of mind over matter that was not of this world.

As the fame of Jesus and his teachings spread he became known as the 'King of the Jews' among followers. The Jewish clergy objected, insisting that he did not conform to their perception of a Messiah. After all, he was the son of a poor carpenter, born in a stable, who did not have the credentials to call himself King. How, they questioned, could this man Jesus say he was the Son of God? As far as the Jews were concerned, this was blasphemy.

For their part the Romans had no axe to grind on the subject of Jesus or religion; they were more concerned with maintaining law and order and with it the uninterrupted flow of taxes. But Jesus's adversaries conspired to entrap him and the Sanhedrin found him guilty of blasphemy, despite the pleas from Joseph of Arimathea and others.

The Romans, unsure as to what action to take, threw open the fate of Jesus to a referendum where the consensus called for punishment of death by crucifixion. The outcome had not taken Jesus by surprise. The previous night, fearful of the events unfolding, he held a farewell supper with his twelve Disciples:

> Jesus took bread, and blessed, and brake it, and gave to them, and said, take, eat: this is my body. And he took the cup [filled with wine] and when he had given thanks, he gave it to them: and they drank of it. And he said unto them, 'this is my blood of the New Testament, which is shed for many'. (*Mark* XIV, 22–24)

Then Jesus foretold the events overtaking them saying:

> All ye shall be offended because of me this night: for it is written, I will smite the shepherd, and the sheep of the flock shall be scattered abroad. (*Matthew* XXVI, 31)

And he spoke of imminent betrayal from one within the group:

> . . . that the scripture may be fulfilled, he that eateth bread with me hath lifted up his heal against me. . . . Verily, verily, I say unto you, that one of you shall betray me. (*John* XIII, 18–21) [The scripture Jesus was referring to was that from the Old Testament book of Psalms (XXXXI, 9): 'Yea, mine own familiar friend, in whom I trusted, which did eat of my bread, hath lifted up his heal against me'].

Then one of the twelve, called Judas Iscariot, went unto the chief priests and said unto them:

> What will you give me and I will deliver him unto you: And they covenanted with him for thirty pieces of silver (*Matthew* XXVI, 14–15). Then Judas, who had betrayed him . . . repented . . . and he cast down the pieces of silver in the temple . . . and the chief priests took the pieces of silver . . . and bought with them the potter's field, to bury strangers in. (*Matthew* XXVII, 3–7)

Thus fulfilling the Old Testament prophecy:

> They weighed for me my price, thirty pieces of silver. And the

Lord said unto me, cast it unto the potter . . . and I took the thirty pieces of silver and cast them to the potter in the house of the Lord. (*Zechariah* XI, 12–13)

And the high priest arose, and said unto him, 'Answerest thou nothing? What is it which these witness against thee?' But Jesus held his peace. . . . Then the high priest [said] 'What think ye?' They answered and said, 'he is guilty of death'. Then did they spit in his face, and buffeted him with the palms of their hands. . . . And Jesus stood before . . . the Governor . . . and when he was accused of the chief priests and elders, he answered nothing. (*Matthew* XXVI, 62–67; XXVII, 11–12)

He is despised and rejected of men; a man of sorrows . . . he was wounded for our transgressions, he was bruised for our iniquities . . . He was oppressed and he was afflicted, yet he opened not his mouth: he is brought as a lamb to the slaughter, and as a sheep before her shearer is dumb, so he openeth not his mouth. He was taken from prison and from Judgement . . . he was cut off out of the land of the living: for the transgressions of my people was he stricken. (*Isaiah* LIII, 3–8)

And they crucified him . . . And they that passed-by reviled him . . . 'he saved others; himself he cannot save' . . . And about the ninth hour cried with a loud voice, 'My God, my God, why has thou forsaken me?' (*Matthew* XXVII, 35–46)

My God, my God why has thou forsaken me? . . . he trusted on the Lord that he would deliver him: let him deliver him . . . I am poured out like water and my bones are out of joint . . . my tongue cleaveth to my jaws, and thou has brought me into the dust of death . . . they pierced my hands and my feet . . . they part my garments among them and cast lots upon my vesture. (*Psalms* XXII, 1–18)

Now there was a vessel full of vinegar: and they filled a sponge with vinegar, and put it upon a hyssup, and put it to his mouth . . . When Jesus had therefore received the vinegar he said 'it is finished' and he bowed his head and gave up the Ghost . . . When they came to Jesus, and saw he was already dead . . . one of the soldiers with a spear pierced his side and forthwith came there out blood and water. And he that saw it bare record, and his record is true . . . for these things were done that the scripture be fulfilled; A bone of him shall not be broken. And again another scripture saith; they shall look on him whom they pierced. (*John* XIX, 29–36)

Many are the afflictions of the righteous: but the Lord delivereth him out of them all. He keepeth all his bones: not one of them is broken. (*Psalms* XXXIV, 19–20)

When the even was come, there came a rich man of Aramathea, named Joseph, who also himself was Jesus' Disciple: he went to Pilate, and begged the body of Jesus . . . he wrapped it in a clean linen cloth, and laid it out in his own tomb, which he had hewn out of the rock. (*Matthew* XXVII, 57–60)

Jesus taught that the hidden purpose of life was to purify the heart (figure 28). A pure heart purifies the soul and a pure soul goes to Heaven

The Pure of Heart

Figure 28. Jesus, pointing to his exposed pure heart that radiates light. The halo around his head carries the four-sector solar cross.

to experience peace, joy and bliss with the creator. The way to a pure heart was through love, sacrifice and suffering.

3–5 Dimensions This is another way of saying that the electromagnetic energy of God, the soul—detached from its godly source—must always be in a state of permanent disequilibrium while inside the body—as a raised rock will always be attracted to the ground, so the pure soul will always be attracted back to Heaven, from whence it came.

Many believe that the Egyptian practise of mummification facilitated the reincarnation process should the soul of the deceased return to Earth. But the Egyptians also preserved the internal organs, apart from the heart and the brain, and in so doing explained that an old brain in a new life is of no value, because a new brain has an empty memory. In the same way, a new heart has no emotional memory. In the next life our intellectual and emotional life start from the beginning, not from where we left off. Reincarnates cannot benefit from previous knowledge which, as we have already heard, is why the ancients encoded their knowledge into their treasures for themselves to rediscover should they not make it to Heaven this time around.

The inference here is that the heart, too, *must* have memory, 'emotional memory'. The brain remembers facts and figures, the super-science of the Sun, but it is the Heart that remembers the love given and gained, won and lost. Indeed, when we review our lives, our successes and failures, it is not the houses, cars or jobs that come to mind but the regret, remorse, joy and happiness of the relationships with living things.

A computer memory stores data by electronically processing information and stacking it in memory cells that retain the electrical charge for later retrieval. The heart therefore must store emotional information in the heart organ using electrical charge in the same way. There are documented accounts from modern heart-transplant patients who have experienced recall of how the heart donor died, perhaps by being shot dead, or killed in a car accident. The heart is a dynamic organ that can take us to Heaven.

The late-Celtic Rinnagan Crucifixion plaque (figure 29), a beaten bronze plaque from the cover of a lost seventh-century theological manuscript, was found in a churchyard in County Roscommon, Ireland. It shows the Crucifixion of Christ with Longinus—the Roman soldier who pierced the side of Christ with a sword—and Stephaton, to his

The Crucifixion of Christ

Figure 29. The bronze Rinnagan Crucifixion plaque, found in a churchyard in County Roscommon, Ireland, now kept in the Celtic collection of the National Museum of Ireland in Dublin. The scene shows the Crucifixion of Christ with, on his right, Longinus, who pierces the side of Christ with his sword. Stephaton, to his left, carries the vinegar-soaked sponge on a reed to the lips of Christ. The two angels above represent the twin-star (planet) Venus, the morning star and the evening star.

left, offering a vinegar-soaked sponge to the lips of Christ. Either side of his head two angels appear as the morning star and the evening star. The treasured Celtic relic is nowadays kept in the National Museum of Ireland in Dublin. Archaeologists are perplexed as to why the plaque shows Christ with Celtic spirals swirling around his chest, and around his head, and why they also feature on the angels either side of him.

The Lost Meaning of the Celtic Spiral

The Bhagavad Gita states that God is light. God, therefore, must be the Sun. The human soul, as part of God, must therefore also be the Sun in a slightly different form (as water might be steam or ice). Figure 30a shows the magnetic structure of the Sun. Figure 30b shows the positive and negative distribution of magnetic energy present in a cross-section slice taken around the equatorial region. The energy spirals carved into the heart centre of Christ on the Rinnagan Crucifixion plaque (figure 30c) correspond exactly to the Sun's energy (figure 30b): two quadrants each composed of a two-part spiral, the yin and yang, the dark and light principles of energy that the ancient Chinese believed to be inherent in all living things.

As we have seen, the Sun's equatorial region (figure 30a) rotates once every twenty-six days (twenty-eight days to an observer on Earth) and the Sun's polar magnetic caps rotate once every thirty-seven days (forty-one days to an observer on Earth). At the same time, the Earth moves around the Sun once every year. The effect of the 'differential rotation' of the Sun's magnetic fields means that every calendar month, one of the solar equatorial field sectors will be enlarged at the expense of its adjacent neighbour (figure 30b) resulting in the two equal quadrants (of yin and yang, mentioned above) and, in addition, two unequal quadrants.

The two-part yin and yang spirals (figure 30b) rotate in opposite directions, indicating the respective positive and negative field polarities undisturbed by the polar field during one particular month. The two unequal quadrants consist of three-part spirals, each representing the adjacent field sectors that *are* disturbed by the rotating polar magnetic field each month. In this way the energy spirals featured on the heart of Christ, on the Rinnagan Crucifixion plaque (figure 30c), are hence shown to be identical to those of the Sun.

The Crucifixion of Christ (II)

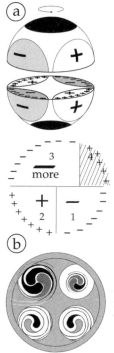

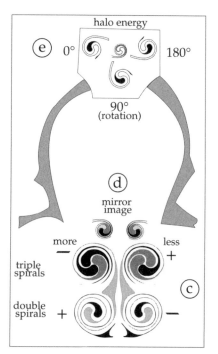

Figure 30. (a) Sun's magnetic fields. (b) Plan view of (a): cross-section of the Sun's equatorial magnetic fields showing the four unequal quadrants of magnetic activity that change monthly. Box-framed: schematic of energy centres on the Rinnagan Crucifixion plaque. (c) The heart chakra energy of Christ corresponds with the Sun's magnetic fields. (d) Soul (mirror image) marker—indicating that the heart chakra energy represents the soul in man. (e) The halo chakra differs from the crown chakra in that each spiral is rotated by 90° to its neighbour (unlike the soul energy in the heart, which is a mirror image—that cannot be obtained using rotation).

The magnetic interaction (for the month under examination) makes one heart-spiral quadrant more positive (shown as grey-grey-black) and the other more negative (shown as black-black-grey). The appearance of the spiral schematic on the heart of Christ shows that Christ's energy, the soul, is the same type of energy as the Sun and that the energy resides in the heart. That this is a reasonable interpretation of the Christ heart-spiral arrangement is supported by the appearance of the two miniature triple spirals that appear above the four heart spirals; these two three-part spirals are mirror images of each other, suggesting that the heart spirals represent the soul energy, the mirror-image energy, in man.

Another distinction is emphasised by energy spirals located in the halo of Christ; these three two-part spirals are obtained by simple rotation, suggesting that the energy is something other than mirror-image energy. Moreover, the tiny centre three-part halo spiral integrates the three two-part spirals into one three-part spiral.

The spiral markers on the Rinnagan Crucifixion plaque therefore highlight the difference between soul energy and godly energy; soul energy is godly energy (solar energy) which is attached to the heart of man whereas halo energy is pure godly energy, light.

The spiral, or whorl, is a central feature in Celtic art, meaning that the Celts were preoccupied with purification of the soul—the conversion of soul energy to halo energy [the conversion of 666 to 999], the super-science of the Sun, and the higher orders of spirituality.

The re-distribution of energy (figure 30b) can be analysed more simply, as in figure 31: here the reduced quadrant is considered 'neutralised' (N) each month. This is to say that an observer on Earth sees only three of the four quadrants in any one month (30.4375 days). The radiation of solar particles (positive and negative charges) leads to twelve different sequences of magnetic modulations of the Earth's magnetic field, resulting in twelve types of genetic mutations in early impregnated ovum and the consequential development of twelve different personality types each year (Sun-sign astrology). In addition, the radiation patterns are detected by the human brain causing varia-

The Celts and Sun-sign Astrology	Monthly equatorial field sector disturbance caused by poles	Radiation pattern sequence: neutralised by poles	Month	Element	Astrological Sign
	1234	123N	1	Fire	Aries
	1234	12N4	2	Earth	Taurus
	1234	1N34	3	Air	Gemini
	1234	N234	4	Water	Cancer
	1234	123N	5	Fire	Leo
	1234	12N4	6	Earth	Virgo
	1234	1N34	7	Air	Libra
	1234	N234	8	Water	Scorpio
	1234	123N	9	Fire	Sagittarius
	1234	12N4	10	Earth	Capricorn
	1234	1N34	11	Air	Aquarius
	1234	N234	12	Water	Pisces

After 1 month, the solar pole slips backwards by 90° with respect to the solar equator.

Figure 31. The equatorial region of the Sun spins every 26 days. The polar magnetic caps spin once every 37 days. The Earth orbits the Sun every 365.25 days. This interaction causes neutralisation of a different equatorial field sector every month. The resulting solar wind radiation sequence travels to Earth and is trapped in the Van Allen radiation belts, causing the Earth's magnetic field to vary at ground level (figure 8). The magnetic modulations affect the production of oestrogen and progesterone in females, regulating the menstrual cycle and causing genetic mutations in early impregnated ovum—by rearranging sections of DNA—producing twelve different personality types throughout each year, which is why the ancients worshipped the Sun as the god of fertility and the god of [Sun-sign] Astrology.

tions in levels of the timing hormone melatonin and variations in the production of the fertility hormones oestrogen and progesterone, and the consequential regulation of menstruation and fertilty in females—which is why the ancients worshipped the Sun as the god of astrology and the god of fertility.

The four-part heart spiral was represented by the Hallstatt Celts as the reverse swastika (figure 32ai). The tri-part halo energy spiral arrangement refers to the solar wind after equatorial field sector neutralisation. Those who increase their own soul voltage during their lifetime on Earth go to Heaven. The tri-part spiral was depicted by

The Secrets of the Celtic Spirals

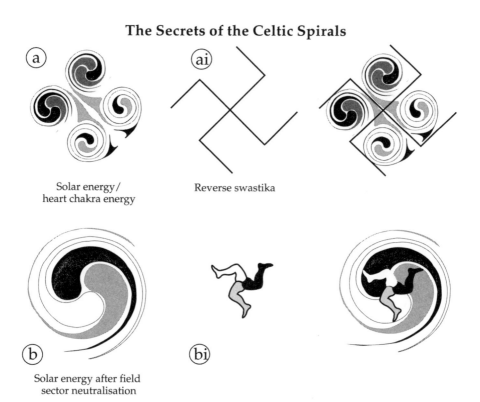

Solar energy/
heart chakra energy

Reverse swastika

Solar energy after field
sector neutralisation

Figure 32. (a) Solar equatorial magnetic energy fields. (ai) Reverse swastika of the Hallstatt Celts depicting the solar radiation pattern, as seen from Venus, before field sector neutralisation caused by interaction with the polar fields. (b) Solar radiation pattern from the solar wind, as seen from Venus after field neutralisation caused by interaction with the polar fields. (bi) The Celtic symbol for Man, from the (Celtic) Isle of Man (a Dependency of the United Kingdom).

the Celts as the three-legged symbol of Man (figure 32bi), the national emblem of the Celtic people, the Manx, of the Isle of Man.[35]

After the Crucifixion

Following the Crucifixion, the body of Jesus was laid to rest in the tomb previously prepared for Joseph of Arimathea. Pontius Pilate, fearful of claims of martyrdom should the body be taken, arranged for the opening of the sepulchre to be blocked by a large rock and for two Roman Centurions to stand guard.

The next day Mary Magdalene—who some say was the closest of anyone to Jesus—visited the tomb. The Centurions were dead. The large rock that had blocked the tomb had been rolled away exposing the open entrance:

> . . . And behold there was a great earthquake for the angel of the Lord descended from Heaven and came and rolled back the stone from the door and sat upon it . . . and for fear of him the keepers [guards] did shake and became as dead men . . . and the angel said unto Mary . . . fear not ye: for I know that ye seek Jesus which was crucified. He is not here for he has risen . . . come see the place where the Lord lay . . . And go quickly and tell the Disciples that he is risen from the dead . . . and behold he goes before ye into Galilee, there shall ye see him. (*Matthew* XXVII 1–8)

> Mary ran quickly towards Jerusalem and, as the angel had foretold, met the resurrected Jesus; be not afraid, go tell my bretheren that they go into Galilee, and there they shall see me. (*Matthew* CCVII, 10)

Verse 16 goes on to describe how he met with his eleven Disciples. John XX, 25, says that there were two meetings around this time, the first with ten Disciples present, the second with eleven, including Thomas, who had missed the first and doubted what they had told him, hence the expression 'doubting Thomas':

> Jesus told them all to 'go ye into the world and preach the Gospel to every creature . . . he that believes will be saved. (*Mark* XVI, 15)

John XX1, 14 mentions a third meeting between Jesus and the Disciples:

the third time that Jesus showed himself to his Disciples after he had risen from the dead.

The book Acts of the Apostles says that Jesus remained on Earth for forty days following the resurrection:

> ... the Apostles whom he had chosen ... To whom also he showed himself alive after his passion by many infallible proofs, being seen of them forty days ... (*Acts* I, 2–3)

Acts then records how the Disciples gathered together and prayed to God, asking for guidance in selecting a replacement for the dead Judas Iscariot, saying:

> ... [who shall take part] ... in this ministry and Apostleship, from which Judas by transgression fell? ... and they gave forth lots; and the lot fell upon Mathius, and he was numbered with the eleven Apostles. (*Acts* 24–26)

The names of the Apostles, given in the Acts of the Apostles, thus differ from other accounts in the Gospels:

- Peter
- James
- John
- Andrew
- Philip
- Bartholomew
- Matthew
- Thomas
- James (the son of Alphaeus)
- Judas, the brother of James [Thaddaeus; Jude Thaddeus]
- Simon Zelotes (the Zealot)
- Mathius, who replaced Judas Iscariot

This appears to be the last time that the Disciples met with the resurrected Jesus. But Acts goes on to say that the Holy Spirit visited them on the day of Pentecost.[36] There, the tongues of the Apostles, before the gathered multitude, were confounded, allowing them to speak in many languages and thereby spread the teachings of Christ throughout the world.

The Gospel of Mark, the first of the four to appear, was set down by Mark in around AD 70. The Gospel of Matthew appeared shortly after, written in Greek, and then the Gospel of Luke (AD 80 or 90), who also compiled the Acts of the Apostles. The Gospel according to John was the last to appear, according to fragments of a papyrus discovered in around AD 100 that contains part of the eighteenth chapter.

The Appearance of St. Paul

In the years immediately following the Crucifixion, sixty others were called to the Apostleship including St. Paul—the convert Saul who was born in Tarsus (Turkey) and obtained Roman citizenship. In the early days he was involved in stoning the Christians, but after experiencing a vision of Jesus (on the road to Damascus) he was transformed into a Christian.

After the Crucifixion and ascension of Christ Paul travelled widely around the eastern Mediterranean making at least fourteen missionary journeys to: Cyprus, Attalia, Tarsus, Iconium, Antioch, Asia Minor, Troy, Philippi, Thessaly [near Macedonia], Athens, Corinth and Crete before returning to Jerusalem. There, the Jews accused Paul of blasphemy leading to his arrest by the Romans who imprisoned him (Acts XXV). Paul was then shipped to Rome (Acts XXVII) in AD 64 where he may have been acquitted and released before being re-arrested and executed at [modern-day] Tre Fontane in Rome in AD 67.

The life and times of Paul were set down in letters written by him from around AD 51: the Epistle of Paul the Apostle to the Romans [abb. Romans], the First Epistle of Paul the Apostle to the Corinthians [abb. Corinthians I], the Second Epistle of Paul the Apostle to the Corinthians [abb. Corinthians II], the Epistle of Paul the Apostle to the Galatians [abb. Galatians], the First Epistle of Paul the Apostle to the Ephesians [abb. Ephesians], the Epistle of Paul the Apostle to the Philippians [abb. Philippians], the Epistle of Paul the Apostle to the Colossians [abb. Colossians], the First Epistle of Paul the Apostle to the Thessalonians [abb. Thessalonians I], the Second Epistle of Paul the Apostle to the Thessalonians [abb. Thessalonians II] and the Epistle of Paul the Apostle to Philemon [abb. Philemon]. The Epistles of Paul to the Hebrews, Titus and Timothy are not ascribed to him but are believed to have been written after his death. All of the Epistles were written in Greek.

Other Epistles in the New Testament, the authorship of which is uncertain, appeared in the fifty years that followed: the General Epistle of James, Peter (I and II), John (I, II and III) and Jude.

Revelation, the last book of the New Testament, was written by St John on the Greek island of Patmos where he had been banished by the emperor Domitian. It tells of a Revelation to St. John. Its meaning is unknown and allegorical containing visions, nightmares of Heaven and Hell, prophecies about the end of the World and the final day of Judgement. It contains the enigmatic numbers of 666 and 144,000 that appear in the treasures of all of the other Supergods (described in chapter 1) and ends with Jesus saying 'I am the bright and morning star' and warns no one to change, add, or take away any word of what has been written.

Collation of the New Testament

By now the Gospels, Epistles, and Revelations were lost in a canonical free-for-all of forgeries, wishful thinking and speculation. A standard text was sorely needed, one that had sorted the wheat from the chaff: an arrangement of the holy works in a single collection along the lines of the Old Testament.

The delay was due to difficulty in several areas, among them: the selection of material that should be included and uncertainty in regard to who or what authority was qualified to judge.

In around AD 150 a wealthy businessman named Marcion was having his own say in his local town of Sinope on the Black Sea. He believed that God had sent his son Jesus to Earth to deliver mankind from the God of the Jews, Jehovah, and decided that the true God was not the evil Jehovah but the all new, all loving, all forgiving God proclaimed by Jesus. He thus sought a complete break from the past, from the Old Testament and from the history and beliefs of the Jews. His father, the local bishop, was so unimpressed that he banished his *heretic* son from the town. Undeterred, Marcion decided to go to Rome and donate his fortune to the Church in the hope that he could put together

87

a New Testament—according to Marcion—that might be accepted by the emerging Christian Church.

He began by throwing out the Gospels of Matthew, Mark and John, preferring that of Luke. He decided to exclude the Jews and anything Jewish; after all, he believed that they had brought about the trial and consequent Crucifixion of Jesus. Part I of his Canon thus consisted of the Gospel of Luke and Part II of just ten of St. Paul's Epistles. Nothing else qualified for inclusion as far as he was concerned. Then he revised both parts, removing any reference to the Jews.

Christians, unimpressed with Marcion's version of events, decided to ignore him and the first attempt at compiling a 'New Testament' was left to gather dust.

The second attempt at consolidation came from a Christian martyr named Justin who died in Rome in AD 165. He issued a critique on what might be true and what might be false in the teachings of the day and in so doing became a forefather of what might in future be included in any New Testament.

In the eighteenth century some fragments of an early (c. AD 200) manuscript named the 'Muratorian Fragments' (after the name of the librarian who discovered them) surfaced in the library of Milan. They contain a dissertation, in poor Latin, on the efficacy of Christian literature; the Gospels are classified as genuine as are the Acts, Revelation, the Epistles of Paul, John and Jude, but not Hebrews, Peter and James or John III. The unknown author writes in extremely poor and primitive Latin that often degenerates into slang containing grammatical mistakes, suggesting that he was either uneducated or that the manuscript was poorly transcribed.

In the second century Irenaeus, the bishop of Gallia, quoted from the four Gospels, the Epistles of Paul, the Acts, Revelation, the Epistles of Peter I and John I and II.

Around the same time a Syrian Christian named Tatian attempted to synthesise the four Gospels into one story written in Modern Greek for the layman. His version found favour for the next 200 years until at least AD 360 when the scholar Ephraim commented upon it. But in AD 450 the priest of the Syrian church, Theodore of Antioch, declared it invalid in favour of four separate Gospels.

The Gospel of Truth, one of the Gnostic writings found at Nag

Hammadi in 1947, suggests that a New Testament along the lines of the one of today existed in around AD 150. Gnosticism—divine knowledge based on a combination of Christianity, Greek philosophy, Hinduism and Buddhism—was an early rival of orthodox Christianity.

In AD 254, in Alexandria, the early Church Father Origen reconfigured writings into a New Testament in Greek which was later augmented by the bishop of Caesarea (in Palestine), Eusebius Pamphilli, in AD 314.

Persecution of Christians prevailed from the date of the Crucifixion until the reign of Constantine the Great (AD 285–337) in Rome. In AD 306 he succeeded his father as joint Roman emperor, in York, England. In AD 312, during a victorious battle outside Rome, he saw a vision of the cross-of-Christ on the face of the Sun which inspired his conversion to Christianity. A year later he issued his 'Edict of Tolerance', extending religious tolerance to all faiths and in AD 324 became the first Christian Roman emperor to rule the whole of the Roman Empire.

The developing Church in Rome modelled itself on the structure of the empire. The dioceses were structured along the lines of Roman administration; city-based bishops met in Synod in the capitals. Roman bishops shared power with those of Constantinople and Alexandria, and Antioch and Jerusalem in the East. At the same time a significant number of Christians chose a life of renunciation by retreating into monasteries established under the monks Pachomius (AD 290–346) and Basil (c. AD 330–377) in the east and Benedict (c. AD 480–550) in the west.

The Christian community in Britain was steadily growing in numbers and martyrs began to appear. St. Alban, a prominent Roman citizen of Verulamium (present-day St. Alban), was the first English martyr to be executed—beheaded on a hill thirty miles north of London where the modern-day church of St. Alban now stands. The British Church must have been organised into dioceses by at least AD 314 when the bishops of York, London and Lincoln are known to have attended the Council of Arles in AD 314. Early churches were established in Silchester in AD 360 and Caerwent.

The first Ecumenical Council to represent the whole of the Christian Church met at Nicaea in AD 325. In AD 367, Athanasius, bishop of Alexandria, included Revelation into the New Testament and declared, in his Festive Letter of Athanasius, the New Testament to be fixed and unalterable. Other ecumenical councils followed in Constantinople (AD 381), Ephesus (AD 431) and Chalcedon (AD 451).

The development of the Latin version of the New Testament, preferred by Rome, differed from the Greek version. In Italy the early Church Fathers Cyprian, Hilarius and Ambrose preferred a version along the lines of the Muratorian fragments until in 382 Pope Damascus commissioned the Christian scholar Jerome to make a new version of the Bible in Latin. At first he worked from Rome before moving to a monastery in Bethlehem where he translated the Old Testament, direct from the Hebrew, and the New Testament from the Greek version. His version, the Vulgate (the book of the people), became the most popular Latin version of the Bible from the seventh century but was not adopted as the official Catholic Bible until 1546 by the Council of Trent.

In Syria Tatian's integrated Gospels were favoured until the fifth century when Syrian bishops developed the standard Bible, the *Peshitto*, which was brought into line with the Greek and Latin versions in the sixth and seventh centuries. The earliest known version of the New Testament comes from an early *Peshitto* manuscript precisely dated as being written in AD 464.

Joseph of Arimathea who had acquired and hidden the Holy Grail used by Christ at the Last Supper was imprisoned in Palestine. It is said that the holy powers of the Grail sustained him during his period of imprisonment. After his release, legend says that he sailed with Lazarus—who was raised from the dead by Jesus—Mary Magdelene and the Apostle Philip, from Palestine to Marseilles in France. Mary and Lazarus stayed at Marseilles while Joseph, the Grail and twelve followers of Christ continued on the voyage to Glastonbury. Legend says that on landfall Joseph climbed a local hill and thrust his rosewood staff, grown from Christ's holy crown of thorns, into the ground where it miraculously took root on Wearyall Hill where, to this day, it blossoms every Christmas. In AD 60 Joseph purchased land on Glastonbury Hill upon which he built the first wood and wattle Christian church named Vetusta Ecclesia where he was later buried together with the Holy Grail.

The recovery of the Grail became the great quest of the Knights of the Round Table. The Grail, so one version of the Arthurian story recalls, was handed over by Joseph to the knight Sir Galahad who 'took our Lord's body between his hands more than 300 years after Joseph's death, and then he died'.[37]

Collapse of Roman Rule

In AD 330 the capital of the Roman Empire was transferred to Byzantium—modern Istanbul—by Constantine the Great who renamed it Constantinople, the capital of the Byzantine Empire.

By the end of the fourth century Rome came increasingly under attack from barbarians and as a result recalled troops from the outposts of the empire. By 406 the Romans had gone from Britain leaving a power vacuum in their wake. England was overrun by barbarian Picts from Scotland and Celts from Ireland. A new Celtic leader named Vortigern (active 425–450) emerged from the Welsh border-lands to rally the English Celts and, under pressure, appealed for Roman help to repel the invaders. At first the Romans responded with troops but eventually, realising the futility of their contribution, withdrew, leaving Vortigern to go it alone.

Vortigern met with the Council of British Kings who agreed to call in mercenaries from Germany. The Angles, Saxons and Jutes sent three longboats full of fighters across the Channel in return for gold. According to the English historian Bede the first consignment arrived in AD 449 led by the Saxon brothers Hengist and Horsa.[38] At first the arrangement worked well, so much so that the daughter of Hengist was married to Vortigern who bequeathed to him the land of Kent. But Hengist wanted more and the treachery began; he arranged a banquet of 300 British noblemen together with 300 Angles and Saxons who, on the orders of Hengist, drew their daggers and killed the British. It was known as the 'night of the long knives'. Much of southeast England was now in the hands of the Angles and Saxons who pushed what remained of Vortigern's men westwards. But many areas of England, to the west and southwest, remained free from Saxon control.

St. Patrick

St. Patrick (AD 389–461) was an Englishman, a one-time slave in Roman-occupied Britain who was sold to a landowner in northwest Ireland in around AD 404. He passed the days of his youth tending sheep in prayer and contemplation of God. After six years he escaped to return home across the Irish Sea. Travelling by night, to avoid detection, he walked the 321 km (200 miles) to the southeast of Ireland and begged a passage on a small boat to France. His Irish experience had raised the possibility in his mind of a divine mission to convert the Irish Celts to Christianity, but to do that he would firstly need the authority of the Church.

For twenty-one years Patrick studied Christian theology in the French monasteries of Lerins and Auxerre and during that time experienced a visionary dream calling him back to Ireland to continue his

St. Patrick

Figure 33. Statue of Saint Patrick (Timoleague, West Cork, Ireland) carrying the crook, the symbol of spiritual leadership.

mission. In AD 432, as a fully ordained bishop in the Church of England, he returned to Ireland to fulfil the divine order, firstly by winning over the hearts and minds of local kings and then by preaching to the Druids in the language of Mayo-Irish. In the years that followed he established a Celtic-Christian Church across Ireland. His teachings were seen as divergent, raising suspicion from the English bishops who, claiming him to be heretic, tried and failed to excommunicate him.

Patrick built the first churches and established the earliest practises of worship in Ireland. Legend says that he had divine protection; one day a powerful king was sent to ambush him and his fellows but, miraculously, they all became invisible. The king could see only a group of stags before him, and he heard voices chanting:

> *Christ be in me, Christ before me,*
> *Christ beneath me, Christ above me,*
> *Christ at my right, Christ at my left,*
> *Christ in my lying down, Christ in my sitting,*
> *Christ in my rising,*
> *Christ in the heart of everyone who thinks of me,*
> *Christ in the mouth of everyone who speaks to me,*
> *Christ in every eye that sees me,*
> *Christ in every ear that hears me.*

The prayer became known as the *Deer Cry*.

Patrick is credited for introducing the Irish shamrock [the three-leafed clover] to Ireland, to represent the Holy Trinity of the Father, the Son and the Holy Ghost, but no evidence exists to support that view.

CHAPTER THREE

The Monasteries

Havens of Refuge

The spread of Christianity inspired the building of new monasteries throughout Europe and the Middle East. Devotees flocked to subscribe to the new Christian ethos of chastity, obedience and poverty.

The reason for chastity was twofold: those who chose a life of physical replication—having children—would find it difficult to purify their own soul because they would love their own children more than their neighbour's, contrary to Christian teaching that, first and foremost, demanded love of one's neighbour—which includes the neighbour's children. It says nothing about becoming attached to one's own children, nothing about preferring them to the children of others. The second reason is physiological: ejaculation of high-protein sperm in males depletes the body of a vital resource. The body then needs to use energy to replace the sperm, instead of using the energy to increase the voltage of the soul within; energies in the body should flow up the spine to make a halo, not down the spine to make sperm—which is why circumcision, as an inhibitor to masturbation, proved so popular among the Jews:

> And certain men which came down from Judaea taught the Brethren, and said 'Except ye be circumcised after the manner of Moses, ye cannot be saved'. (*Acts* XV, 1)

In avoiding fornication St. Paul writes:

> It is good for a man not to touch a woman, nevertheless, to avoid

fornication, let every man have his own wife, and let every woman have her own husband. (*Corinthians* VIII, 1–2)

He preferred the life of the ascetic, of the monk and the celibate priest, defaulting to marriage only when the will is weak:

But if they cannot contain [their desire] let them marry for it is better to marry than to burn. (*Corinthians* VII, 9)

'To burn', here, refers to the insatiable self-inspired pain born of lust and desire that distracts the mind from peaceful thought. It arises from misperception in the minds of those who desire to possess, control, consume and discard—triggering a self-sustaining drama in which the participant volunteers to engage and ends, inevitably, in self-destruction. It differs substantially from the positive attributes of *suffering*.

Suffering arises from outside stimuli over which the victim has little or no control. It causes pain in the mind. The wrestling mind leads to pain in the heart. Pain in the heart leads to searching of the soul and searching of the soul leads to the purging of impurity, as the wringing of a wet rag purges it of water. In this way pain purifies the heart which purifies the soul in preparation for entry into Heaven. Herein lies the heart of Christian teaching.

When we pay for our own mistakes we suffer—because we have to work longer and harder to earn the money to pay for the mistake. The mind suffers, the heart suffers and the soul purifies and goes to Heaven. The fool, who prefers others to pay for his mistakes, simply sends them to Heaven and at the same time consigns his own soul to oblivion. The wise man therefore *eagerly* pays for his own mistakes and *readily* pays for the mistakes of the fool. This is the way to Heaven. By paying for the mistakes of others Christ took the sins of the world upon himself, suffered, purified his soul and ascended to Heaven. The Theory of Iterative Spiritual Redemption (figure A20) illustrates the choices and the outcomes available. We choose our own destiny.

It becomes clear that some individuals seldom pay for their mistakes and are therefore denied access to Heaven this time around. It is the client who pays for the incompetence or ineptitude of a lawyer or barrister. It is the innocent convict who pays for the incompetence or ineptitude of the judge. In this way the innocents suffer and become pure while the guilty consign their own souls to Hell.

Herein lies the heart of the law of karma, the Universal law of action and inaction that automatically makes all wrongs right.

> But many that are first shall be last; and the last shall be first. (*Matthew* XIX, 30)

> It is easier for a camel to pass through the eye of a needle than for a rich man to enter into the Kingdom of God. (*Matthew* XIX, 23–24)

Retreat to the monasteries amounted to self-imposed exile where the spiritually predisposed could escape from *normal* people who are driven by desire to replicate and self-destruct. They had read the story of how normal people had nailed a perfectly innocent man to a cross, and they preferred to have none of it.

They turned their backs on the normal way of life and flocked to the monasteries that became havens of refuge and centres of prayer, work and education for those seeking salvation. There they spent their time in contemplation of God, replicating his work: carving and decorating stone into crosses and monuments, transforming precious metals and gemstones into liturgical vessels and compiling the first *illuminated* copies of biblical texts through years of toilsome work and study.

The need for texts brought with it a need for words that progressed from simple strings of capital letters to mixed texts of capital and lower-case letters. Scribes progressed, laying text onto parchment or vellum (calfskin)—using straight guidelines and dividing pages into two or three rubics.[39] Sheets were then stitched together into an early form of book, a codex.

The *Codex Argentus*, the 'silver codex', emerged in the sixth century from an Italian monastery. The bilingual *Codex Carolinus*, laid out in two columns—one Gothic, the other Latin—appeared shortly after. In AD 746 the English Benedictine monk St. Boniface (AD 680–754), who was charged with taking Christianity to Germany by Pope Gregory II, carried the Latin *Victor Codex*, of Fulda, to Germany.

Biblical manuscripts often ran to several volumes leading to the appearance of shorter versions containing just the Psalms or the Gospels beautifully decorated with coloured inks often bound with chased metal and leather. There were also portable versions of the books known as the 'Pocket Gospels' carried by monks on their missions. Production of texts continued by hand until the advent of paper and the development of printing around 1250. By 1440 simple woodcut blocks appeared and the introduction of moveable type in 1450 allowed a new versatility of book production hitherto unseen.

In AD 597 Pope Gregory I sent St. Augustine (d. AD 605) to England to formally convert the English to Roman Catholicism. He baptised King Ethelbert of Kent shortly after arriving at Ebbsfleet and went on to become the first archbishop of Canterbury.

The quasi-independent Celtic Christian Church established by Patrick in Ireland was by now set in its own ways and fundamental differences between the two Churches, first noticed during Patrick's time, began to deepen. The Church organisation in Ireland differed from the Episcopal system organised by bishops throughout Europe. In Ireland the monasteries were often founded by families to ensure that their own family members subsequently ruled as abbots who performed baptisms, mass and funerals and were regarded superior to bishops. Another difference concerned the dating of the Easter festival that celebrated the resurrection of Christ: Rome preferred the moveable feast falling on the first Sunday *following* the full moon after the spring equinox whereas the Celts preferred their own date.[40]

In AD 431 Pope Celestine sent Bishop Palladius to Ireland, presumably to build upon Patrick's work.[41] One of the first Irish monasteries was that of St. Enda, on Arainn (Inishmore, Aran Islands). St. Finnian's at Clonard, County Meath, became a school for monastic-founding monks who would spread the word to other parts of Britain and the Continent.

The Irish abbot St. Columba (Colm Cille, AD 521–597), who was born in County Donegal of royal descent, established several monasteries in Ireland including one at Durrow, near Tullamore, County Offally. The seventh-century scholar Adomnan (AD 628–704), the ninth abbot of Iona (AD 679–704), in his *Vita Columbae* (the *Life of Colm Cille*) c. AD 697, describes him as:

> . . . a perfect disciple chosen by God who experienced prophetic revelations, the power to work miracles . . . experience angelic visitations . . . who devoted himself to the Christian life . . . who

> with God's help studying wisdom and keeping his body chaste
> . . . spent thirty-four years as an island-soldier of Christ. (*Vita
> Columbae*, Adobnan [quoted from *The Encyclopaedia of Ireland*, Gill
> & Macmillan, 2003])

This refers to the time he spent after sailing from the northern tip of
Ireland in AD 563 with twelve companions to build the monastery on
the Scottish island of Iona. From there he made missionary journeys to
the mainland that played a major part in the conversion of Britain to
Christianity.

In AD 635 another Irish monk, St Aidan (AD 600–651), a prodigy of St
Columba, established a Christian monastery on causeway-connected
Lindisfarne (Holy Island) just off the coast of Northumberland, northeast England. Aidan, like Patrick in Ireland before him, did not person-
ally recognise the Church of Rome and refused to speak Latin.

It was not until AD 664 that King Oswey of Northumbria, at the
Synod of Whitby, decided to adopt the Roman form of Christianity in
Britain [later repealed during the Reformation]. Papal authority was
established in Ireland at the same time allowing inspiring bishops from
both sides of the Irish Sea to make regular visits to the pope in Rome.

The Works of Angels

It was towards the end of the seventh century that monasteries on
the islands of Lindisfarne and Iona produced the finest of the Celtic-
style illuminated manuscripts. The Romans, during their occupation
of England, had subdued and suppressed Celtic art in favour of their
own. But the Romans never reached Ireland where the Celtic tradition had continued unbroken. With the Romans gone and Irish monks
flooding into Britain, the Celtic La Tène style, favoured by monks, was
given a new lease on life. Lavishly illustrated manuscripts adorned
with Celtic animals (figure 34), decorative calligraphy (figure 35), and
Celtic interlaced continuous-line knot-work (figure 37)—already established on ancient stone monuments—began to appear in manuscript
form; the twelfth-century writer Gerald of Wales could only describe
them as 'the works of angels'.

> The Lord hath filled him with the spirit of God, in wisdom, in

Celtic Mythology

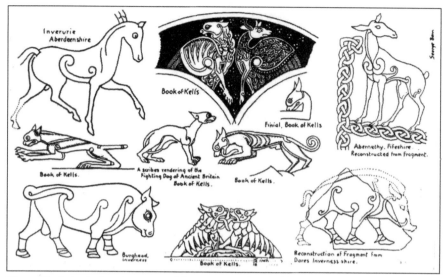

Figure 34. Animal drawings, carved into stone and copied into manuscripts, feature widely in Celtic art. (From George Bain's *Celtic Art—Methods of Construction*)

Celtic Continuous-line Interlacing

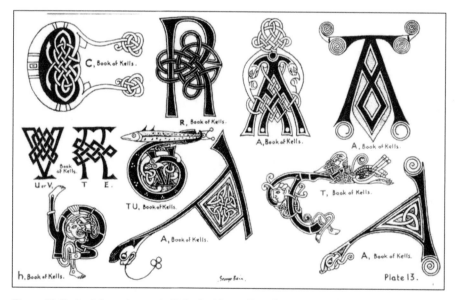

Figure 35. Textual characters embellished with scrolls and continuous-line drawing were used extensively in the early Christian manuscripts. (From George Bain's *Celtic Art—Methods of Construction*)

understanding, and in knowledge, and in all manner of work-manship and to devise curious works, to work in gold, and in silver, and in brass, and in the cutting of stones, to set them, and in the carving of wood, to make any manner of cunning work. Them hath he filled with wisdom of heart, to work all manner of work, of the engraver, and the cunning workman, and of the embroiderer, in blue, and in purple, in scarlet and in fine linen, and of the weaver, even of them that do any work, and those that devise cunning work. (*Exodus* XXXV, 31–35)

We know that the [so-called] Book of Lindisfarne was written in around AD 698 because Aldred, the later provost of Chester-le-Street in around AD 950, added a gloss [a commentary] in English—the earliest surviving translation of the Gospels in English—and a colophon [a publisher's imprint] naming Bishop Eadfrith of Lindisfarne as the maker of the original:

Eadfrith, Bishop of Lindisfarne Church [in AD 698] originally wrote this book for God and St. Cuthbert and jointly for all the saints whose relics are on the Island. And Ethewald, Bishop of Lindisfarne Islanders impressed it on the outside and covered it, as he well knew how to do. And Billfrith, the anchorite, forged the ornaments which are on the outside and adorned it with gold and with gems and with gilt-silver. And Aldred, unworthy and most miserable priest, glossed it in English between the lines.

The format of the illuminated monastic books from Lindisfarne, Iona, Kells and Durrow vary but, generally, they all contain the texts of the four Gospels with portrait illustrations of the Apostles, carpet pages and initial pages. Layout and illustration were constrained by the format; there were no sentences or paragraphs, just long strings of letters that had to be separated by larger initial letters that helped readers find their way around the text. Carpet pages were purely ornamental and played no part in the stories but separated sections. The initial page of each Gospel was extravagantly decorated with Celtic patterns (plate 16) inspired from earlier designs found on Celtic weapons, jewellery and horse-trappings. Portraits of the Apostles in the books of Kells and Durrow were Romanised in style rather than Celtic, no doubt because they were based on portrait versions sent out from Rome.

The earliest theological texts to arrive in Britain and Ireland came with the missionaries during Roman times and were written in formal Roman *uncial* [with round letters not joined together] and *half-uncial* [with distinct ascenders and descenders].

The oldest surviving Irish manuscripts, dating from the end of the sixth century, include the *Springmount Bog* writing tables, the *Codex Usserianus Primus* (Gospel book fragment) and the *Cathach*, all written in what has since become known as *insular majuscule* [Island script—formed with distinctive triangular wedge-shaped serifs on the verticals]. The script was written with a chisel-edged quill held parallel to the page, producing solid letters consisting of thick downstrokes and thin horizontal strokes. This gave the text a highly horizontal appearance that was later adopted and developed by the island monasteries at Lindisfarne (plate 16) and Iona.

Where the Book of Kells was written is uncertain. Many believe it derived from the monastery of Iona, Scotland, in around AD 795. Church transactions copied into it prove that it must have been in Kells by the eleventh century.

Lindisfarne monks, fleeing raids from Vikings, carried their manuscripts along with other precious liturgical artefacts to Iona for safekeeping. When the monk Alcuin heard of the first devastating raid on the monastery at Lindisfarne on 8th June AD 793, he wrote a warning letter to Ethewald, bishop of Lindisfarne:

> Consider [them] carefully, brothers, and examine [them] diligently, lest perchance the unaccustomed and un-heard of evil practice [ensnares you] . . . Consider the dress, the way of wearing the hair, the luxurious habits of the princes and people. (Letter from Aluin to Ethewald, *The Annals of Ulster*, AD 793)

But the refuge was not to last. Iona was pillaged in AD 795, 802 and again in 806, forcing the monks across the Irish Sea to the new monastery at Kells [which was completed in 814]. Shortly after, the Vikings mounted assaults on Irish monasteries, once again forcing the monks to abandon their sanctuaries and to hide or bury their treasures. From AD 840 onwards the Vikings established coastal and lakeside settlements in Ireland.

The Book of Kells consists of 340 vellum folios [680 pages] written by at least three scribes in insular majuscule. The Gospels are based on the Latin Vulgate preferred by Rome (commissioned by Pope Damascus from St. Jerome in AD 404) mixed with parts from the less reliable Old Latin translation. These were accompanied by preliminary texts, including a list of Hebrew names, *breves causae*—headings, Gospel sections, the *argumenta*—brief lives of the Apostles, and the highly decorated *Canon tables*—that divided the text into numbered sections and enabled the reader to cross-reference between Gospels.

The colourful design of the book was probably created by three artists using a variety of styles derived from Celtic, Germanic, Pictish [early Scottish] and Mediterranean influence. It is revered as the most colourful of the illuminated manuscripts and features full-page illustrations of Christ, Christ with the Virgin Mary, miniatures of the Temptation and the Arrest, and a page with symbolic portraits of the four Apostles: Mark as a lion, Matthew as an angel, John as an eagle and Luke as an ox, referring to passages from the Bible:

> As for the likeness of their faces, they four had the face of a man, and the face of a lion on the right side; and they four had the face of an ox on the left side; they four also had the face of an eagle. (*Ezekiel* I, 10)

> And before the throne there was a sea of glass like unto crystal: and in the midst of the throne, and round about the throne, were four beasts full of eyes before and behind. And the first beast was like a lion, and the second beast like a calf and the third beast had the face of a man, and the fourth beast was like a flying eagle. (*Revelation* IV, 6–7)

> And they sung as it were a new song before the throne, and before the four beasts, and the elders; and no man could learn that song but the hundred and forty-four thousand, which were redeemed from the Earth. (*Revelation* XIV, 2–3)

Generally speaking, the four symbols represented Christ as a lion—the King [of the jungle], as the sacrificial ox, as the eagle—ascending to Heaven, and the Holy Spirit in Heaven—the angel [although in the book of Durrow, John is shown as the lion].

The oldest surviving insular majuscule illuminated manuscript is contained within the Psalter *Cathach of St. Columba*, compiled during the times of St. Columba, which contains few enlarged initials while a few remaining vestiges of a Gospel book, found at Durham, England, contain early plait-work previously only encountered on stonework.

The first fully illuminated book to contain the Gospels was the Book of Durrow, from around AD 680, which contains an inscription saying that it was copied out by St. Columba, suggesting that it had been written before that of Kells or Lindisfarne. It appeared in the Columban monastery at Durrow, Ireland, in around AD 680 but was not written there. It seems likely, from the style and decoration, that it was written at Lindisfarne or at least another monastery in Northumbria, England, founded by St. Columba, who probably carried it to Durrow. It contains 248 leaves of vellum and measures approximately 245 x 145 mm (9.65 x 5.7 inches). Again, it contains St. Jerome's fourth-century Latin Vulgate translation of the Gospels and prefaces from him, interpretations of Hebrew names, and Canon tables. The text is written in insular majuscule and some of the illustrations derive from the earlier Old Latin Vulgate. Eleven full-colour pages emblazoned with red, yellow, green and brown inks include symbols, rather than portraits, of the Apostles and the carpet pages are richly decorated with biting animals, roundels (solar crosses), spirals within spirals (like those of figure 30, representing solar radiation) linked to each other by a flowing motif known as a trumpet spiral—all contained within an elaborate interlaced continuous-line pattern.

The Book of Lindisfarne reaches a watershed in Celtic illumination with a new, higher level of decoration and sophistication. It contains the four Gospels of the Latin Vulgate, each opening with a picture of the Apostle and his symbol. The portraits of the Apostles are less stylized than those of the Book of Kells and contain classical and Byzantine influence; the Apostles appear in Greek-style clothing and their names appear in Latinised Greek. Like the others the book also contains Canon tables, prefaces, argumenta and material on the feasts of saints. The five initial pages, one at the beginning and one between each of the Gospels, and the carpet pages are lavishly decorated with fine interlaced fretwork and running borders containing parades of intertwining bird and animal heads each snapping at the one ahead.

Decoding the Celtic Designs—Continuous-line Drawing

The links with the Sun and the scriptures are patently evident in the illuminated manuscripts and it is clear that the painstaking efforts of the monks, singing praise to God, have been duly rewarded in the quality of the works. But why spend such a disproportionate amount of time and effort on Gospel decoration that might have been better spent converting the fallen? Such consideration implores us to re-arrange the words of Rabbi Moses Maimonides quoted earlier:

> Every time you find in a *book a decoration or a pointless embellishment which appears to defy reason and common sense* then be sure that it contains a profound allegory veiling a deeply mysterious truth; and the greater the absurdity *of the pattern,* the deeper the wisdom of spirit. [author's amendments in italics]

Continuous-line drawing is not unique to the Celts, as the *Lost Tomb of Viracocha* observed:

> Maria Reiche was not the first or last to notice that each of the Nazca desert line drawings [see figure 36, the monkey, herein] was made by one single continuous line that circumscribed the [drawing of the] creature . . . A similar technique is used in a common children's game where one of the *rules* of the game requires that the pencil should not be lifted from the drawing surface until the picture is completed in its entirety.
>
> There are other characteristics of the drawings . . . The first is that there must have been a *reason* for the *rule,* for not lifting the pencil . . . from the paper (desert) and, moreover, that this reason must have had something to do with either the *method used to construct* the lines or the *message* which was intended to be conveyed by the lines (or both). Engineers familiar with electrical circuits will immediately note a similarity here; early facsimile machines used either electro-sensitive or thermal recording paper. Generally, the underside of the roll of recording paper connects to one side of an electrical circuit whereas the signal-carrying pen makes contact with the topside surface of the paper.
>
> Whenever a signal appears on the pen it flows through the paper to the other side of the circuit, burning a black mark into the

paper sandwiched between the two conductors. It goes without saying that if ever the pen should cease to make contact with the paper then current would be forced to stop, and the paper-marking (drawing) would also stop, irrespective of the presence of a signal on the tip of the pen. This means that the pen must be in contact with the paper at all times; it must not be lifted from the paper during the period the drawing is taking place. The *continuous-line* characteristic of the lines of Nazca tells us that whoever drew the lines understood this principle; that *a continuous current-like process was actually employed in the line-drawing process.* If we recall, it was *the continuous flow of ultraviolet light (the current) from the Sun on the surface of the* [Nazca] *basin that oxidised the rocks* [on the ground] *in the first place* and allowed the lines to be created the way that they were. This draws our attention to understanding the nature and capabilities of solar radiation. In

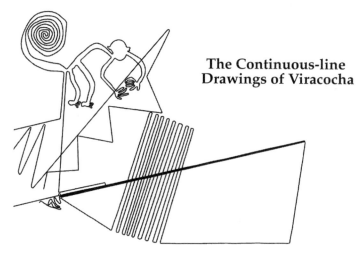

The Continuous-line Drawings of Viracocha

Figure 36. Picture of a monkey, one of the continuous-line drawings scraped into the desert sands of Nazca in Peru in around AD 500. One of the rules of this style of drawing precludes lifting the pen from the paper. The drawings were hence generated using an uninterrupted (constant-flow) process; this tells us that solar radiation oxidised the surface pebbles, turning them blackish-brown, in contrast to the lighter-coloured subsurface pebbles of which the lines consist (figure A25 shows two more drawings from Nazca). The monkey in this drawing has four fingers on the right hand and five on the left; one finger is missing from the hands, just like the Viracocha bas-relief carving from the Gateway of the Sun at Tiahuanaco (figure A6f). The monkey embraces the largest of three identical shapes (triangles) and the statue of Viracocha is the largest of the three standing statues in the Temple of the Stone Heads at Tiahuanaco (figure A2a). The monkey desert line drawing tells us, therefore, that the pictures were also created (drawn) by the hand of Viracocha.

> using the continuous-line technique the ancients were attempting to draw our attention to the power of the Sun. (*The Lost Tomb of Viracocha*, Maurice Cotterell, Headline, 2001)

The section concluded with an analysis of the creature patterns recognising that they could only have been created by a miracle, by Viracocha, the son of God who walked the lands of Peru in around AD 500.

In the same way, by using the continuous-line technique the Celts were attempting to draw our attention to the power of the Sun and to the fact that the continuous-line drawing of the Celts could only have been enabled by God, on Earth.

Moreover, the dedicated scribe-monks no doubt sought salvation through work, always keeping their pen on the paper, always vigilant:

> Watch ye therefore: for ye know not when the master of the house cometh, at even or at midnight, or at the cock-crowing or in the morning: Lest coming suddenly he find you sleeping. (*Mark* XIII, 35–36)

It was their way of getting to Heaven.

Decoding the Celtic Knot-work Patterns

The Scottish artist and scholar George Bain, born in Scrabster, Caithness, Scotland, in 1881, devoted his life to studying and teaching the rudiments of construction of Celtic interlacing patterns and knot-work found in Celtic stonework and, later, in the illuminated manuscripts. For his efforts he became known as the 'father of modern Celtic design'. After he died in 1968 his family donated his works to the Groam House museum in Rosemarkie. William McLellan & Co., of Glasgow, published his book *Celtic Art—the Methods of Construction* in 1951.

In the introduction Bain comments:

> This elementary textbook is prepared especially for use in elementary and secondary schools. It will also serve to give instruction to Art Students, Artists, and Art workers in a multitude of crafts. There is much that will be useful to the archaeologist and the historian, although I have refrained from dealing with such problems,

Encoding of Celtic Numbers

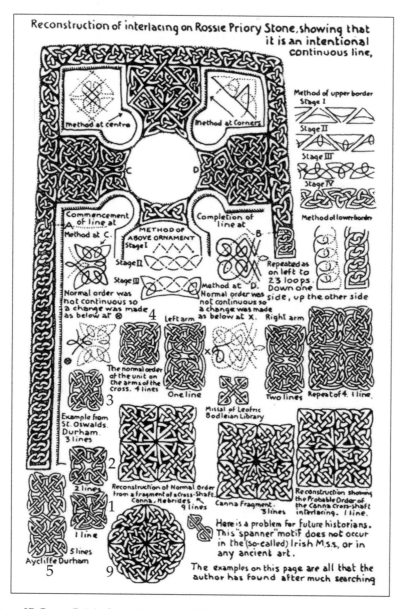

Figure 37. George Bain's observations showed that Celtic continuous-line interlacing patterns comprise either 1-, 2-, 3-, 4-, 5- or 9-line construction. No 6-line pattern has been found. Celtic *pattern-numbers* thus stop after 5, apart from the 9-line pattern (the Sun), drawing attention to the importance of the numbers 6 and 9 [666 and 999] and the Sun, showing once again that the Celts were aware of the super-science of the Sun and the higher orders of spirituality. (From George Bain's *Celtic Art—Methods of Construction*)

for the primary purpose of this book is to give to others the results of my many years of research into the methods used by the ancient artists . . . Realising the meagreness of the written language, especially when used by me as a medium for the clear transmitting of instructions on the partly artistic, partly geometrical and partly mathematical method peculiar to many forms of Celtic Art and particularly to that of the Pictish School, I have put the onus of understanding upon the student by compelling the close observation of every stage of the methods with *very few words* to hinder or to assist. Many years of experimenting have led me to believe that when once this slight initial difficulty has been overcome in this manner of reading, *to dispense with words is beneficial.* [author's italics]

With genuine humility, gained by years of research into the possible methods of the great intellectual artist and craftsmen of the Pictish nation, who produced the great art of the cross-slab stones of East Pict and their counterparts in the Books of Durrow, Kells and Lindisfarne, the Tara Brooch, the Ardagh Chalice and other masterpieces of the Celtic jewellers art, I present the result of my studies . . . The extreme minuteness of the art of the illuminated manuscripts and the impossibility of ordinary eyes perceiving much of its contents show, conclusively, that the artists did not display their skill for human eyes and human applause.

They were imbued with the idea that the eyes of God would detect errors and worked solely to glorify him. Their aids to eyesight and the tools that enabled them to draw a line with exactness beyond the skill of moderns may never be known. Referring to a page of the *Book of Armagh,* one of the 'pocket gospels', Professor J. O. Westwood wrote:

In the space of about a quarter of an inch . . . I counted with a magnifying glass no less than one hundred and fifty-eight interlacements of a slender ribbon pattern formed of white lines edged with black ones upon a black background. No wonder that tradition should allege that these unerring lines should have been traced by angels. (*Celtic Art—the Methods of Construction*, George Bain, William McLellan & Son, Glasgow, 1951)

Bain sketched profusely the designs found on the standing-stones and

in the manuscripts. Figure 34 shows some of the animal figures he cat-
alogued from Scottish stones and the Book of Kells. His investigations
are revealing. The sketch of the 'fighting dog' (figure 34, centre) from
the Book of Kells is identical to the cast-bronze ones that feature on the
Basse Yutz flagons (plate 14) that date to the much earlier period of 400
BC, meaning that the beast must have been favoured by the Celts in
decorative art for over 1,000 years.

He also noticed that the interlaced Celtic knot-work patterns
fall into groups consisting of 1-line designs, 2-line designs, 3-line
designs, 4-line designs, 5-line designs and 9-line designs (figure 37).
Curiously [at least it must have been to him], he never found any
designs made up of 6 individual lines or 7, or 8, although this did not
seem to trouble him. Bain must be congratulated for his incredible
achievements, but it never occurred to him that the patterns might
amount to Celtic representations of the *numbers* of 1, 2, 3, 4, 5, and 9.
After all, if they did represent numbers, why would the numbers 6,
7, and 8 be missing?

To the esoteric Celt the fact that the numbers stop after 5 and
restart at 9 was important. It announced to the world that the Celts
were acutely aware of the body (6) and the Soul (9), and given that the
pattern for the number 9 resembles the Sun (figure 37), they must have
been preoccupied with the Sun and its effects on Earth.

Figure 38 recalls a section of the numbers matrix from the Pyramid
of Inscriptions at Palenque (figure A17). The numbers of 6, 7, 8 are
likewise missing from the matrix and can only be found by decoding the beads in the jade necklace that adorned the neck of the dead
Lord Pacal in his sarcophagus. When the beads are counted and rationalised the missing numbers appear, not as themselves but as factors
of other compound numbers. The message of the matrix of Lord Pacal
was hence twofold: there was no place for the number 666 in his tomb
and the completed matrix (which finishes with 99999) multiplied by
the cycles of time used by the Maya [20 days, 260 days, 360 days, 7,200
days and 144,000 days] throws up the Birth of Venus number, 1,366,560
days.

Figure 38 likewise shows that the Celts encoded the same information into their knot-work numbering system and the analysis may be
continued to reveal the same and additional information (figure 39);

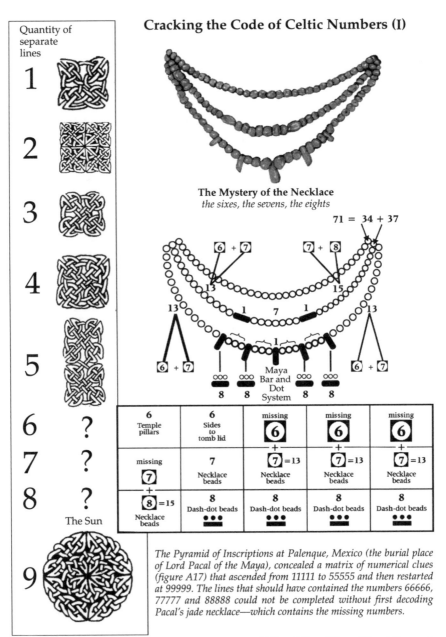

Quantity of
separate
lines

1

2

3

4

5

6   ?

7   ?

8   ?

The Sun

9

The Mystery of the Necklace
the sixes, the sevens, the eights

71 = 34 + 37

6 + 7   7 + 8

13   15

13   1   7   1   13

1

6 + 7   Maya   6 + 7
                     Bar and
                     Dot
8   8   System   8   8

6 Temple pillars	6 Sides to tomb lid	missing 6	missing 6	missing 6
		+	+	+
missing 7	7 Necklace beads	7 = 13 Necklace beads	7 = 13 Necklace beads	7 = 13 Necklace beads
+				
8 = 15 Necklace beads	8 Dash-dot beads ●●●	8 Dash-dot beads ●●●	8 Dash-dot beads ●●●	8 Dash-dot beads ●●●

The Pyramid of Inscriptions at Palenque, Mexico (the burial place of Lord Pacal of the Maya), concealed a matrix of numerical clues (figure A17) that ascended from 11111 to 55555 and then restarted at 99999. The lines that should have contained the numbers 66666, 77777 and 88888 could not be completed without first decoding Pacal's jade necklace—which contains the missing numbers.

Figure 38. (a) Celtic continuous-line patterns consist of 1-line, 2-line, 3-line, 4-line, 5-line and 9-line arrangements. Continuous-line numbers 6, 7 and 8 are missing, just like in the numerical matrix of Lord Pacal at Palenque. Celtic 'pattern-numbers' hence, like the matrix of the Pyramid of Inscriptions, stop at 6 (666) and restart at 9 (999). In this way the Celts drew attention to the Body (666) and the Soul (999) and to the fact that 666 had no place in Celtic ecumenical thinking—just like it had no place in the tomb of Lord Pacal.

when the missing numbers of 678 are subtracted from the number of the body [666] (figure 39a), the result is –012. When the *mirror image* [representing the Soul] of the missing numbers (876) is subtracted from the number of the soul [999], the result is +123. This immediately tells us that the body (–) is of the opposite polarity [voltage] as the soul (+) as earlier hypothesised in the Theory of Iterative Spiritual Redemption (figure A20).

Continuing the resulting numerical series: 012, 123 . . . produces the number 234. The same sequence of 234 was also found in the troop formations of Pit number 3 of Ch'in Shi Huangdi's terracotta army in China [there were 2 troops in one chamber, 3 troops in another, and 4 troops in another when read according to instructions in the tomb]. In that case it was followed by a zero [there were no troops in the northeast corner of the chamber]. Here again we have the same sequence 234 followed by nothing, giving 2340. 2,340 revolutions of the planet Venus (seen from Earth) of 584 days = 1,366,560 days—the Maya Birth of Venus number which recognises that Lord Pacal, like Jesus, was Venus.

The illuminated manuscripts of the Celts thus contain the super-science of the Sun and the higher orders of spirituality.

There are other, lesser-known illuminated works, not yet mentioned; the Celtic missionary St Willibrord embarked on an evangelical mission to the Frisian Islands, off northwest Holland, in AD 690 and was appointed archbishop there in AD 695. Three years later he founded a monastery at Echternach, Luxembourg, where monks at the scriptoria made copies of illuminated manuscripts. One of these was the Echternach Gospels. The colophon says the text was copied from an original that had been revised in AD 558 by Eugippius, the abbot of a monastery near Naples.

The Lichfield Gospels was produced in around AD 740, between the appearance of the books of Lindisfarne (in AD 698) and Kells (c. AD 795). It is not known where it was written but an inscription at the end of St Matthew's Gospel reads:

> Gelhi the son of Arihtuid brought this Gospel from Cingal and gave him his best horse for it . . . and Gelhi donated his purchase to the church of Llandeilo Fawr [in South Wales].

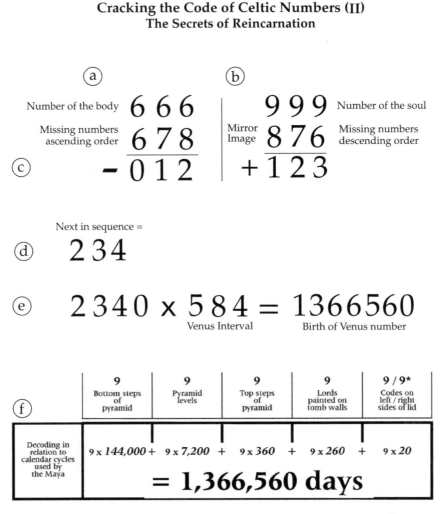

Figure 39. The numbers 6, 7 and 8 are missing from the Celtic numerical sequence (figure 38). The Celtic number sequence stops at 6 (666—representing the body) and restarts at 9 (9996 representing the soul). (a) When the soul is in the body (666) its voltage is able to increase (represented by the ascending numbers that are missing: 6, 7, 8). (b) When the soul is in Heaven (999) its voltage can only ever decrease [if it returns to Earth] (represented by the descending missing numbers: 8, 7, 6). When the missing numbers and the mirror image (the soul) of the missing numbers are subtracted from the body and soul (c) the sequences of – 012 and +123 appear, indicating, firstly, that the voltage of the body is negative (–) and that the voltage of the soul is positive (+). Secondly, continuing this new series of numbers produces the sequence 234. (d) 234 is significant because (e) 2,340 revolutions of the planet Venus amount to the Birth of Venus number worshipped by the Maya, 1366560, the same figure produced in the numerical matrix (f) from the Temple of Inscriptions, Palenque. The same number, 2340, was encoded into the arrangement of terracotta warriors in Pit number 3, at Xian, by the first emperor of China, Ch'in Shi Huangdi [*the Son of Heaven*—see *The Terracotta Warriors*].

By the tenth century the considerably damaged book had found its way into the hands of St Chad at Lichfield. It has much in common with the Book of Lindisfarne—for example, in the layout of the carpet page and the Apostles' symbols, but the style of the Apostolic portraits are more in keeping with those from the Book of Kells.

CHAPTER FOUR

A Land Without a King

The Arthurian Legends

The period following the exodus of the Romans and the arrival of the Anglo-Saxons in Britain was one of turmoil. Their departure gave way to a free-for-all where the Angles and Saxons routed the southeast of England and it was during these so-called 'dark ages' that the legendary figure of King Arthur emerged.

It is not known for certain if Arthur was a warrior-king as he is portrayed. The earliest mention of him comes from the sixth-century writer Gildas who credits him with a victory in c. AD 500 at the battle of Mons Badonicus (Mount Badon) where a confederation of British kings fought and beat the Saxons, a victory that led to fifty years of peace. But no one knows where the battle took place, nor who fought it nor, give or take fifty years, when it was fought: only that a victory of the kind had been won.

In the ninth century the monk Nennius describes twelve of Arthur's battles in his *History of Britain*. But again no hard evidence exists to substantiate the accounts. Nennius describes Arthur as *a dux bellorum*, a Romano-British cavalry commander who must have lived, therefore, at least fifty years earlier [c. AD 450] before the arrival of the Saxons. A seventh-century Welsh poem, *The Book of Aneirin*, describes Arthur, historically, as a great warrior.

The legends of Arthur appeared in the twelfth-century works of the French writer Chrétien (Christian) de Troyes, Geoffrey of Monmouth, and in the fifteenth-century work of the English author Thomas Malory.

Arthur is believed to have been born at Tintagel Castle in Cornwall and eventually buried at Glastonbury Church.

Chrétien de Troyes wrote several accounts of the Arthurian legends: *Perceval ou le conte du Graal* (c. 1182), *Lancelot, ou le Chevalier de la Charrette* (c. 1178), *Erec* (c. 1170) and *Yvain, ou le Chevalier au Lion* (c. 1178).

In *Perceval ou le conte du Graal* the hero, a young knight named Perceval, chances upon a mysterious castle near a river. The lord of the castle is known as the Fisher King, ostensibly because he is crippled and therefore incapable of walking or running and able only to fish. Inside the castle Perceval beholds a vision of a procession led by a young man carrying a white lance that drips blood onto his hands. He is followed by two men carrying candelabra and a beautiful girl who carries the Holy Grail, or *Sang Royal* (French for *Holy Blood* of Christ) in a cup. The light from the cup illuminates the whole room. A maiden carrying a carving dish is the last in the line. The procession moves past Perceval and out of the room. Perplexed, he fails to enquire who or what the procession was meant to represent. When he rises the next day the castle is deserted and as he attempts to leave the drawbridge rises by itself. He survives the ordeal and is later told that he should have asked the question 'whom does the Grail serve?' If he had asked the question then the Fisher King would have been cured and could have walked again.

This version of the Grail differs substantially from the others. This one, in isolation, appears to be an allegorical tale about Christ, the Fisher King who is symbolised by the sign of the fish, the vesica pisces, the geometric symbol of Christianity which is constructed from two overlapping circles (plate 3) that represent the twin planet Venus (plate 3c). The blood dripping from the lance likely represents the sword of the Roman soldier Longinus who pierced the side of Christ on the Cross and thus had 'blood on his hands'. The candelabra carriers represent those who seek the light and the beautiful girl takes the part of Salome, the daughter of King Heroditus Antipas who demanded and received the head of John the Baptist on a silver plate:

> And when Salome, the daughter of Heroditus had come in, and had danced, and pleased Herod and them that were at table with him, the king said to the damsel: Ask of me what thou wilt, and I will give it thee ... Who when she was gone out, said to her mother,

what shall I ask? But she said: The head of John the Baptist. And when she was come in immediately with haste to the king, she asked, saying: I will that forthwith thou give me in a dish, the head of John the Baptist. And the king was struck sad. Yet because of his oath, and because of them that were with him at table, he would not displease her: but sending an executioner, he commanded that his head should be brought in a dish: and gave it to the damsel, and the damsel gave it to her mother. (*Mark* VII, 21-28)

Failure by Perceval to question the meaning of what he saw means that the Fisher King, Jesus [the so-called cripple], would not walk again, meaning, allegorically, that Perceval, the one who failed to ask the question, would not find the Grail, would not drink the Holy Blood, and would therefore not enable the blood of Jesus to walk (live) again.

Chrétien's account therefore allegorically attempts to propagate the story of Jesus who was anointed by John the Baptist and speared in the side with a lance. Only those who ask the right questions will find the Grail, the blood of Christ, and when they do they will find the light and meet Jesus who lives again in Heaven.

Some accounts maintain that Joseph of Arimathea used the Grail to catch the spilled blood of Christ at the Crucifixion, but no biblical texts exist to support the claim. And why would anyone carry a cup to an execution? The reference to the cup that held the blood of Christ derives from the Gospel accounts of the Last Supper:

Jesus took bread, and blessed, and brake it, and gave to them, and said, take, eat: this is my body. And he took the cup [filled with wine] and when he had given thanks, he gave it to them: and they drank of it. And he said unto them, 'this is my blood of the New Testament, which is shed for many'. (*Mark* XIV, 22–24)

The expression from Mark refers to the wine as blood, as in the Eucharistic [Greek, *thanksgiving*] sacrament, the most important Christian ceremony in which bread and wine—the metaphorical bones and blood of Jesus—are consumed in commemoration of his tortuous death and sacrifice.

The account of the Arthurian legend from the Welsh priest Geoffrey of Monmouth (c. 1100–1114) appears in his *History of British Kings* (c. 1139). In it he claims that his Latin version is based on a translation from an 'older text in the British tongue' leading some to believe that it derived from an earlier Celtic version. The book includes a section on *Vita Merlini*, the fabled magician mentor of Arthur.

Merlin in Welsh Celtic myth is known as Myrddin and also Emrys, an ancient rendering of the Greek name Ambrosia (*immortal*), the food of the gods, indicating that Merlin was regarded by the Celts as an immortal or one of the gods.

According to Geoffrey of Monmouth, Merlin was the illegitimate son of a Welsh nun who was overshadowed by an angel (Merlin's father) and left with child; this is to say that Merlin's mother was a virgin and that his father was angelic energy, suggesting that Merlin must have been born through an Immaculate Conception.

Sir Thomas Malory (c. 1410–1471), a Warwickshire landowner and writer, published his *Le Morte d'Arthur* [The Death of Arthur—written in English, despite the title] in around 1485 giving his own version of many of the earlier legends of King Arthur, the Knights of the Round Table, the magical sword Excalibur and the search for the Holy Grail.

Merlin appears in Malory's version as the mentor of the warrior-king Uther Pendragon. Uther appeals to Merlin for help in battle and Merlin summons the sword Excalibur from the lake. Using the magical properties of the sword Uther rises to share power with Gorlois (the Duke of Cornwall) over the lands in the southwest of England and the two leaders meet at Tintagel Castle to celebrate the union. It is there that Uther meets Queen Igraine, Gorlois's wife. Consumed with lust and desire he vows to have her and war between Uther and Gorlois breaks out again. Uther begs Merlin to help him achieve his ambition over Igraine.

Merlin draws Gorlois from the castle allowing Uther's troops to kill him. Using trickery and deception Merlin transforms Uther into the image of Gorlois and arranges the sexual union of Uther and the Queen Igraine in a deal where Uther agrees to hand over any resulting offspring in return for the satiation of Uther's lustful desires over her. Nine months later Merlin visits Queen Igraine and collects the child— Arthur. Soon after Uther is mortally wounded in battle and as he dies he thrust his sword Excalibur into a large boulder in the forest saying 'he who draws the sword from the stone shall be [the next] King'.

Merlin passes Arthur to the noble family of Sir Ector who foster and rear the child as one of their own, for around eighteen years.

After Uther's death England had no king and noblemen of the times met regularly in jousting tournaments to decide who should have the title. Merlin reminds them that only 'he who draws the sword from the stone' shall be eligible to become king. Many knights try to draw the sword from the stone but all fail. Some years later Arthur journeyed to London to watch a tournament in which his guardian knight was taking part. Realising he had mislaid his sword the knight instructed Arthur to find one, whereupon Arthur effortlessly 'pulled the sword from the stone' to become King of England and, using the powers of Excalibur, the greatest warrior-king in the land.

One day Lancelot, 'the bravest knight from a land overseas', meets Arthur on a bridge that covers a stream and challenges his right to be King. A sword fight breaks out during which Lancelot questions Arthur's irrational passion saying 'who are you Sir, who will fight to the death for a stretch of road you could easily ride around?'

Using the powers of Excalibur, Arthur wins the fight but accidentally breaks the magic sword into two, effectively breaking that which legend says 'could not be broken'. Arthur, filled with remorse, recognises that the sword has been taken from him because of his own ego, pride and anger. He had misused the powers of the sword on a good man. Falling to the ground, he begs God for forgiveness and apologises to Lancelot. Merlin appears and summons a new sword from the lake and Lancelot pledges allegiance to Arthur.

This is the heyday of Arthurian rule. He marries Guinevere, the daughter of the knight Leon de Grance, and establishes a 'Round Table' of sun worship at his magnificent mediaeval castle in Camelot where fellow knights, inspired by courage, truth, duty and sacrifice, meet to enjoy the days of peace and tranquillity.

There is no consensus for the number of knights who joined Arthur at his Round Table. Malory's version gives twenty-six, representing the twenty-six-day rotation rate of the Sun's equatorial magnetic field. In other versions (plates 17 and 19) there are nine knights, the highest number that can be reached before becoming one with God.

All is well at the Round Table until Lancelot meets Guinevere. The couple fall in love and betray Arthur. Arthur, devastated, discovers them entwined. Unable to forgive them, he thrusts Excalibur into the ground next to their naked bodies, thus banishing them both from the land.

The Mummies of China

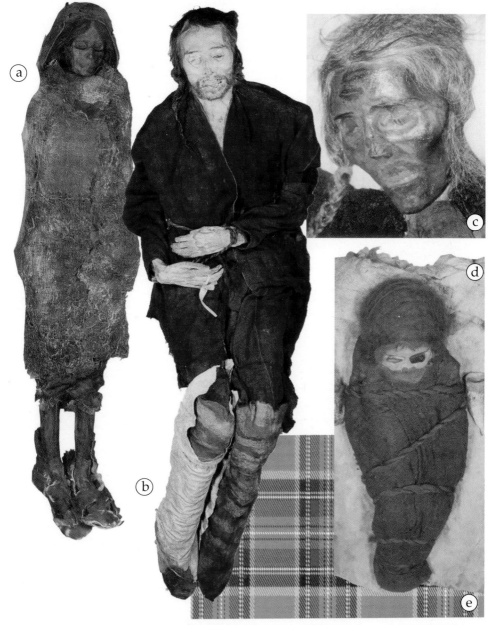

Plate 1. In 1994, J. P. Mallory and Victor H. Mair announced the discovery of Caucasian-type mummies—up to 4,000 years old—buried in the wastelands of China's Tarim basin in the Taklamakan Desert, the second largest desert in the world. The dry sand had perfectly preserved the bodies and the fabrics they wore: (a) Loulan mummy, known as the 'Beauty of Loulan', c. 2000 BC, from Qawrighul, Chinese Gumugou, Cherchan. (b) Fifty-five-year-old white, bearded male found near Cherchan, c. 1000 BC, buried with three females (tomb 2, Urumchi Museum). (c) Blonde-haired Zaghunluq mummy c. 1000 BC. (d) Zaghunluq baby (tomb 1) c. 1000 BC (aged around three months) wearing a dyed blue felt bonnet and a woolen shroud secured with a blue and red tie cordóidentical to that in (b). Blue lapis lazuli stones cover the eyes. (e) A plaid twill similar to one found near Qizilchoqa c. 1200–700 BC.

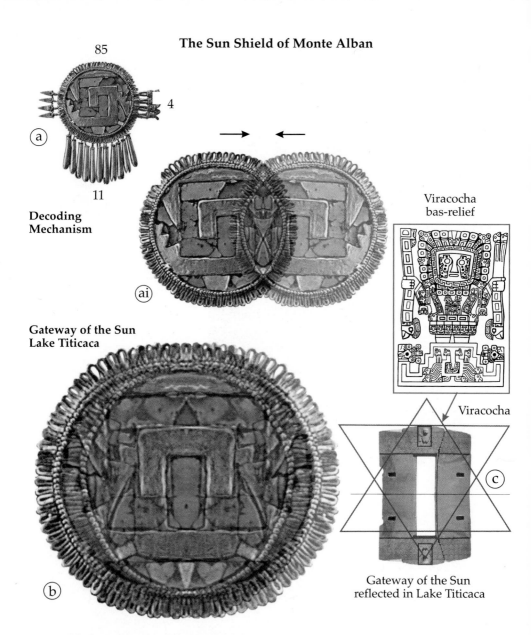

Decoding
Mechanism

Gateway of the Sun
Lake Titicaca

Viracocha
bas-relief

Viracocha

Gateway of the Sun
reflected in Lake Titicaca

Plate 2. (a) The magnetic field of the Sun shifts every 1, 366,040 days: 1,366,040 ÷ 365.25 = 3,740 years, exactly. This gold and turquoise sun shield from Monte Alban, Mexico, encodes this period: 4 (arrows) x 11 (pendants) x 85 (gold loops) = 3,740 [20 sunpot cycles of 187 years]. The four arrows symbolise the four previous ages of the Sun which all ended in catastrophic destruction. The 85 loops around the perimeter represent magnetic field loops of sunspots on the Sun's surface. Closer inspection of the sun shield reveals another Mayan transformer (ai), which when decoded reveals a composite picture (b) of the Gateway of the Sun at Tiahuanaco and its reflection in the waters of Lake Titicaca—all inside a Star of David, the geometric symbol of Judaism. (c) The Gateway of the Sun from Tiahuanaco, Bolivia [mirror imaged to show the reflection in the water], contained within a Star of David. Other orientations of the transparencies reveal more pictures (see plates 3 and plates 6–13). Figure 9 reveals the geometric symbolism behind the Star of David.

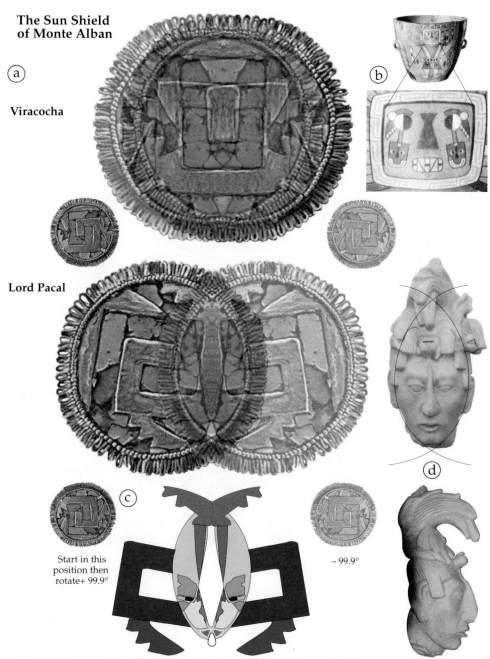

The Sun Shield of Monte Alban

(a)

Viracocha

(b)

Lord Pacal

(c)

Start in this position then rotate+ 99.9°

− 99.9°

(d)

Plate 3. (a) Composite picture of the head and face of Viracocha. (b) Comparable picture of Viracocha, from the Viracocha vase of Tiahuanaco c. AD 500, Peru. (c) Composite picture of Lord Pacal, of Mexico (with the distinctive hairstyle), regurgitating a pearl [the symbol of the wisdom and the rebirth of Venus] inside a vesica pisces [the fish], the geometric symbol of Christianity. (d) Head of Lord Pacal, c. AD 750, from his tomb in the Pyramid of Inscriptions, Palenque, shown inside a vesica pisces. These secret pictures reveal that Viracocha, Lord Pacal and Christ were all different incarnations of the same spiritual energy (God) on Earth at different moments in history. [Compare (c) to the head and shoulders of Lord Pacal, appearing as Xipe Totec in the Mural of Bonampak transformer (plate 4)].

The Mural of Bonampak

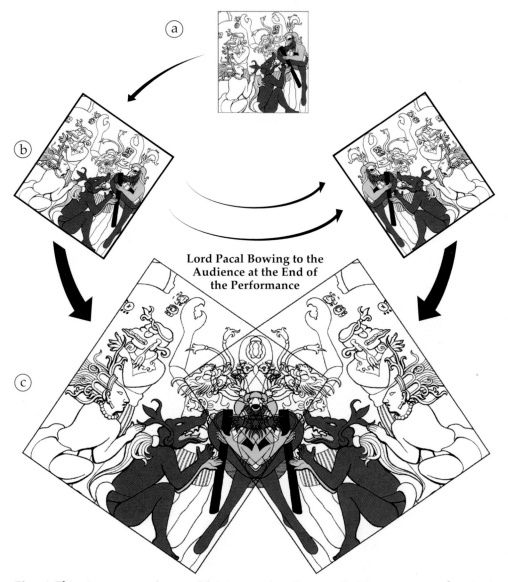

Plate 4. This picture, part of a mural from a temple at Bonampak, Mexico, contains hundreds of hidden pictures, just like the Amazing Lid of Palenque (plate 5b and figure A10). Using the same decoding process, the secret pictures are revealed. These tell stories that are enacted, like a theatre production, by the gods of the Maya. This decoded scene, obtained when the transparencies are juxtaposed by 66.6° ['. . . here is wisdom, let him that hath understanding count the number of the beast; for it is the number of a man and his number is 666', Revelation XIII, 18] is the final one in the story of Xipe Totec, Lord of the Stags, God of the East, Fire and Sacrifice. It shows Xipe Totec, half-stag, half-man, carrying two sticks—which he used to rub together to make fire—bowing to the audience of two stags, who applaud the end of the performance. This finale, where the actors appear on stage and bow to the audience, is a common feature of these decodable pictures, which appear in many forms—carvings, paintings and jewellery—and are collectively known as Mayan transformers. The stag was associated with the Sun and worshipped by the Celts and other sun-worshipping civilizations.

The Sun-Kings of Mexico and Peru

'I saw an angel come down from Heaven . . . and a rainbow was upon his head and his face was, as it were, the Sun . . . and he set his right foot upon the sea and his left foot upon the earth'. Revelation X

Plate 5. (a) Stucco head of Lord Pacal. (b) Decoded picture from the carving on his tomb lid (the Amazing Lid of Palenque) that corresponds to the stucco head. A bat mask—the sign of death—covers his mouth. Covering the bat mask, a small man, wearing a hat, raises his arms and exposes his pure heart. (c) A small man wearing a hat with raised arms, from the tomb of Viracocha Pachacamac, Peru, c. AD 300. (d) Golden crab-man from the tomb of Viracocha, c. AD 500. The crab, which lives in the foam of the sea (on land and in the water), is a metaphor for the *perfect human being*—who is simultaneously in touch with the air, water, fire [sunshine] and earth. (e) Reconstruction of Viracocha Pachacamac (from the Museum of Archaeology, Lima, Peru). Inca accounts tell of two great leaders that walked the lands of Peru performing miracles, Viracocha *(foam of the sea)* and Viracocha Pachacamac '. . . a great leader, a white man of large stature and authoritative demeanour who took the highland route north from Tiahuanaco and followed the coast from Nazca to Sipan, performing miracles on the way. He spoke with great kindness, giving men instruction on how to live, admonishing them to love one another and show charity to all. They called him Viracocha Pachacamac which, in their language, means *'God of the World . . .'* (Cieza de Leon, *Cronica del Peru, part II*, chs. 4 and 5)

Lord Pacal as the Stag

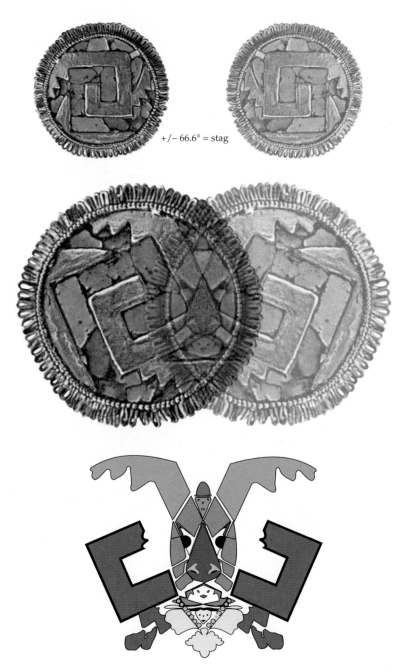

+/− 66.6° = stag

Plate 6. Lord Pacal as the stag, a personification of Christ. The small man with the hat from Peru appears between his antlers—which become his wings. A baby bird, representing Quetzalcoatl, covers his mouth. Another bird hangs on a chain from around his neck. The small man with the hat also appears with wings in a scene from the mosaic mask of Palenque (plate 24).

The Birth of Christ

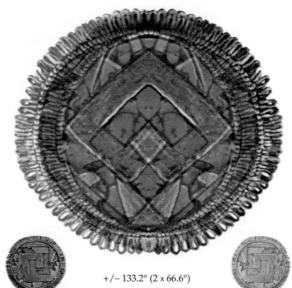

+/− 133.2° (2 x 66.6°)

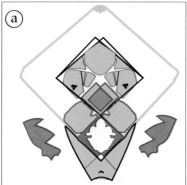

Character wearing Arab-type (or Indian-type) headgear saying, and gesturing, 'come closer and see'.

Plate 7. This complex series of pictures shows: (a) an Arab-type (or perhaps Indian-type) character who can hardly contain his excitement as he invites the onlooker to 'come and see'; (b) a white man with a beard, in the heavens [with a star in his mouth] with a small baby between his legs; (c) the baby's body rises from a bat god (in the knee area) suggesting that he rises from the dead, the re-birth of Jesus on Earth—the baby can be identified as Jesus from the marks that cover the picture; (d) three sets of compasses, the cross of Christ and the squareóthe picture thus shows God giving birth to Jesus. The whole series of pictures is covered by the square of virtue.

God, in the heavens, blowing his breath—the Holy Ghost—to create the baby Jesus who emerges from between his legs [God giving birth to Jesus].

Baby Jesus in mummy-type pose with hands across chest—Jesus rising from the dead.

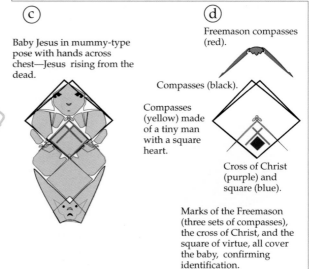

Freemason compasses (red).

Compasses (black).

Compasses (yellow) made of a tiny man with a square heart.

Cross of Christ (purple) and square (blue).

Marks of the Freemason (three sets of compasses), the cross of Christ, and the square of virtue, all cover the baby, confirming identification.

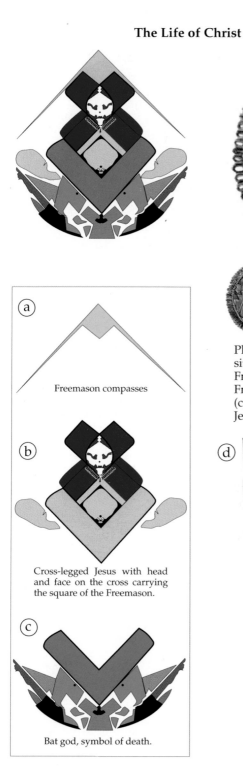

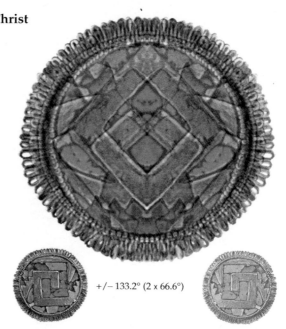

+/− 133.2° (2 x 66.6°)

Plate 8. Composite picture showing: (a) Jesus sitting cross-legged beneath the compasses of the Freemason; (b) he carries the square of the Freemason, representing virtue and purity and is (c) carried away by the bat god—meaning that Jesus was a Freemason who died a virtuous man.

(a)

Freemason compasses

(b)

Cross-legged Jesus with head and face on the cross carrying the square of the Freemason.

(c)

Bat god, symbol of death.

(d)

Christ as the Great Architect of the Universe, using the compasses of the Freemason. (*Bible Moralisée* c. 1235–1245, Laborde facsimile, 1911–27, British Library)

Death by Crucifixion

+ 48°   (angular difference = 96° [999, 666])   − 48°

Jesus as the Sun

Sun God from the Amazing Lid of Palenque.

(b) (c) (d)

Jesus, with a halo of sunspot loops. (*Bible Moralisée* c. 1235–1245, Laborde facsimile, 1911–27, British Library)

Sun God from Aztec calendar stone.

Plate 9. (a) Composite picture showing Jesus as the Sun God, with an extended tongue, and sunspot loops on his head, inside a vesica pisces (the geometric symbol of Christianity). He is seen with the cross of the crucifixion across his forehead, the favoured location for the cross of baptism.

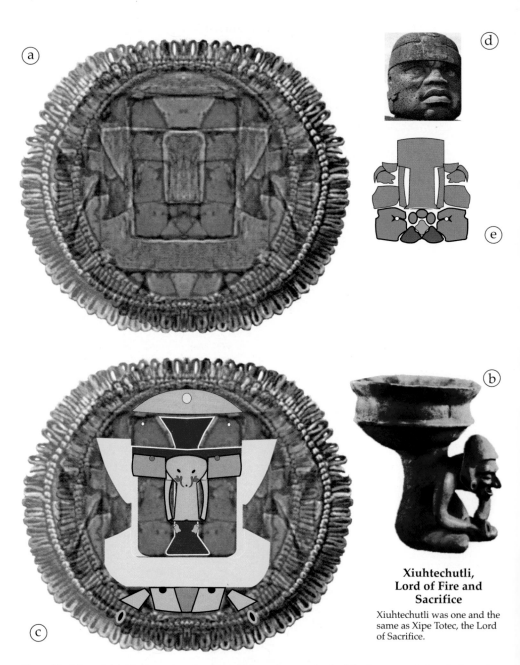

**Xiuhtechutli,
Lord of Fire and
Sacrifice**

Xiuhtechutli was one and the
same as Xipe Totec, the Lord
of Sacrifice.

Plate 10. (a) and (c) Composite picture of a bat, the symbol of darkness and death, hanging from the Christian cross, revealing that Viracocha (plate 3) died on the cross. (b) and (c) The scene is carried by Xiuhtechutli, who carried the sacrificial brazier of cremation on his back. The Sun and Venus, representing God and Jesus, shine above his head. An Olmec head (d), an earlier incarnation of Viracocha, watches over him [inside the brazier, (e)] during the sacrifice.

Christ on the Cross

Plate 11. An even closer examination of the composite of the bat hanging from the cross reveals more complex pictures inside the bat: (a) a Christlike figure; (b) a Lord Pacal–type figure and (c) an Oriental-like figure. [The images are much more persuasive when displayed on the computer using maximum zoom]. Thus a picture of Christ is shown dying on the cross. [To see the Christlike figure, gaze at the eyes, just below the hood, and wait for the picture to snap into consciousness].

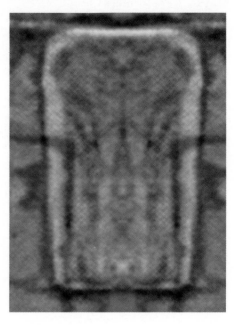

Terracotta figure of a white man with a beard, from a Han tomb, c. AD 400–600, in China. The serrated edge down the spine resembles the step pattern on the sun shield.

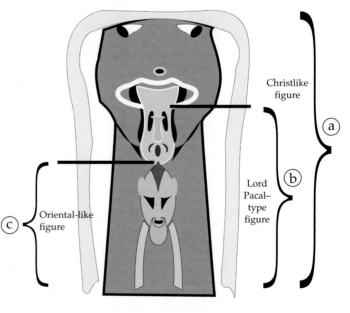

Christlike figure

(a)

(b)

Lord Pacal– type figure

(c) Oriental-like figure

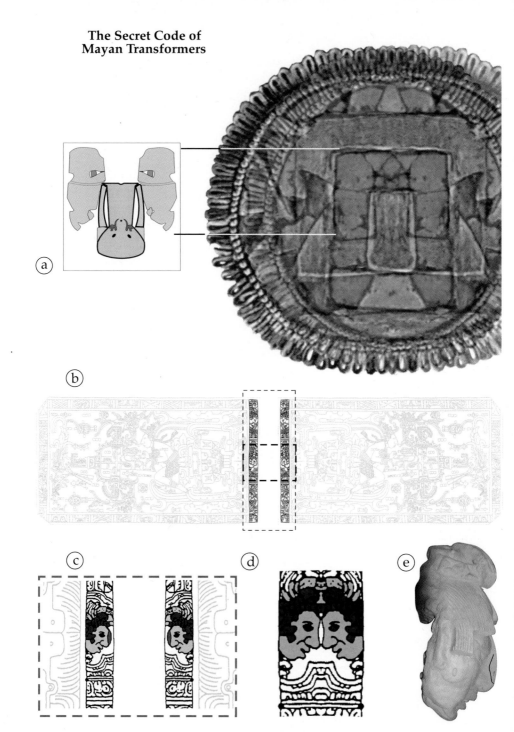

Plate 12. (a) Composite picture of Lord Pacal, as the twins (Venus) in profile. The bat covers both noses, referring to the secret (darkened) instructions encoded into the Amazing Lid of Palenque, (b), (c) and (d), that reveal the Mayan transformer decoding process. (e) Stucco head from Pacal's tomb showing the same 'decoding' mark on the nose (emphasised).

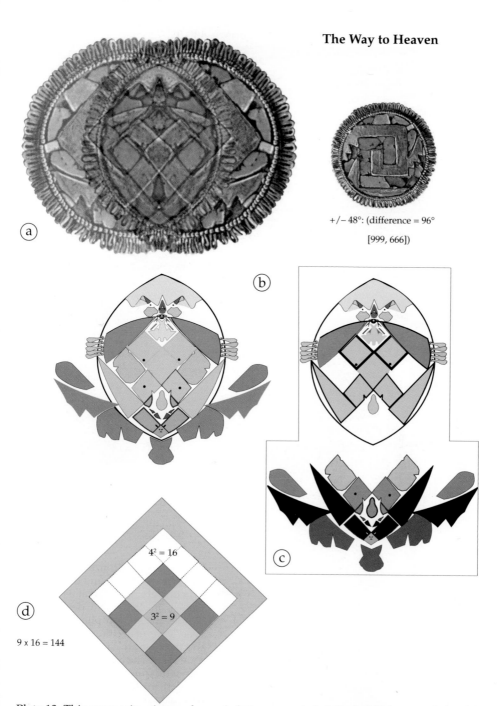

+/− 48°: (difference = 96°

[999, 666])

$4^2 = 16$

$3^2 = 9$

9 x 16 = 144

Plate 13. This composite picture shows (what appears to be) God, (b) his curved shoulders representing the Earth's horizon. His mouth appears to be the rising Sun, his eyes the rising star and the falling star. He opens his cloak and in so doing exposes his naked body and so is carried away by the bat, (c) meaning that those who live by the body (a physical life) find only death and darkness, the place of the bat. (d) The 3, squared, and the 4, squared: $3^2 = 9$, $4^2 = 16$; $3^2 \times 4^2 = 144$, an abbreviation of the 144,000 from Revelation. The non-physical, who are numbered among the 144,000, find eternal life.

Plate 14. (a) Bronze Basse Yutz flagon, c. 400 BC, found during construction of a new road at Basse Yutz, France, in 1927. The design style typifies the second phase of the La Téne style of Celtic art. The spout and the base are circumscribed with coral inlay. The lid contains a beautiful semispherical bronze stud, detailed in (b), which is patterned with a tracery of bronze wire infilled with coloured enamel (moulten glass), the earliest known appearance of the technique in Europe. (c) Second vase of the pair [almost the same size as (a)].

The Long Journey of the Israelites

Plate 15.

Plate 16. Initial page of the Gospel according to Saint Mark, from the Lindisfarne Gospels, known to date from AD 698. The names of the saints appear in Latinised Greek. The distinctive font is identical to the one used in the names of the saints carved on the Ardagh Chalice (discussed shortly), but there the names appear in Latin.

The Arthurian Legend of the Holy Grail

Plate 17. King Arthur (with crown and staff) together with eight of his knights (*Summoned to the Quest by a Damsel*, Edward Burne-Jones, c. 1898, tapestry) commemorating the Last Supper. The mysterious empty seat, known as the *Siege Perilous* (next to Arthur), belonged to his 'right-hand man', the knight who would one day return with the Holy Grail. The inscription on the fabric over the empty chair reads 'CCCLIII - Hiemius Peractis . Post . Natum . Umn . Nostrum - I - C . Oportet . Hanc . Sede . Compleri'; *In the year of our Lord AD 453 winter is over. It is right and proper for this seat to be occupied*', meaning that 'the dark days are over, the Holy Grail [the cup of light] has been found'.

Plate 18. This painting, *Fair Rosamund*, by John W. Waterhouse, 1916, is typical of those from the Pre-Raphaelite school of art that flourished in England from around 1850 to 1925. To the uninitiated it appears to show a simple picture of a princess waiting anxiously for her knight in shining armour. It actually contains secret information from the book of Ecclesiastes, in the Bible, explaining the mysteries of life—of Heaven and Hell (see figure 42).

The Arthurian Legend of the Holy Grail and Excalibur [the Sword of King Arthur]

Plate 19. King Arthur (seated centre) together with his nine knights at the Round Table (after a fifteenth-century manuscript). Arthur also appears in time lapse, in the left-hand-panel window, drawing the legendary sword from the stone. The Holy Grail (flanked by two anthropomorphic golden dragon-angels, centre) is shown as a chalice, identical to the Ardagh Chalice, with light radiating through a samite pall that carries the cross of Christ.

The Secrets of the Tara Brooch (I)

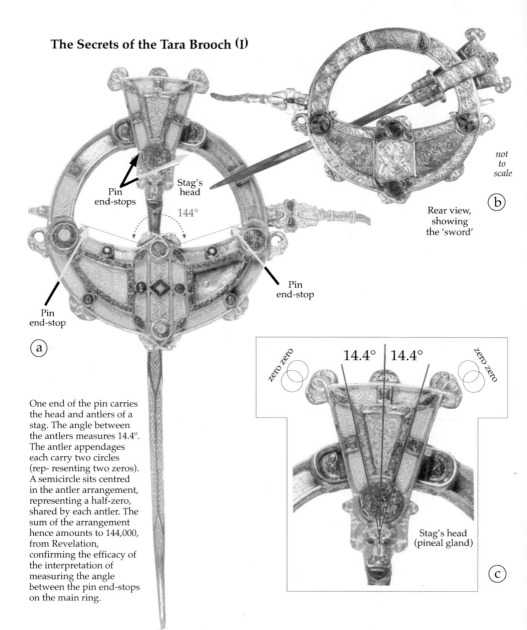

not to scale

Pin end-stops

Stag's head

144°

(b)
Rear view, showing the 'sword'

Pin end-stop

(a)

Pin end-stop

zero zero | 14.4° | 14.4° | zero zero
Zero

Stag's head (pineal gland)

(c)

One end of the pin carries the head and antlers of a stag. The angle between the antlers measures 14.4°. The antler appendages each carry two circles (rep- resenting two zeros). A semicircle sits centred in the antler arrangement, representing a half-zero, shared by each antler. The sum of the arrangement hence amounts to 144,000, from Revelation, confirming the efficacy of the interpretation of measuring the angle between the pin end-stops on the main ring.

Plate 20. The Tara brooch contains secret knowledge of a very high scientific and spiritual order, associating its sister artefact, the Ardagh Chalice, with the same provenance. It also contains an account of the Arthurian legend of Excalibur. The stag's head can be slid around the ring until it reaches one of the pin end-stops. The pin (the sword) can then be removed from the stone set into the ring, by swinging it backwards, away from the brooch. Then the angle between the pin end-stops 144° [an abbreviation of the sacred number 144,000, from the book of Revelation in the Bible] can be measured. Hence the expression: 'he who draws the sword from the stone [who understands the meaning of the expression "144,000"] will be a King in Heaven' [from the Arthurian legend]. Clearly, the esoteric code of the Tara brooch was also broken by King Arthur, giving him knowledge of where to find the Grail. Later the story became part of the Arthurian so-called 'legend', which is actually fact.

The Tara Brooch (II—detail)

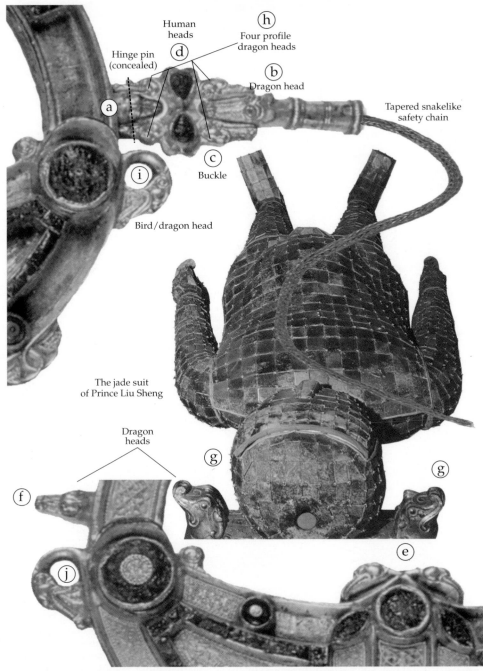

Human heads

Four profile dragon heads

Hinge pin (concealed)

Dragon head

Tapered snakelike safety chain

Buckle

Bird/dragon head

The jade suit of Prince Liu Sheng

Dragon heads

Plate 21. Tara brooch detail: (a) and (f) a pair of dragon heads; b) dragon head safety chain to buckle connector; (c) Buckle (connected to ring by hinge pin); (d) two glass human heads (black); (e) two entwined vulture heads; (g) dragon heads from the tomb of Prince Liu Sheng; (h) four profile dragon heads; (i) and (j) bird/dragon heads.

The Secrets of Tara Brooch (III)

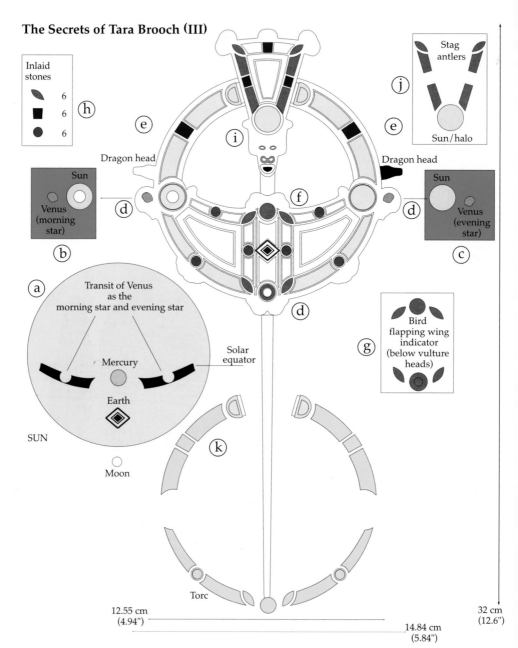

Inlaid stones (h)
- 6
- 6
- 6

Stag antlers (j)
Sun/halo (e)

Dragon head (e)
Dragon head

Sun — Venus (morning star) (d) (b)
Sun — Venus (evening star) (d) (c)

(i)
(f)

Bird flapping wing indicator (below vulture heads) (g)

(a) **Transit of Venus as the morning star and evening star**
Mercury
Solar equator
Earth
SUN
Moon

(d)

(k) **Torc**

12.55 cm (4.94")
14.84 cm (5.84")
32 cm (12.6")

Plate 22. The Tara brooch contains the super-science of the Sun and the higher orders of spirituality. (a) The main ring represents the disc of the Sun. The planet Mercury appears closest to the Sun. The twin-star (planet) Venus is seen in both of its manifestations (as the morning star and the evening star) transiting the face of the Sun along the solar equator [also shown in (b) and (c)]. The Earth, represented by the square [in China], is shown beyond Venus, and the moon is shown in its orbit around the Earth. (d) Bird/dragon heads (also shown in plate 21i and 21j). (e) Dragon head astronomical data indicators (also shown in plate 21a and 21f). (f) and (g) Flapping wing vulture indicators. (h) The number 666 represented by inlaid stones. (i and j) The stag [the mark of Cernunnos—Christ] (figure 22) wearing a halo and antlers [containing the number 144,000 (plate 20c)]. (k) Torc of Cernunnos [Venus] (figure 22).

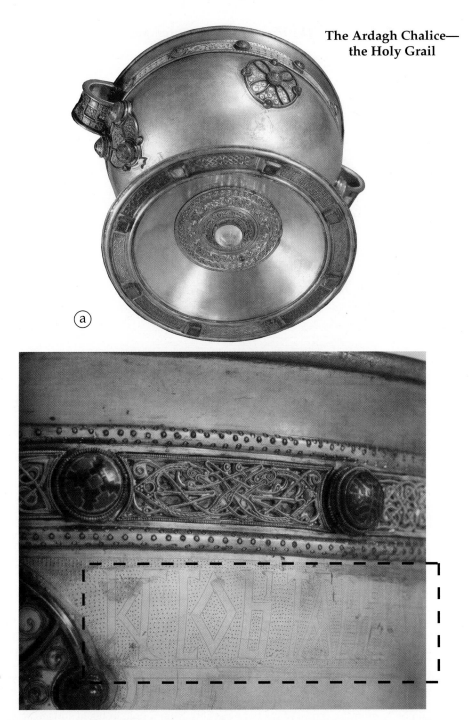

**The Ardagh Chalice—
the Holy Grail**

(a)

(b)

Plate 23. (a) The so-called Ardagh Chalice. A solar cross features in between the handles on both sides of the bowl. A ring of 12 enamelled studs, inlaid with bronze and silver wire—to produce twelve individual patterns—circumscribes the cup beneath the rim. The name of an Apostle is engraved beneath each of the studs. (b) The ones seen here (box-framed) read IACOBI [James] and TATHEVS [Thaddeus (Jude Thaddeus)].

The Mosaic Mask of Palenque
The First Picture of God (I)

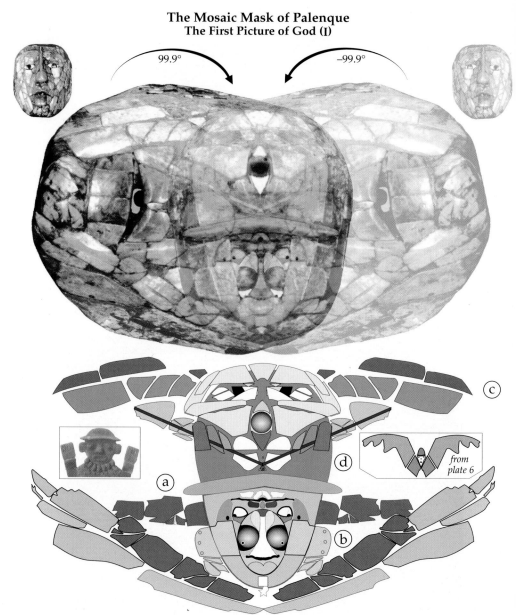

Plate 24. The mosaic mask of Palenque transparencies, set to 99.9°, reveal a complex picture confirming that Lord Pacal (who made the mask), Viracocha and Christ were all one and the same spiritual energy. (a) The main character is the man with the hat from the tomb of Viracocha Pachacamac [box-framed] in Peru. (b) Viracocha also appears as a crab (purple) across the man's face. The [egg-shaped] face of the bat god [with appendages on the forehead] in turn covers the face of the crab (hence the three sets of eyes). The soul of the man can be seen in the centre of his hat emerging from a hole in his head (see also plate 21g). (c) The soul is caught in the open beak of an eagle who carries it away to the heavens. (d) Just beneath the soul a Christlike figure stands, emulating the Crucifixion, carrying the compasses of the Freemason in his hands (his face and ankles are coloured red to help identification). The eagle carries away the compasses and the Christlike figure in its claws. The man with the hat takes flight as his spirit flies away (see also figures 65 and 66).

At around the same time, Arthur's evil stepsister Morgan-le-Fay seduces Arthur, using sorcery and trickery partially learned from Merlin, and becomes pregnant, in the hope of prising the crown from Arthur's lineage to her own.

Without Excalibur the land falls into decline and Arthur, depressed, sends his knights on a quest for the Holy Grail in the hope that the powers of the Grail will compensate for the loss of the sword. All of the knights search for the Grail without success and find only death. In Malory's version the knight Perceval sees the Grail but is unable to retrieve it. Following Perceval's attempt one seat is left empty at the round table, the Siege Perilous [*the seat of peril*]. Merlin ordains:

> . . . in the Siege Perilous there shall no man sit therein but one, and if there be any so hardy to do it he shall be destroyed, and he that shall sit there shall have no peril.

As we have already heard, another version says that the Grail passed in a line of stewardship from Joseph of Arimathea eventually to the knight Sir Galahad who 'took our Lord's body between his hands more than 300 years after Joseph's death'.

Arthur, worn out and weary from a broken heart after years away from his beloved Guinevere, forgives her in his heart and mind. She then meets with Arthur and returns Excalibur, which she has treasured and kept safe during their years apart.

During the years of the quest Arthur's son by Morgan-le-Fay, Mordred, grows to manhood and challenges Arthur to hand over the crown. Refusing, the two armies go into battle on Salisbury Plain where both Arthur and Mordred are mortally wounded. Two surviving knights, Lucan and Bedivere, help Arthur to a chapel by the sea. Arthur asks that Excalibur be tossed into a lake, saying, 'one day a king will come and raise the sword again'. Arthur's body is then carried to his final resting place in Glastonbury where the inscription on his tomb reads 'here lies Arthur king that was, king that shall be', referring to the fact that he would be born again: a king in Heaven.

Like Chrétien's account of the Arthurian legends (*Perceval ou le conte du Graal*), Malory's version must surely be allegorical allowing us, once again, to reconsider the quotation from Rabbi Moses Maimonides:

King Arthur (Lineage)

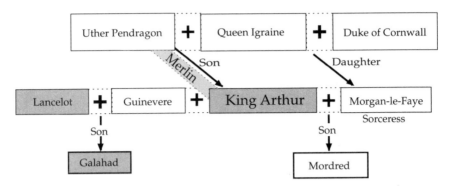

Figure 40. Lineage of King Arthur and his associates. Merlin, the magican, was the mentor of King Uther who summoned the magical sword Excalibur to help Uther win battles and become king. Using trickery and deception he arranged the union between Uther and Igraine that resulted in the birth of Arthur. After Uther's death Merlin counsels Arthur as king.

The Knights of the Round Table

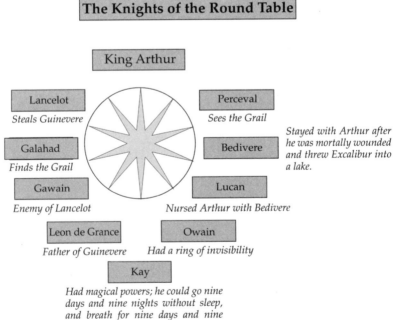

Figure 41. Arthur established the Round Table in thanks to God for giving the land one king, peace and prosperity. The warrior-knights were a bretheren of Freemasons who met regularly to discuss the secrets of the Sun and the higher orders of spirituality. These names feature in Malory's version of the Arthurian legend but other accounts include other knights.

Every time you find in . . . a tale, the reality of which is repugnant to both reason and common sense, then be sure that the tale contains a profound allegory veiling a deeply mysterious truth; and the greater the absurdity of the letter, the deeper the wisdom of spirit. (*Hidden Wisdom in the Holy Bible*, vol. 1, G. Hodson, Wheaton, Ill.: Theosophical Publishing House)

Malory was trying to convey that Excalibur, the magical double-edged sword of truth and courage, was the only thing that could bring peace to the land—meaning, more specifically, that only truth and courage will bring peace. Lord Krishna gives the same message to the soldier Arjuna in the Bhagavad Gita before the battle of Kurukshetra begins. During the discourse Lord Krishna tells Arjuna that the battle should be fought not because it might be won or lost but out of duty, because it needs to be fought. If he wins, he will become a king on Earth and should he lose he will become a king in Heaven, because he has performed his duty.

The Bhagavad Gita then considers the nature of attachment:

In this world there is a two-fold path. There is the path of wisdom for those who meditate and the path of action for those who work. No man can refrain from activity by refraining from action; nor can he reach perfection by refusing to act. He cannot remain inactive because Nature will compel him to act or not to act. All honour to him whose mind controls his senses; because he is thereby beginning to practise 'karma-yoga', the path of right action, keeping himself always unattached. Do your duty as prescribed; for action for duty's sake is superior to inaction . . . let your acts be done without attachment, as sacrifice only . . . he who does not help the revolving wheel of sacrifice but instead leads a sinful life, rejoicing in the gratification of his senses, O Arjuna! He breathes in vain. (*The Bhagavad Gita*, chapter III, Shri Purohit Swami, Faber & Faber, 1935)

And in regard to desire:

Desire leads to frustration, frustration to anger, anger to delusion and delusion to self-destruction. (*The Bhagavad Gita*, chapter II, Shri Purohit Swami, Faber & Faber, 1935)

King Arthur had broken the sword in a fit of vanity, ego and rage fighting a pointless battle with Lancelot who questioned what the fight was about: 'you will fight to the death for a piece of road that you could easily ride around'. Arthur repents and asks for forgiveness and in return Merlin summons a replacement sword. This part of the tale reassures us that if we repent, we will be restored to our previous position.

But, in time, his desires fulfilled, Arthur forgets about the importance of the sword (truth and courage) and, sliding into a life of ease, comfort, inaction and attachment, relegates the importance of the sword to second place in his life, preferring instead the affections of Guinevere. She is thus taken away from him, into the arms of Lancelot who might more deserve her affections because he lacks the ego, vanity and passion earlier displayed by Arthur. Again driven by ego and anger Arthur, unable to forgive, thrusts Excalibur into the ground alongside the sleeping lovers as an expression of dismay. His land, his alliance with the Knights of the Round Table and his health now all begin to slip into oblivion, until he finds it in his heart to forgive Guinevere and Lancelot. He searches for Christ (the blood of Christ in the Grail). Finding the Grail, he finds it in his heart to forgive Guinevere and Lancelot. Then Excalibur, truth and courage, return to him. Finally, he falls, to rise again a king in Heaven.

Therein lies the allegory in the tale. But how could the allegory be saved, written down and preserved for future generations to help those on the narrow path to get to Heaven next time around? As before, it could be set down in pictures or numbers as well as myth.

The Pre-Raphaelites

The pharaohs of the Old Kingdom were the first in our present cosmic cycle to encode the secret teachings into the pyramids. Tutankhamun, Solomon, Ch'in Shi Huangdi, the Viracochas and Lord Pacal continued the tradition in their own times. During the Middle Ages mediaeval Freemasons encoded the knowledge into the architecture of the cathedrals that blossomed throughout Europe. And then, the Pre-Raphaelite artists, a body of Freemasons known as the Brotherhood, continued the ancient tradition encoding the secrets for themselves, in paintings, tapestries and stained glass as their forefathers had done before them.

William Morris, one of the great Pre-Raphaelites, was born in 1834, the son of a wealthy copper-mining industrialist in Victorian England. In 1853 he moved to Oxford to study theology at the University but soon switched to architecture. There, he befriended Edward Burne-Jones, who became one of the most famous Pre-Raphaelites. In 1853 the two teamed up with the painter Dante Gabriel Rosetti and the colloquial 'Brotherhood' was born. John Everett Millais, John W. Waterhouse, Arthur Hughes, Ford Maddox-Brown, William Holman Hunt, Edmund Blair, Leighton Frank Dicksee, William Frank Calderon and others soon joined them.

As before, their aim was to sing the praise of God in their works, believing that the soul of man could be raised to Heaven through artistic expression. They longed for a bygone romantic age—the age of chivalry, courage, duty and truth enshrined in the Arthurian legends.

One of the first collaborative projects undertaken by Morris, Burne-Jones and Rosetti was the painting of the ceiling of the Oxford University Union building with water-colour frescoes of the much loved Arthurian legends. One of the last, by Burne-Jones and Morris, was the design and production of a series of six 'Holy Grail' tapestry panels that had been commissioned by an Australian mining engineer, William Knox D'Arcy, to decorate the walls of Stanmore Hall. The series consisted of: 1. The Knights of the Round Table Summoned to the Quest by a Damsel (plate 17); 2. The Arming and Departure of the Knights; 3. The Failure by Sir Lanceleot to enter the Chapel of the Holy Grail; 4. The Failure of Sir Gawaine; 5. The Ship; and 6. The Attainment.

It took Burne-Jones three years to finish the design of the scenes that he started in 1890. Morris, who by that time had become the foremost designer and producer of tapestries, wallpaper, stained glass and furniture in England, then wove the tapestries. The six magnificent tapestries featuring the Arthurian legends are now kept in the Birmingham Museum and Art Gallery in England. Another complete set was woven for William D'Arcy's partner, Mr. McCulloch, for his house in Queen's Gate, London, and a handful of individual panel repeats were produced for other clients.

The fact that they referred to themselves as the Brotherhood implies that they must have inherited their esoteric knowledge from their Freemason fathers. Plate 18, *Fair Rosamund*, by John W. Waterhouse

(1916) and its schematic, figure 42, demonstrate how they went about encoding esoteric information into their works.

The art lover sees only a good-quality picture of a princess anxiously waiting for her knight in shining armour to pass by. It seems that the chambermaid has been ushered behind the curtain, to take a break from spinning—just in case, if fate dictates, the knight decides to stop at the window and strike up a conversation. After all, he could hardly be frank and honest about his intentions or feelings if he believed that someone might be listening.

The art expert may have more to say. He might begin by explaining the romantic symbolism contained in Pre-Raphaelite paintings: how, in the painting, the rose clinging to the wall by the window symbolises the princess's desire to cling to her prospective lover. He might go on to explain how her right hand anxiously clutches her left wrist, carefully avoiding contact with the red fabric of the vest she wears beneath her dress—a metaphor that says she 'no longer wishes to hold on to her virginity'. Indeed, a closer look at the floor shows the faintest glimpse of red creeping from beneath her dress, symbolic of the blood from her first loving encounter. And the maid looks on, furtively, realising that these may be the final moments of her employment if the desires of her mistress are fulfilled.

The esotericist will labour longer, in the knowledge that only a human being filled with God could produce such a beautiful piece of art. He would appreciate instinctively that no individual achieves anything. It is the godly energy within the individual that achieves. A swallow cannot fly through the branches of a tree at 100 miles per hour. It is not the bird that flies. It is not the bird brain that achieves. It is God within the bird that flies so miraculously. The esotericist understands the true purpose of life, the higher knowledge, the super-science of the Sun and the higher orders of spirituality. He is eager to share his knowledge with the like-minded and at the same time protect it from the profane. He exists in the spiritual dimension above and away from the profane. It is as though the intellectual body hitches itself to the spiritual and in so doing experiences consciousness free of physical or emotional restraint. This capability is not open to lower initiates but only to the higher adepts who have progressed through disciplined study of the sacred sciences, years of devotion and probation.

The Secrets in the Painting

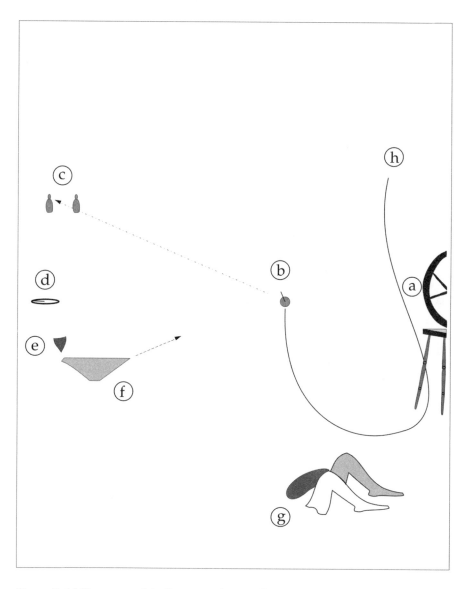

Figure 42. (a) Compasses of the Freemason (set at 66°) representing God, the Great Architect of the Universe. (b) The Sun, on its axis. (c) Twins, representing Venus, the morning star and the evening star. (d) Vagina. (e) Bikini line. (f) Arrow pointing to the vulva of the Princess, the Sun and Heaven. (g) Lovers entwined. (h) Silver thread, the cable tow. The painting contains a secret story explaining the mysteries of life.

Temporary evacuation of the soul from the body results from a three-fold technique obtainable only by disciplined meditation and ritual which teaches men how to function away from the physical body at will. They teach that the spiritual nature, the soul, is attached to the physical form at certain points, symbolised by the three nails of the Crucifixion. Through initiation they are taught to withdraw the nails, enable the divine nature of man to come down from the cross and thereby release their own soul from their body into another dimension. Out-of-body experiences are possible only once the emotional, intellectual and physical bodies are at peace and equilibrium which in turn is achieved through the meditation and ritual.

During an out-of-body experience the soul leaves the body through a mythical silver thread that, with practice, extends from the navel. The journeying soul can leave the body safely, providing the higher intellect holds this umbilical cord tight to provide a return path to the body. The practise is dangerous, as breakage of the silver thread precludes its return to the body. Should this happen, then the initiate would die. Ecclesiastes, in the Bible, says this:

> Man goeth to his long home and the mourners go about the streets: or ever the silver cord be loosed or the golden bowl (halo) be broken . . . then shall the dust return to the Earth as it was; and the spirit shall return to God who gave it. (*Ecclesiastes* XII, 5–7)

The reason for the look of fear and trepidation on the face of the maid behind the curtain now becomes clear. The silver thread, passing as it does through the open legs of the spinning wheel, adds to the story; she is fearful that her princess will submit to desire, fearful that the knight will find Heaven between her legs. She fears that her mistress will sell her soul to desire and attachment and perish. She too sees the passionate embrace on the floor, beneath her long flowing dress, wrestling in each others arms and holds tight to the silver cord that extends from her navel in a vain attempt to tether her mistress to Earth—one last-gasp effort to save her mistress from selling her soul to oblivion as the Holy Ghost, her veil, clings to her head for dear life. Her desire, like King Arthur's, can only lead to anger, delusion and self-destruction.

So the painting has more to say to the spiritually pre-disposed than first meets the eye.

In the same way, the Pre-Raphaelite painting *Summoned to the Quest by a Damsel* by Edward Burne-Jones, 1898 (plate 17), has more to say. To the art lover it is simply a gathering of King Arthur and eight of his knights commemorating the Last Supper of Christ. The mysterious empty seat, known as the Siege Perilous (next to Arthur), as we have heard, belonged to his 'right-hand man', the knight who would one day return with the Holy Grail. However, close inspection of the scene reveals that the sheet, draped over the chair, carries a mysterious inscription, in Latin, that reads CCCCLIII - Hiemius Peractis . Post . Natum . Umn . Nos trum - I - C . Oportet . Hanc . Sede. Compleri': 'In the year of our Lord AD 453 winter is over. It is right and proper for this seat to be occupied'—meaning 'the dark days are over, the Holy Grail [the cup of light] has been found'.

Edward Burne-Jones, as part of the Brotherhood, would not have included the quotation in the picture if it were meaningless. The picture is, once again, another classic example of artistic beauty and the artist again clearly filled with godly energy. In the scene a damsel beckons, by the side of the returning knight's horse, saying 'come and look at the Grail'.

The date of AD 453 fits in with the version of events that says Galahad 'took our Lord's body between his hands more than 300 years after Joseph's death, and then he died'. Joseph likely died in around AD 64, after building the church at Glastonbury. If the inscription on the fabric over the chair is correct, then it supports the account, AD 453 being '*more than* 300 years after the death of Joseph of Arimathea'.

It is not just the Pre-Raphaelites who have more to convey; plate 19 shows a mediaeval painting featured in the French manuscript *Livre de Messire Lancelot du lac* (by Gautier de Moap, Ms. Francais 120 fol. 524v). This one is even more revealing in regard to the legends of King Arthur. Again we see Arthur at the Round Table, this time accompanied by his nine knights. They behold the cup of light in the middle of the table. The cup is flanked by two golden anthropomorphic dragon-angels and light radiates from the cup in all directions. The floor within the circular table is again chequered and squared, indicating esoteric importance.

Curiously, and enigmatically, Arthur appears *twice* in the same picture—*at the same time*—as though in time-lapse, in the left-hand-panel

window. He wears the same clothes at the table as he does outside—
at the same time. Outside he can be seen pulling a sword from the stone.
Now the Arthurian legends fuse together. The story of worshipping
the Grail is *inextricably linked* with the event of pulling the sword from
the stone, which can only mean that the act of pulling the sword
from the stone *led to the discovery* of the Grail. This understanding is
crucial if we are to understand the esoteric significance of the Arthurian
so-called legends. Moreover, if we recall, Malory suggests that the
Grail was found only after Guinevere returned Excalibur—which
could only happen *after* Excalibur had firstly been removed from the
stone.

The Secrets of the Tara Brooch

The Tara brooch (plate 20) is one of the most famous of more than fifty
known Celtic brooches. It was found on the beach at the mouth of the
river Boyne near Bettystown, County Meath, in 1850 and passed to a
firm of jewellers, Waterhouse and Company, of Dublin, who named
it Tara (after the name of the ancient Irish seat of kings located northwest of Dublin) simply to enhance its value. Archaeologists believe
the brooch must have been manufactured in around AD 700 because
the artistic style is similar to that embodied in the illuminated manuscripts. But this need not be the case, as we shall see.

There are two styles of brooch, thought to have been used as cloak
fasteners from around AD 450 to AD 950. Figure 43 demonstrates the
different principles of the various mechanisms. The penannular (figure
43a) type of brooch varies in size but is typically 5–10 cm (2–4 inches)
in diameter, consisting of 'almost a ring' which is split at the lower
part to facilitate the through passage of a swinging pin and the second
version, thought to have appeared later, the ring brooch (figure 43b)
where a piece of metal bridges the split in the ring or, alternatively, like
the Tara brooch, where the ring continues unbroken along the entire
circumference.

Clearly the two types of mechanism operated differently. The small
pin on the penannular was firstly stabbed through the two pieces of
fabric toward the chest and then back through the fabric away from
the chest to the front side. The pin could then be passed through the

Celtic Penanular and Ring Brooches

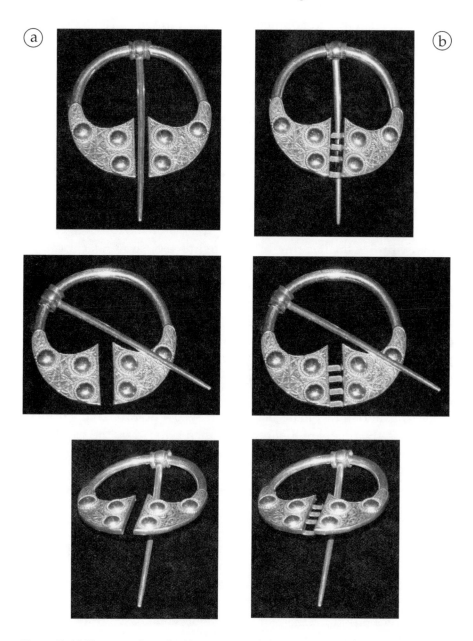

Figure 43. (a) The penanular style of brooch was broken at one point of the ring facilitating the through passage of the fastening pin. (b) The ring brooch was either a continuous ring or, as shown here, bridged by connecting bars. The pin could not pass through the ring, although it could be flipped over (for demonstration purposes) when not in use, as shown here (right).

gap in the ring and then slid around the ring, the end of the pin rest-ing, stressed, on the ring of the brooch. The pin thus fastened the two pieces of fabric together.

The later ring brooches are, generally, much larger than the simple penannular ones. The pin on the Tara brooch, for example, is 32 cm (12.6 inches) long [*Treasures of the National Museum of Ireland,* Gill and Macmillan, 2002] and the ring diameter [scaled from the computer using the 32-cm (12.6-inch) pin as a reference] measures 14.84 cm (5.84 inches) [although the diameter given in the *Treasures of the National Museum of Ireland* is 8.7 cm (3.42 inches) which, following visual inspec-tion of the brooch, cannot be correct].

The pin on the Tara brooch is far too large to stab through the fabric without causing substantial damage to the material. However, experi-ments with the smaller ring brooch (figure 43b) show that it can be used to hold two pieces of fabric together using a different method to that used by the penannular. The same method could therefore be used with the Tara brooch: starting with the brooch in front of the chest, one of the triangular ends of a cloak is firstly passed from the front through the ring, under the pin and back out through the front of the ring. The large pin is then slid around the ring so as to crush the fabric already in the ring (thus opening-up an empty gap on the other side of the ring). The second corner of the cloak is now passed through the empty gap in the ring, under the pin (as before) and again out through the front of the ring. Both corners of the fabric are then gripped by the hands and pulled apart, from centre to shoulders, which forces the larger parts of the cloak into the ring where they jam tight. The main pin is thus required to travel around the ring, within limits, and to move forwards and backwards.

This demonstrates that the enormous Tara brooch could, theoreti-cally, be used as a cloak fastener, the idea being that once fastened, the cloak is pulled sideways so that the brooch settles below the shoulder. Which is all very well, unless the wearer should fall over and become impaled on the massive 32-cm (12.6-inch) pin. Immediately, the ratio-nal observer questions the real purpose of the massive so-called ring brooches.

The main ring and pin of the Tara brooch are made of gold-plated silver, the gilt being much worn with time. The front consists of several recessed panels decorated with gold filigree interspersed with *stones* of glass, enamel and amber. One of the panels is missing, revealing a tiny metal stud that holds a back panel in position. Solid surfaces are finely engraved.

The ring carries several cast animals and birds; two baby dragon heads project outwards from the horizontal centre-line of the main circular ring (plates 21a and f, and 22e). One dragon head (plate 21a) grips a carved cast swinging buckle hinged between its teeth. The other side of the buckle attaches to a tapered snake-like zoomorphic-style safety chain made of woven gilt wire, the head end of which grips the buckle between its teeth (plate 21b). The head of the creature is similar to the dragon head that Cernunnos carries in his left hand in the Gundestrup Cauldron [c. 100 BC] (figure 22). The buckle itself sports two tiny black glass human heads, vertically mirror imaged (plate 21d). Two entwined vulture heads hang over the centre of the ring (plate 21e and plate 22f). Two more heads project from either side of the main ring (plate 21i and j). The heads at first appear to be dragon-like but the associated long neck is smooth, without scales, more like the neck and head of a bird, perhaps a pelican. In any event they are 'feathered snakes'; another pair, without the neck loop (plate 22d), are seen entwined on the lower ring.

The lower part of the wedge-shaped brooch pin is decorated with the head and face of a stag with stylised antlers (plates 20a and 22j) comprising several engraved panels, each separated with stones of different shape, style and colour.

Clearly, the brooch has many spiritual associations: the appearance of the stag's head has much in common with Cernunnos, the Celtic god known to have been worshipped in around 100 BC who is associated with Christ: the dragon-like safety chain again associates the piece with Cernunnos and the feathered snake (part bird, part snake and part stag). And the brooch has astronomical associations: the two tiny black mirror-imaged glass heads on the buckle, with the twins of Venus; the vulture heads, with those of Tutankhamun (who was also known as the feathered snake, the 'Son of God' who carried the vulture on his forehead); and the dragon/pelican heads (if that is what they are) with the feathered snake and the constellation of Orion [in Peru] and resurrection.

Indeed, closer examination of the main-ring dragon heads (plates 21a and 21f) shows them to be identical to a pair (plate 21g) found on the jade headrest of Prince Liu Sheng, the nephew of Ch'in Shi Huangdi (the Son of Heaven, whose insignia was the dragon), the first emperor of China. The hole at the top of the jade burial suit allowed for the release of the Soul.

In *The Terracotta Warriors* I showed how the arrangements of jade platelets in the spherical headgear concealed the super-science of the Sun (figure 44). Here again, in the Tara brooch, a baby dragon head looks out from either side of a circular ring, suggesting that the Tara brooch might likewise conceal astronomical information beyond the obvious already mentioned.

With this in mind the brooch can be examined in greater detail (plate 22). The central ring (plate 22a) represents the Sun. Mercury, the closest planet to the Sun, can be seen closest to the solar equator. Moving outwards, away from the Sun, the next to appear is Venus, in

Jade Headgear of Prince Liu Sheng

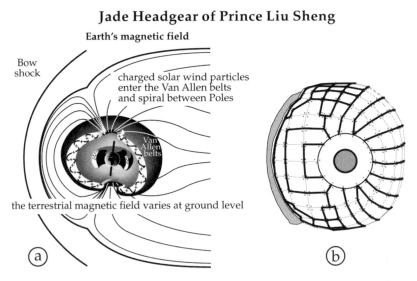

Earth's magnetic field

Bow shock

charged solar wind particles enter the Van Allen belts and spiral between Poles

Van Allen belts

the terrestrial magnetic field varies at ground level

(a) (b)

Figure 44. (a) Schematic of the Earth's magnetosphere compressed on the sunward side by the solar wind corresponds with (b) lines on the head of the jade suit, created by intersections between the jade platelets. The circular head rests on a jade pillow that carries two dragon heads, one either side of the circular head—and the jade head itself (the circle) contains the super-science of the Sun. In the same way, the Tara brooch carries a dragon head either side of the main ring (plate 22 [red])—indicating that the main ring, in some way, might likewise contain the super-science of the Sun.

its manifestation as the twin planet, a circle either side of Mercury on the solar equator. Moving out from Venus the Earth is shown as a blue *square*, as it is in China. The Moon can be seen below in its orbit around the Earth.

The looping dragon/pelican neck and heads (plate 22d—either side of the main ring) contain within them the manifestation of Venus in both of its emanations as the morning star and the evening star in the heavens (also shown inside boxes plate 22b and 22c) either side of [the main ring] the Sun.

A downward 'flapping-wings' symbol is created by three stones (shown in brown) beneath the entwined vulture heads (plate 22d). A similar symbolic flapping-wing arrangement appears above the lower pair of dragon/pelican heads (plate 22d), and both pairs are shown boxed in plate 22g, confirming that the juxtaposed creatures are indeed meant to be interpreted as birds (vultures and pelicans).

Altogether there are six [brown] wing shapes, two in each of the bird symbols and another two in the pin-end arrangement. There are also six blue square shapes and six circular green shapes (plate 22h), revealing the number 666.

Plate 22i and j show detail of the stag's head with a halo on the crown chakra, at the top of the head, and the arrangement of antlers, in brown.

Closer examination (plate 20a) shows that the centre pin contains end-stops that correspond to end-stops on the stag's head, inviting the observer to slide the pin around the ring in either direction until it comes up against an end-stop. There must be a reason for this because the pin would stop anyway, of its own accord, as it crashed into the ring. The end-stops, thus, at first appear unnecessary and surplus to requirements. But we have to remind ourselves that the ancients never did anything without a good reason. This amounts to an invitation to slide the pin around the ring and measure the angle between the pin end-stops.

Sliding the pin around the ring between the end-stops (plate 20a) reveals the angle of 144°, representing the esoteric number of 144,000, the number destined for Heaven, mentioned in Revelation.

That this abbreviated figure was intended to be conveyed and interpreted in this way is confirmed by measuring the angle between the antlers of the stag [Christ]. Plate 20c shows that the angle from the crown chakra (the pineal gland) of the antler arrangement to the vertical centre-line of the antler arrangement measures 14.4°. The antler appendages terminate in double zeros and in between these lies a semicircle (like the setting Sun) shared by both antlers. The antler arrangement thus yields 144,000, confirming the efficacy of measuring the angle between the pin end-stops.

Moreover, when the pin is swung backwards, to facilitate the measurement of the angle of 144° from each pin end-stop position, we notice that the pin (which resembles a sword, plate 20b) moves, naturally, *away* from the [largest] stone fixed either side of the brooch front. This means that—by removing the pin (the sword) from the stone—the angle of 144° can be measured or 'he who draws the sword from the stone—and understands what is happening—becomes one of the 144,000, destined to be a king in Heaven'.

This all sounds familiar. In the Arthurian legend, whoever 'pulled the sword from the stone would become a king on Earth'. Arthur pulled the sword from the stone and became a king on Earth 'who would live again' in Heaven. Which surely means that King Arthur must have decoded the Tara brooch in the same way. The information contained within the Tara brooch must be the foundation that supports the so-called myth contained in the Arthurian legend, which must actually be fact.

The rear of the brooch (plate 20b) is altogether more austere. Figure 45 enables analysis in greater detail. The four profile dragon heads (plate 21h) are on the obverse transformed into bony dragon skeleton heads, forming an immediate association with death. Two black semicircular stones, partially eclipsed by the main ring (figure 45a), show the rise and fall of Venus, but this time only as the 'black' *evening* star, emphasising darkness and death. The two large circular stones (figure 45b) are made of black glass, inlaid with 6 pieces of red glass [6, and again 6] and altogether there are 6 circular black stones (five circular + two semicircular), making 666 from the black circular stones on the obverse. The centre of each inlaid stone also embraces an equilateral triangle (666).

The flapping-wing bird indicators on the obverse this time appear only in black, referring to the bird of the night, the bat, and death. Venus appears yet again (figure 45c) in the ring panels (figure 45c) as two tiny white studs in a sea of Celtic swirling blackness.

The Tara Brooch (rear)

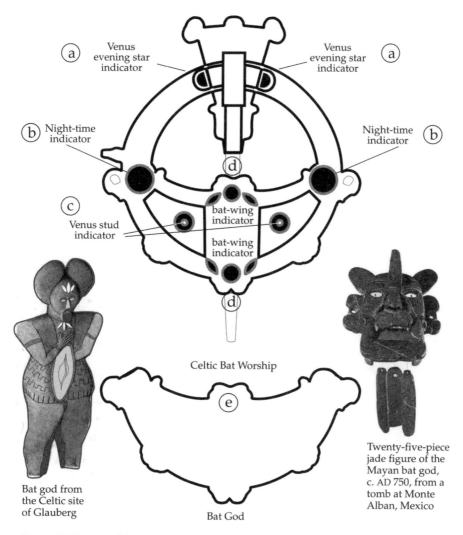

(a) Venus evening star indicator

(a) Venus evening star indicator

(b) Night-time indicator

(b) Night-time indicator

(c) Venus stud indicator

bat-wing indicator

bat-wing indicator

(d)

(d)

Bat god from the Celtic site of Glauberg

Celtic Bat Worship

(e)

Bat God

Twenty-five-piece jade figure of the Mayan bat god, c. AD 750, from a tomb at Monte Alban, Mexico

Figure 45. The rear of the Tara brooch is much more austere and sombre than the front. The four profile dragon heads on the front (plate 21h) become bony skeleton heads on the obverse, forming an immediate association with death. (a) The semicircular stones, either side of the pin, represent Venus rising and setting, but now only as the black evening star, in the darkness. The large black and red stones (b) likewise represent Venus as twin black planets and Venus appears yet again (c) as two tiny white studs in a sea of swirling blackness in the panels. (d) The brightly coloured flapping-wing indicators on the front now appear on the back in black, representing the wings of the bat, creature of the night, and (e) the outline of the entire brooch now becomes the outline of a bat, representing death. The Tara brooch thus represents light and life on the front and darkness and death on the back, revealing the choices between everlasting life, for those who understand the super-science of the Sun and the higher orders of spirituality, and death, for those who do not.

135

The Tara brooch thus represents light and life on the front, for those who understand the super-science of the Sun and the higher orders of spirituality, and darkness and death on the back, for those who do not, revealing the choices between everlasting life or death.

The Tara brooch is not the only large ring brooch; several others have been found in Ireland and Scotland, like the Roscrea brooch and the Loughmoe brooches of Tipperary, the Kilmainham brooch, the Ardagh hoard brooches, the Cadboll brooch and the Hunterston brooch of Scotland among them. But the Tara brooch is the largest, the most spectacular, the most beautiful, the most exquisite, the most ornate and the most sophisticated. It is the only one to carry pin end-stops, on the main pin and on the ring, that are capable of making contact with each other. It is the only one to contain the super-science of the Sun and the higher orders of spirituality; it is the only one to feature a stag, a dragon, a snake and a torc (plate 22k), and it is far too large and dangerous to have been worn as a brooch.

The Ardagh Hoard

The Ardagh hoard was found in September 1868 under a stone slab beneath a hawthorn tree in a disused earth-fort at Reerasta Rath (near Ardagh, County Limerick, Ireland) by Paddy Flanagan and Jimmy Quinn while digging potatoes for Jimmy's mother, who rented twenty acres of land from nuns who owned the site. The treasure had been deliberately hidden and concealed at some time in antiquity. It consisted of a magnificent chalice that has since become known as the Ardagh Chalice (plate 23), a smaller undecorated simple copper-alloy chalice and four silver brooches, all said to date, by their style, from around AD 750 for the Ardagh Chalice and to around AD 950 for the brooches.

Two things become clear on inspection of the Ardagh hoard. The Ardagh Chalice did not belong with the other items found; they had simply all been buried together. Secondly, archaeologists agree that whoever made the Ardagh Chalice *must have made the Tara brooch*, because the style, metalwork, design, craftsmanship and sophistication are unparalleled in Celtic artistic achievement elsewhere. This means that the Tara brooch and the Ardagh Chalice were once kept together and must have become separated.

A quick glance at the chalice is revealing:

- There are twelve stud mounts in the girdle that runs beneath the rim of the main bowl but only eleven studs, suggesting that one is missing. The eleven enamelled studs (plate 23a) are similar in style to the enamelled stud on the Basse Yutz flagons (plate 14), which archaeologists date around 400 BC.
- The name of an Apostle has been crudely engraved—as though with the tip of a large nail—beneath each of the stud mounts, a strange thing to do given the quality of workmanship in the rest of the piece.
- The name of Judas Iscariot, who betrayed Jesus, is missing.
- The name of Mathius, who replaced Judas, is also missing.
- The name of St. Paul, who was not at the Last Supper, appears as one of the twelve names.
- The dating of the chalice was agreed at around AD 750 because the style is identical to the Tara brooch and because the names of the Apostles have been carved in insular majuscule script, the very same script used in the Lindisfarne Gospels (plate 16)—meaning, say archaeologists, that the chalice *must* date from the same period (AD 698). [But this need not be the case, as we shall see].

And the chalice, like the Tara brooch, contains an unusually large amount of esoteric information:

- Two large solar crosses dominate the main bowl—immediately associating the piece with the super-science of the Sun.
- The pattern of name carving continues around the chalice, running into a Celtic knot-work continuous-line pattern beneath each solar cross and onwards, to carvings of two dragon heads, one either side of the chalice beneath each of the handle escutcheons—and the dragon represents the feathered snake, a Supergod.
- An unusual interlaced maze-like pattern [identical to one found on the Hallsatt scabbard (figure 4)—dating back to 600 BC—and identical to another, one that circumscribes the head of Viracocha (figure A6f)—dating back to AD 500] circumscribes the base of the chalice.
- Beneath the base a large quartz crystal (which, as we shall see later,

is synonymous with light) dominates the design and sits underneath, in the dark.

- Decorative glass studs in the foot of the chalice are arranged as a pentagon and an octagon—known Freemason symbols.

We know that the Tara brooch is intimately associated with the Arthurian legend. We know that the Arthurian legend is associated with the Holy Grail, used by Christ at the Last Supper. And we know that the Tara brooch and the Ardagh Chalice were once kept together.

Take another look at the Grail legend illustration, plate 19:

- In the illustration King Arthur pulls the sword from the stone, at the same time as he worships the Holy Grail at the Round Table—the illustration shows them together, in the same place at the same time.
- In the illustration the Grail radiates light—and the Ardagh Chalice (as we shall see shortly) radiates light (from the quartz crystal in the foot-cone).
- In the illustration the Grail is flanked by two dragon-angels and two dragons are engraved on the chalice, either side of the main bowl.

And the names of the Apostles, the followers of Christ, are engraved around the bowl. Surely, the inference is obvious. The so-called Ardagh Chalice *must* be the Holy Grail used by Christ at the Last Supper.

We need to examine the chalice carefully, to confirm the hypothesis.

CHAPTER FIVE

The Holy Grail

The Ardagh Chalice

It seems that Paddy Flanagan found the Ardagh hoard but Jimmy Quinn wanted to take all of the credit for the discovery. The dispute caused the two to fall out, forcing Paddy Flanagan to quit Mrs Quinn's employment. Soon after, he died, impoverished, and was laid to rest in a pauper's grave in Newcastlewest. Jimmy Quinn fared no better; he died after emigrating to Australia, where he was buried. Mrs Quinn sold the hoard to the bishop of Limerick, Dr Butler, for fifty pounds. Butler examined the chalice with the antiquarian Lord Dunraven before selling it to the Royal Irish Academy for £500 in 1873.

More than a hundred years later, the Irish Academy published *The Treasures of Ireland* and noted:

> The Chalice . . . is . . . a form well known from Byzantine silver hoards . . . it is inspired by eastern Mediterranean prototypes . . . the ultimate La Tène style [La Tène III, 150–50 BC] is well represented. (*The Treasures of Ireland*, p. 124, Royal Irish Academy, 1983)

And, according to *The Treasures of the National Museum of Ireland*:

> The Ardagh Chalice is quite unlike other European chalices of the early mediaeval period . . . its closest companions are in fact, to be found among Byzantine chalices of the Eastern Church. (*The Treasures of the National Museum of Ireland*, p. 178, Gill and Macmillan, 2002)

The Irish claim jurisdiction for the writing of the Book of Kells, although the consensus today prefers that it was written at Iona. It is understandable that they should want to claim jurisdiction over the manufacture of the chalice, given its beauty, the quality and the craftsmanship evident in the piece. And, after all, the experts say, the carving of the names of the Apostles uses the very same insular majuscule script found in the Lindisfarne Gospels, which means that it *must* date to AD 698. Of course, they have no idea that the person who engraved it was different from the one who manufactured it. And they have no idea that the appearance of the chalice inspired a whole new generation of inferior look-alikes. So there's no harm in describing the chalice as it actually appears; they have nothing to lose, because it *has to* date to AD 698. It's easy to see why they believe what they want to, despite the evidence:

- The La Tène style [150 BC–50 BC] is well represented; in other words, it seems to date from around 150–50 BC.
- It is influenced by the Byzantine style [AD 350+]—which itself was influenced by the earlier La Tène style [150–50 BC].
- It is inspired by eastern Mediterranean prototypes, meaning that it was probably made in the eastern Mediterranean.
- It is quite unlike other European chalices of the early mediaeval period, meaning that it is unlikely to be European.

Whether the Irish will prefer to deny that they now hold the Holy Grail, the most precious, the most treasured, the most sought-after liturgical relic of the Christian Church, in their own collection at the National Museum of Ireland, remains to be seen.

Construction of the Grail

The Irish Academy passed the chalice to a jeweller named Johnson, who took it apart for cleaning and re-examination. Johnson's findings were incorporated into a report, written by Dunraven in the 1874 *Transactions of the Irish Academy*. The two investigators reached the conclusion that there are 354 separate parts to the chalice and that the bowl, stem and foot-cone were held together by a single iron bolt attached to the bowl.

The last Druidic calendar known to have been used (chapter 1) is the one found at Coligny near Bourg-en-Bresse in France dating from the reign of Augustus (63 BC–AD 14). That was the last time, as far as we know, that the Druidic year of 354 days was used (although it might have been used by the Druids who defied the Romans at Ybys Mon until as late as AD 70). If the chalice was made by Christian monks during the Lindisfarne period, as archaeologists suppose, then why encode the ancient calendar of pagan Druids into the arrangement? Why not encode the 365.25-day figure used by the Lindisfarne monks at the time?

In 1961 the chalice had become loose at the stem and was sent to the research laboratory at the British Museum, in London, for repair and restoration. The anticipated restoration encountered many problems, not least of which was the re-organisation of the British Museum, which entailed shifting departments between different buildings during the period the chalice was there, and the whole job took much longer than expected. At one point it was hurriedly re-assembled, placed in an exhibition, in 1962, and then taken apart again for the restoration job to continue.

In 1970 the Museum of Fine Arts, in Boston—intending to demonstrate how modern scientific techniques could be used to study ancient archaeological artefacts—scoured museum inventories around the world for a suitable example to investigate. As fate would have it, they chose the Ardagh Chalice and in 1970 produced a paper called *Application of Science in Examination of Works of Art*, edited by William J. Young.

The objectives of the scientific investigation were, firstly, to find a way of permanently re-securing the loose neck (also referred to as the 'stem'); secondly, to check Dunraven's account for reliability and to confirm his finding that 'a square iron bolt' held the bowl, stem and foot-cone together; and, thirdly, to determine the nature of the various materials employed. The final objective was to collate results into a published format. As much evidence as possible was to be recorded photographically and by scaled drawings, whether it was currently understood or not, to facilitate future investigation.

It was agreed that the investigation would progress through various stages: the study and documentation of the chalice as it was received; disassembly of the chalice and the measurement, recording and cleaning of individual components; assimilation of observations and resulting deductions; hypothecation, in regard to a theory to adequately explain the chalice and re-assembly and, finally, re-examination of the entire piece to confirm the theory.

The methods used to study the chalice included observation, through touch; measurement by a scale, callipers, slide gauge, micrometer, micrometer eyepiece (in a microscope) and travelling microscope; direct visual observation and microscope-assisted observation through air, oil films and immersion in liquids. Indirect observations using moulds, wax impressions, silhouettes, shadows cast by straight-edges and by grids of lines. Detailed comparisons were made visually by superimposition of negative images from one component on positive images of another component or by use of a synchrisiscope—an instrument used by ballistic experts for comparing marks on bullets. Non-destructive tests were carried out to determine metallic content and hardness; observations were made on naturally etched surfaces, and on prepared and polished surfaces; and samples were analysed using X-ray diffraction analysis and spectrography (the analysis of light emitted from a source). The recording of details was made primarily by photography, using varying types of light, backgrounds and cameras and a Vickers projection microscope, viewing objects directly and also indirectly through mirrors.

General Description

The entire piece (plate 23a) stands 178 mm (7 inches) high and measures 185 mm (7.3 inches) wide across the outer diameter of the bowl (figure 46). Two handles, fixed on opposite sides of the bowl, increase the outer width to 230 mm (9 inches)—[scaled on the computer from height and width measurements supplied].

The assembly brings together the main silver bowl that carries the [damaged] split-pin fastening bolt (figure 46). The bolt passes through the centre of a stem assembly made of three highly decorated gold-plated bronze pieces consisting of a tubular stem with a concave washer-type interface collar that cradles the bowl above and an identical convex washer-type interface collar that sits on the foot-cone below (shaded in grey in the figure 46 cross-section box).

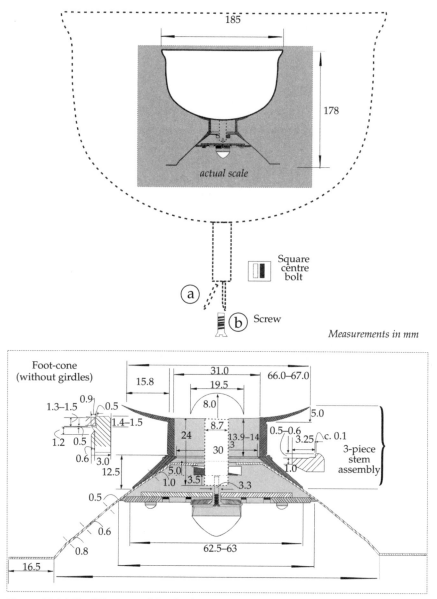

185

178

actual scale

Square
centre
bolt

(a)

(b) Screw

Measurements in mm

Foot-cone
(without girdles)

31.0
15.8
19.5
66.0–67.0
8.0
1.3–1.5
0.9
0.5
1.4–1.5
8.7
5.0
1.2
0.5
24
13.9–14
0.5–0.6
c. 0.1
3.25
3-piece
stem
assembly
0.6
3.0
30
1.0
12.5
5.0
1.0
13.5
3.3
0.5
62.5–63
0.6
0.8
16.5

Figure 46. (a) The 354 pieces of the Grail are held together by a square bolt fashioned into a split-pin beneath the base of the bowl—the legs of which were originally spread apart to hold the assembly together. The damaged pin had been modified in the nineteenth century by the jeweller Johnson, and again, in 1962, by the British Museum, who repaired the worn-out fixing by fitting a screw (b) into the square bolt that carried the pin. The assembled chalice thus relies entirely upon the integrity of the square bolt. The square represents virtue and knowledge for the esotericist.

The Secrets of the Foot-Cone

The foot-cone is described as subconical, meaning that it is cone-shaped to a certain degree but becomes more rounded as it progresses to the cone tip, terminating in the shape of a Gothic arch. It has a foot flange that is sandwiched between two similar rings (figure 47), the so-called upper foot girdle and the lower foot girdle.

The upper foot girdle (figure 47)—the one visible when viewed from above—originally carried eight miniature decorated panels that fit into dedicated slots in the ring. Four of the original eight are missing. The remaining four are made of gold-plated cast bronze, patterned with sharply angular [zigzag] interlaced knot-work. Originally eight almost-square blue glass studs were distributed around the ring in dedicated slots so as to form an octagonal shape. One of the studs is now missing and another damaged. The mass of each stud consists of blue glass. Two are patterned, in the centre, with a red cross surrounded by a yellow L-shape in each of the four corners [such that pairs of L-shapes form brackets around the central cross] and two have the colour scheme reversed.

The lower foot girdle can only be seen when the foot-cone is viewed from below. It is similar in style and construction to the one above; however, the decorative panels differ in decoration and material: four of the eight decorative panels carry the looping knot-work pattern, shown in figure 50b [also found in the bowl girdle] and are made from silver. Another two, made from copper, carry swastika patterns, representing the solar wind as seen from Earth (more on these later).

The Secrets of the Mesh-mat Panels

The remaining two panels are each made from a mesh-mat of very fine wire, one of bronze and the other one of silver. Both are described as 'woven' but appear to have been hand-knitted. Each row contains eight stitches and connects to the next row by a ninth. Figure 48 shows that the pattern is constructed using an equilateral triangle and a semicircle. The secrets in the mesh reveal that the soul and body are knitted together, as one, during a lifetime on Earth—by God (99999).

One of the stones in the lower foot-cone girdle is missing and another damaged.

Upper Foot Girdle: Stone and Panel Mounting

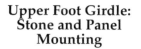

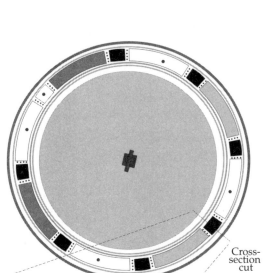

Figure 47. Foot-cone, inside the upper foot girdle, seen from above without the bowl (after re-assembly following restoration). Four decorative panels (here shown simplified in shades of grey) are missing (indicated by the empty circular rivet holes). One stone is missing and one damaged. The square bolt-hole was modified with a cut into the foot-cone, by the jeweller Johnson, in an attempt to tighten the complete assembly with a keyed interface.

Cross-section cut

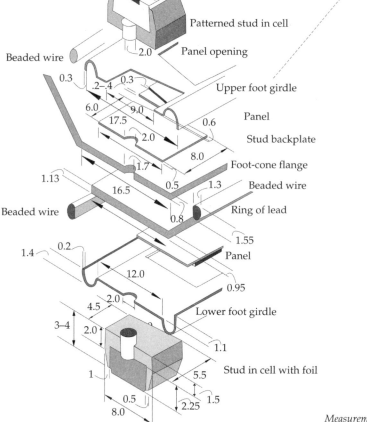

Patterned stud in cell

Beaded wire

2.0 — Panel opening

0.3

.2–.4   0.3

Upper foot girdle

6.0   9.0

17.5   Panel

2.0   0.6

Stud backplate

8.0   Foot-cone flange

1.7

1.13

16.5   0.5   1.3   Beaded wire

Beaded wire

0.8   Ring of lead

1.55

0.2   Panel

1.4

12.0

0.95

2.0

4.5   Lower foot girdle

3–4   2.0

1.1

1   5.5   Stud in cell with foil

0.5   1.5

8.0   2.25

Measurements in mm

145

The Secrets in the Mesh

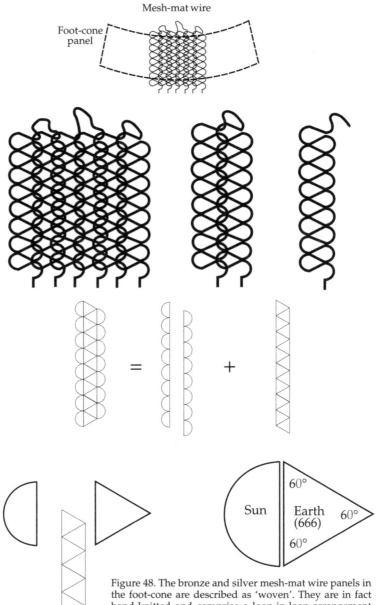

Figure 48. The bronze and silver mesh-mat wire panels in the foot-cone are described as 'woven'. They are in fact hand-knitted and comprise a loop-in-loop arrangement that is itself constructed of an equilateral triangle and a semicircle. The entire pattern thus owes its livelihood to the Sun (999) and the Earth (666) [the soul and the body]. The secrets in the mesh reveal that the soul and the body are knitted together, as one, during a lifetime on Earth.

The fastening bolt turned out to be made of copper, not iron [as claimed by Dunraven], and fixed to the inside of the bowl by a rounded head. It seems that, originally, the copper bolt terminated with a split pin, the legs of which were spread apart beneath the quartz crystal mount to fasten the bowl to the foot-cone. One of the legs of the pin (figure 46a) is now missing. In 1962 the British Museum modified the connecting mechanism by drilling and tapping the central bolt to take a screw to replace the damaged split-pin retention mechanism (figure 46).

The end of the assembled fixing is concealed by another highly decorated gold-plated bronze washer-type interface in the centre of which sits an enormous subconical quartz crystal surrounded by five tiny semispherical studs arranged as a pentagon.

Quartz is intimately associated with light (electromagnetic energy—God). When it is mechanically stressed it generates an electric voltage. Conversely, when a voltage is applied across the crystal it vibrates at a frequency determined by the cut of the crystal. Moreover, when visible light (electromagnetic energy) is passed through quartz, the electrical component of the electromagnetic wave is twisted by 45° towards the magnetic end of the spectrum. We know that magnetic fields affect the manufacture of the timing hormone melatonin, which affects the consequential production of the follicle-stimulating and luteinising hormones in females. These in turn regulate the production of the fertility hormones oestrogen and progesterone and hence fertility in females. Quartz is thus synonymous with light and the twenty-eight-day spinning Sun that regulates fertility in females.

All five tiny semispherical studs were originally patterned with beaded wire but now only two undamaged ones retain the microscopic patterns. They are made primarily of blue glass, enamelled using the champlevé technique found on the other studs but on a much smaller scale.

The five circular blue spherical stones, laid out as a *pentagon* around the central quartz crystal, and the eight square stones, laid out as an *octagon* around the lower foot girdle (figure 49), enable the calculation of the 11.49-year, the 187-year and the 18,139-year solar magnetic cycles (described in appendix 4).

The Secrets of the Bowl and the Bowl Girdle

The bowl and foot-cone are made of beaten lathe-polished silver and the two handles from cast silver are attached to the bowl just above what is described as, on each side, an escutcheon plate [because it resembles a shield with a coat of arms]. To soften the lip of the bowl a gold-plated brass moulded ring is attached to the rim of the bowl.

Two large solar crosses, one either side of the bowl (figure 49), in between the handles, dominate the main bowl decoration. The solar cross describes the magnetic structure of the Sun and is found only in the halo of Christ (figures 2d and e), associating the cup with Christ. The outline of each cross and the compartments within each cross are made from square (viewed in cross-section) silver wire, representing the silver cord or cable tow, which is associated with the soul, discussed earlier. Each aperture of the pattern is decorated with various scroll and double-scroll patterns from beaded wire and then the whole of each aperture has been gold-plated. Four tiny semispherical glass

Foot-cone Sacred Geometry

Figure 49. The eight almost-square blue glass studs, in the lower foot girdle, and the five circular blue studs surrounding the central mount make the geometric shapes of an octagon and a pentagon that together can be used be used to track the 11.49-year, the 187-year and the 18,139-year solar magnetic cycles (see appendix 4).

studs are set into silver-wire mounts spaced at 90° intervals—two blue glass studs and two red ones made of wax—that Dunraven originally described as being made of amber. The four studs hide rivets that attach each solar cross to the bowl.

The bowl girdle, like the foot-cone girdles, is cut with apertures, this time to accommodate twelve enamel stud mounts (figure 50) and ten decorative panels fabricated in the same way: each is made from a thin plate of gold that has been embossed with a pattern. The background of the pattern has then been cut away to provide openwork. Next, a treble layer of beaded wire was soldered on to the pattern ridges and then a copper plate fixed behind each panel, effectively blocking up the holes in the openwork panel. The patterns on the panels vary. Two of the plate patterns are described as ornithomorphic, type-A (figure 50); four carry variations of the knot-work pattern, type-B; and the remaining four panels, described as zoomorphic, type-C (plate 23b), are decorated with a highly complex pattern of interlaced animal, bird and serpent designs that proved, here—along with type-A—far too complex and difficult to sketch. There are no decorative girdle panels beneath the handles.

The ten badly fitting panels were mixed up each time the chalice was restored such that the correct manner of assembly is not known. Archaeologists eventually settled on the arrangement in figure 50a. They also numbered the bowl girdle studs from 1 to 6, from the split in the ring under one of the handles to the front (on the left-hand side) and again from the split in the ring to the front (on the right-hand side). The anachronistic panel arrangement draws attention to the missing panels beneath the handles, the first panel and the last panel; Jesus was the first and the last, the Alpha and the Omega. Jesus thus appears either side of each solar cross (the Sun) on the bowl, as Venus appears either side of the Sun, again specifically associating the design of the cup with Jesus.

The bowl girdle studs (figure 51) are of the low-profile, gently rounded, segmented-arch shape, made of bronze wire in-filled with glass enamel, champlevé style, like the Basse Yutz stud (c. 400 BC), patterned variously with different coloured glass. From visual and photographic inspection one of the studs is clearly missing from a mount adjacent to one of the handles, although this is not mentioned in the

The Mystery of the Mixed-up Bowl Girdle Panels

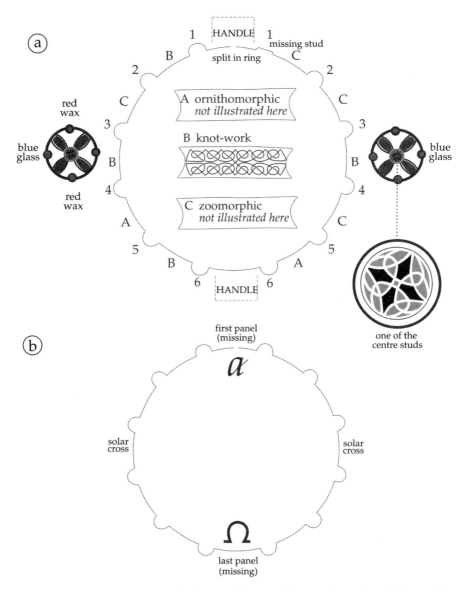

Figure 50. There are ten panels in the bowl girdle: two of the ornithomorphic (A), four of the knotwork (B) and four of the zoomorphic (C) [there are no panels beneath the handles]. The ten badly fitting panels were mixed up each time the chalice was restored such that the correct manner of assembly is not known. Archaeologists settled upon the arrangement in (a) above. They also numbered the studs as shown, from the split in the ring to the front. (b) The anachronistic panel arrangement draws attention to the missing panels, the first and the last. Jesus was the first and the last, the Alpha and the Omega: 'I am the Alpha and the Omega, the beginning and the end, the first and the last', Revelation, XXII, 13. Jesus thus appears either side of each solar cross on the bowl, as Venus: 'I Jesus have sent my angel to testify unto you these things in the churches. I am the root and the offspring of David and the bright and morning star'. Revelation XXII, 16

Bowl Girdle Stud Mounting

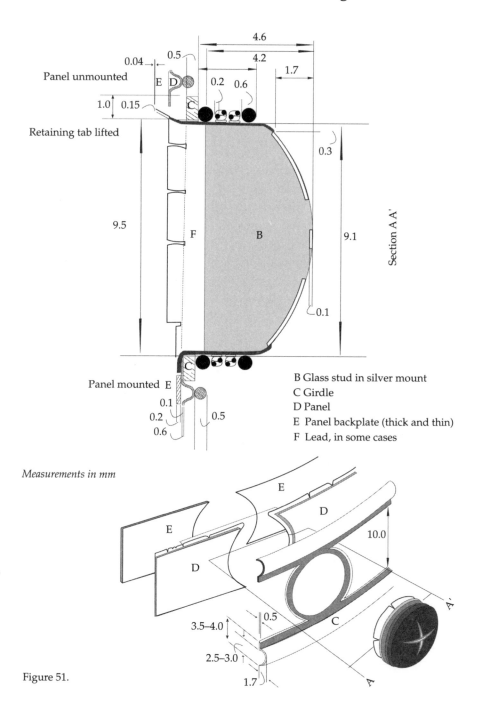

Panel unmounted

0.04

0.5

4.6

4.2

1.7

E D

0.2 0.6

1.0 0.15

C

Retaining tab lifted

0.3

9.5

F

B

9.1

Section A A'

0.1

C

Panel mounted E

0.1

0.2

0.5

0.6

B Glass stud in silver mount
C Girdle
D Panel
E Panel backplate (thick and thin)
F Lead, in some cases

Measurements in mm

E

E

D

D

10.0

0.5

3.5–4.0

2.5–3.0

C

A'

1.7

A

Figure 51.

1970 report. The stud is also seen to have been missing from the earliest known photograph of the chalice, taken by Margaret Stokes, who drew the illustrations for the Dunraven report in 1874. There is no evidence to suggest that this missing stud was ever fitted.

The Meaning of the Missing Stud

The missing stud raises a question: were there meant to be eleven studs in the bowl girdle or twelve? The total number of pieces had already been established as 354 (representing the 354-day Druidic calendar). These two new numbers of 11 and 12 become significant when considering the length of the solar year: $354 + 11 = 365$ and $354 + 12 = 366$. There are either 365 days in a solar year or 366, in a solar leap year, confirming that the 354 pieces must refer to the number of days in a year—and that the cup must have been made by Celts around the time of Christ. It also confirms that one of the twelve rim studs was deliberately left out, in common with the practise used by ancient civilizations, to draw attention to encoded information and also to prophesy the betrayal of Jesus by Judas Iscariot.

The Mystery of the Script

Below each of the studs is carved the name of one of the twelve Apostles. As noted earlier, the names are written in insular majuscule script, persuading experts that the cup was engraved by monks at Lindisfarne. But the names of the Apostles in the Lindisfarne Gospels are written in Latinised Greek whereas on the chalice they appear in Latin. Lindisfarne was established by the Irish monk St Aidan, who, like St Patrick, preferred not to speak Latin [Patrick preferred his Celtic Mayo-Irish]. If the chalice was engraved by the monks of Lindisfarne, why did they not use the same language and convention on the chalice as they used in the Lindisfarne Gospels? Why use Latin on the cup and Latinised Greek in the Lindisfarne Gospels?

The Mystery of the Names

The twelve names as they appear on the bowl also raise questions. The name of Judas Iscariot, the so-called Disciple who betrayed Jesus, is missing, which is understandable. But the name of the Apostle who replaced him, Mathius, is not included. If the monks of Lindisfarne had engraved the cup, they would have known that Mathius had replaced Judas—given that the Lindisfarne Gospels are based on the Latin Vulgate version of the Bible which contains the Acts of the Apostles naming Mathius as the replacement. Instead, the twelfth name on the chalice is that of St. Paul, the one-time Roman Saul, who preached around the Mediterranean during Roman times. The earliest known version of the New Testament comes from the early *Peshitto* manuscript precisely dated as being written in AD 464, after the death of King Arthur. King Arthur, therefore, who died in around AD 450, would not have known that Mathius had replaced Judas. Arthur, however, having lived through the Roman occupation of Britain, would have been aware of the works of St. Paul—the favourite of the Romans after the time of Constantine—and therefore would more likely have believed that the popular Paul had taken the role of the twelfth Apostle.

The Mystery of the Grammar

A linguistic scholar has pointed out that the names contain grammatical errors: ten names appear in the possessive sense but two—the Latin versions of Tatheus and Simon—appear in the nominative. St. Aidan may not have favoured Latin but he was a scholar, as the Lindisfarne Gospels testify. It is unlikely therefore that educated clerics engraved the chalice. If clerics did not engrave the chalice, then who did?

The Secrets of the Carving

The incorrect names of the Apostles support the view that it was Arthur in AD 453 who incorrectly carved the name of Paul on the chalice and not clerics in AD 698.

Arthur would also have had no axe to grind over the use of Latin, unlike the monks, who were at loggerheads with Rome over the dating of Easter and the structure of the Church. He was no educated scholar and therefore more likely to make grammatical errors.

And the carving of the names on the cup is rough and crude (plate 23b) as though it has been done with the end of nail—an instrument intimately associated with the Crucifixion of Christ. It is patently clear that whoever carved the cup wished to convey the fact that they did not possess the skill of whoever manufactured it. But whoever it was, they knew it was the Holy Grail and engraved it to let others know.

The Secrets of the Dragons

The engraving has more to say; it continues in loops around the solar crosses and beneath the handle escutcheons taking the shape of two conjoined dragon heads (figure 52). This 'mark of the Grail'—two anthropomorphic dragon-angels—also appears either side of the Grail shown in the fifteenth-century manuscript (plate 19). Two dragon heads are known, from archaeological evidence, to represent Christ and the Crucifixion, further supporting the association of the chalice with the event. Figure 53 shows an example of a tau cross featuring a scene of the Crucifixion with Christ on the cross together with Mary and St John inside a solar cross envelope inside the conjoined belly of two dragons.

Following the Crucifixion, the Greek letter *t*, or tau, was associated with the cross. The dragons represent sacrifice, after the ancient custom of Silene where the firstborn of every family was (legend has it) sacrificed to a dragon that lived in a swamp. Jesus was, likewise, sacrificed on the cross.

Figure 54a shows another example of a tau cross, this time with Mary and the baby Jesus inside the circular Sun, which carries magnetic loops around the perimeter, again inside the belly of two conjoined dragons. Venus appears either side of the Sun, as a small white circular stud. Figure 54b shows the lid of Lord Pacal at Palenque and figure 54c shows a detailed section of the lid featuring a tau cross, meaning that Lord Pacal is also associated with the tau cross and the Crucifixion of Jesus.

The Secret of the Conjoined Dragons (I)

Tau cross dragon heads

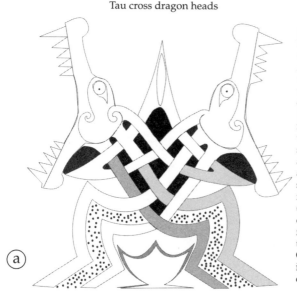

Figure 52. The poor-quality, hand-sketched engraving, detailing the names of the Apostles, continues around the chalice and terminates with a picture of two conjoined dragon heads [shown upside down in this illustration] beneath each of the handle escutcheons. A similar depiction [of two anthropomorphic dragon-angels] also appears either side of the Grail shown in the fifteenth-century manuscript (plate 19). Moreover, two dragon heads are known, from archaeological evidence, to represent Christ and the Crucifixion, further support-ing the association of the chalice with the event.

Tau cross (showing dragon heads)

Figure 53. Tau cross, showing a scene of the Crucifixion with Christ on the cross together with Mary and St John inside a solar-cross envelope, all inside the conjoined belly of two dragons (from a Greek ivory staff, Tarascon, eighteenth century). Following the Crucifixion, the Greek letter *t*, or tau, was associated with the cross. The dragons represent sacrifice, after the ancient custom of Silene where the firstborn of every family was (legend has it) sacrificed to a dragon that lived in a swamp. Hence the association with Jesus who was, likewise, sacrificed on the cross. The staff carried by the time-travelling magician Merlin [counsellor and spiritual guide of King Arthur] was crowned with a Tau cross identical to this one. Merlin was hence aware of the meaning of the Tau cross and its association with Christ and must have, therefore, instructed Arthur to carve the dragons on the Holy Grail to authenticate its provenance.

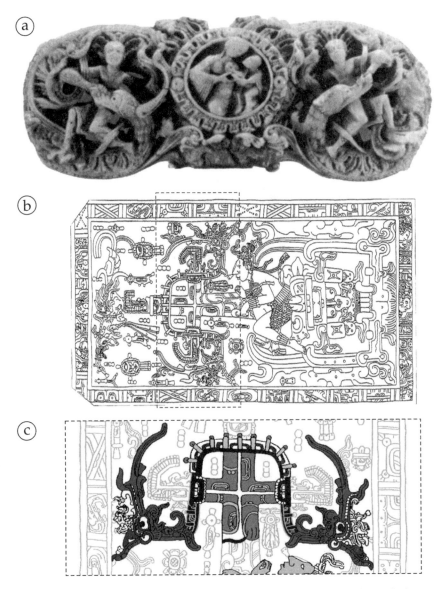

Figure 54. (a) Tau cross, showing Mary with the Christ child inside the Sun, which carries magnetic loops around the perimeter, inside the belly of two conjoined dragons (Walrus-ivory, English, mid-twelfth century). Venus appears either side of the Sun, as a small white circular stud. (b) The Lid of Palenque, the 5-tonne (4.92-ton) limestone lid that covers the sarcophagus of Lord Pacal in his tomb at Palenque. (c) Detail from the lid showing a tau cross, meaning that Lord Pacal was also associated with the tau cross and the Crucifixion of Jesus. The centre cross is covered in magnetic loops, sunspot loops, suggesting that Lord Pacal, like Jesus, was the Sun on Earth.

According to Malory, the staff carried by the time-travelling magician Merlin was crowned with a tau cross identical to the one in figure 53. Merlin was hence aware of the meaning of the tau cross and its association with Christ and must have therefore instructed Arthur to carve the dragons on the Holy Grail to authenticate its provenance.

No one but Arthur or his knights would have engraved two conjoined dragons on the chalice to acknowledge the Crucifixion of Jesus and celebrate the cup's discovery because no one but Arthur or his knights have been featured worshipping the Grail flanked by two dragons. And no one but Arthur or his knights have been featured at the Round Table worshipping the Grail *radiating light*—from the quartz crystal in the foot-cone.

The Secrets of the Chalice Engraving

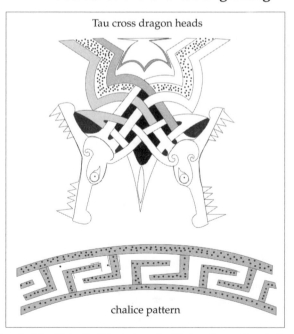

Tau cross dragon heads

chalice pattern

Figure 55. The bowl of the Holy Grail is engraved with two dragon heads, beneath each of the handle escutcheons. The foot-cone is engraved with a maze-like pattern, identical to one found on the Viracocha vase of Tiahuanaco.

The Secrets of the Maze-like Pattern

Another engraving, in the same style as the rest, circumscribes the upper foot-cone, just beneath the dragon heads. By now the reader will be familiar with the pattern. It is the same pattern which is carved on the Hallstatt scabbard (figure 4, alongside the twins [Venus—Jesus] and the reverse swastika of the Hallstatt Celts of 600 BC). It is also the same pattern worn by Viracocha, on his tunic, on the Viracocha vase of Tiahuanaco (figure 56). The vase dates from around AD 500 and was found at the site of Tiahuanaco, on the shore of Lake Titicaca, in today's Bolivia. The pattern therefore must have been in use during the intervening period [between 600 BC and AD 500], around AD 26, the time of the Crucifixion.

As discussed earlier, the sun shield of Monte Alban transformer (plate 2) contains secret pictures of the Gateway of the Sun at Tiahuanaco inside the Star of David, the geometric symbol of Judaism. The bas-relief carving of Viracocha from the lintel of the gateway also carries the same maze-like pattern in the ring around his head. And the sun shield (plate 3c) shows a picture of Lord Pacal regurgitating a

The Viracocha Vase of Tiahuanaco

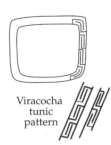

Viracocha
tunic
pattern

Figure 56. The Viracocha vase of Tiahuanaco, Lake Titicaca, ancient Peru, featuring the Sun God Viracocha. The pattern on his tunic is identical to the one on the Grail (see figures 57–59 for analysis).

pearl inside a vesica pisces, the geometric symbol of Christianity. And consider a passage from Revelation in the Bible:

> I saw an angel come down from Heaven . . . and a rainbow was on his head and his face was, as it were, the Sun . . . and he set his right foot upon the sea and his left foot upon the earth. (*Revelation* X)

In isolation, it may seem as though St John was suffering delusions as he wrote Revelation on the island of Patmos in the Mediterranean, at least until we compare the words from Revelation to plate 5e, which shows a reconstruction of Viracocha Pachacamac [from the Museum of Archaeology in Lima, Peru] made by archaeologists using treasures found in his tomb at Sipan. It shows an angel (with a golden halo above his head) with a rainbow on his head and the Sun, as it were [a gold bat mask], across his face. His name is Viracocha, foam of the sea, who would, as his name suggests, stand with one foot in the sand and the other in the sea.

The pattern that circumscribes the foot-cone of the chalice, the sun shield of Monte Alban and the pattern from Viracocha's tunic on the Viracocha vase all reveal that Jesus the Jew reincarnated as Viracocha and that Viracocha reincarnated as Lord Pacal.

Decoding the Maze-like Pattern

The first thing we notice about the maze-like pattern on the tunic of Viracocha is that it is tilted by 23.5° to the vertical (figure 57ai), the same angle as the tilt of the Earth on its axis. Appendix 1 shows that the Viracocha bas-relief found on the lintel of the Gateway of the Sun is actually a Mayan transformer that tells an account of how the Earth has been destroyed on four previous occasions by solar-inspired magnetic reversals that caused the Earth to tilt on its axis. The decoding of the Viracocha transformer also confirms that the same person who encoded information into the Amazing Lid of Palenque, and the sun shield of Monte Alban, used the same Mayan transformer technique to encode information into the Viracocha bas-relief at Tiahuanaco. Given that Viracocha lived in Peru in around AD 500 and that Lord Pacal lived in Mexico in around AD 750, it could hardly have been the same physical person (unless he lived for more than 250 years) and therefore the reincarnation hypothesis is the only one that fits. Viracocha, who used his transformer encoding technique on the bas-relief of the Gateway of the Sun (appendix 1), must have carried the technique to Mexico c. AD 750, in the guise of Lord Pacal.

The Viracocha tunic pattern will now facilitate decoding of the upper foot girdle engraving; figures 57bi and bii show the Viracocha pattern tilted counterclockwise by 23.5° to facilitate analysis. The first thing we notice is that pattern figure 57bi differs from the pattern in figure 57bii: they are mirror images.

Pattern figure 57bi can now be decoded by following the path through the maze-like pattern and, by using arrows, to show the route covered (figure 57c). The arrows reveal the number 666, the number of the beast from Revelation.

But a closer look at the chalice engraving shows that the pattern is identical to the mirror-image pattern, figure 58aii, which does not yield the number 6. Nor does it reveal the number 9, which is what you might expect the mirror image to produce. Viewing the chalice engraving from above (figure 59a) in fact reveals nothing of any numerical significance at all. At least it reveals nothing until we view the chalice maze-like engraving from beneath the foot-cone.

The Secrets of the Quartz Crystal

When we lift the chalice and view the *virtual* pattern, the numbers 99999 . . . now appear (figure 59b) [if it were possible to see through the metal] which tells us that the engraving is intended to be viewed from below, upwards towards Heaven. But it still comes as a surprise that when the pattern is viewed from above the 666 of the physical world does not appear. So, how can 666 be derived from the maze-like pattern around the foot-cone?

The only way to convert the number 666 into the number 999 using mirror imaging is shown in figure 59c. Firstly take the number 666. Then take the *horizontal* mirror image, as shown by the arrow. Then take the vertical mirror image of the result, again shown by an arrow. The same technique can again be used to convert 999 into 666, once again using arrows. What results is a rotating arrow network.

Decoding the Viracocha Pattern (I)

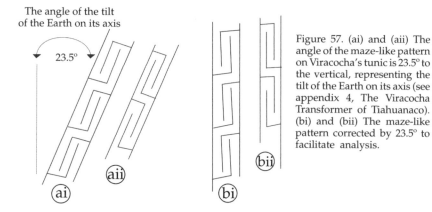

The angle of the tilt
of the Earth on its axis

23.5°

Figure 57. (ai) and (aii) The angle of the maze-like pattern on Viracocha's tunic is 23.5° to the vertical, representing the tilt of the Earth on its axis (see appendix 4, The Viracocha Transformer of Tiahuanaco). (bi) and (bii) The maze-like pattern corrected by 23.5° to facilitate analysis.

Decoding the Viracocha Pattern (II)

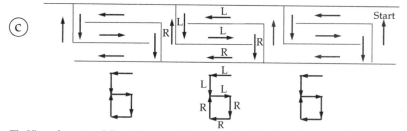

The Viracocha pattern (ai) contains secret information. To follow the path through the maze, the initiate must turn left, left, and then left again (L, L, L), then right, right and right (R, R, R) again. When this instruction is followed—and laid out using arrows (as shown)—the numbers 666 are revealed. The same number, associated with a dragon, is given in the Bible when describing a beast that rises from the sea . . .

> *. . . the dragon gave him his power and his seat and great authority . . . here is wisdom, let him that hath understanding count the number of the beast, for it is the number of a man, and his number is six hundred three score and six [666]. Revelation XIII, 1–18*

Decoding the Viracocha Pattern (III)

Figure 58. (ai) The Viracocha pattern translates into the numbers 666. However, (aii) shows that the adjacent pattern—the identical pattern to that on the Grail—does not yield the number 6. Nor does it yield the number 9. However, it does reveal the mirror image of the number 6 (associating the pattern with the soul).

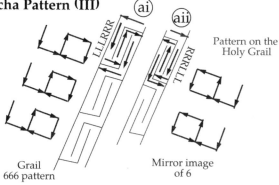

Pattern on the Holy Grail

Grail
666 pattern

Mirror image
of 6

The Secret of the Crystal in the Foot-Cone

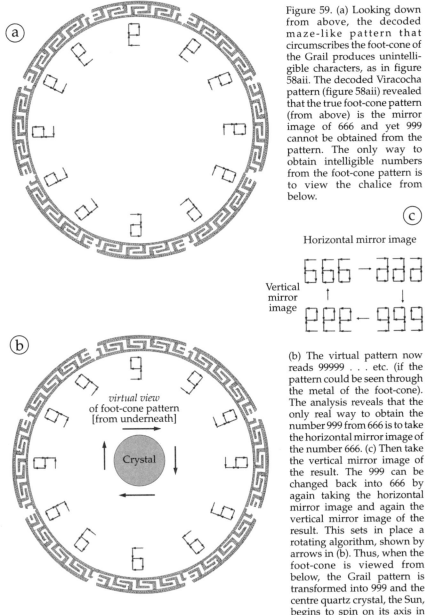

Figure 59. (a) Looking down from above, the decoded maze-like pattern that circumscribes the foot-cone of the Grail produces unintelligible characters, as in figure 58aii. The decoded Viracocha pattern (figure 58aii) revealed that the true foot-cone pattern (from above) is the mirror image of 666 and yet 999 cannot be obtained from the pattern. The only way to obtain intelligible numbers from the foot-cone pattern is to view the chalice from below.

(b) The virtual pattern now reads 99999 . . . etc. (if the pattern could be seen through the metal of the foot-cone). The analysis reveals that the only real way to obtain the number 999 from 666 is to take the horizontal mirror image of the number 666. (c) Then take the vertical mirror image of the result. The 999 can be changed back into 666 by again taking the horizontal mirror image and again taking the vertical mirror image of the result. This sets in place a rotating algorithm, shown by arrows in (b). Thus, when the foot-cone is viewed from below, the Grail pattern is transformed into 999 and the centre quartz crystal, the Sun, begins to spin on its axis in accordance with the arrows. In this way the foot-cone contains the super-science of the spinning Sun and the higher orders of spirituality.

Viewed from below, this attempt [to *intellectually* convert 666 into 999—an attempt to convert the body into a soul] endows upon the centre crystal *circulating arrows*, which in turn cause the centre quartz crystal to *virtually spin*, emulating the Sun as it spins on its axis. This means that the quartz crystal must represent the Sun, confirming the proposition put forward by the Arthurian legends that the Holy Grail *radiates light*, as shown in plate 19—it contains within it the Sun. Only Arthur (who is shown in plate 19 worshipping the Holy Grail radiating light) could have known this and only Arthur could have carved the maze-like pattern on the upper foot-cone to convey this information.

Amazingly, closer inspection of the Hallstatt maze-like pattern (figure 4) shows that it too contains *both* versions of the maze-like pattern, the original and the mirror image [the pattern very cleverly reverses beneath the hands of each of the twins]. Which means that whoever carved the pattern on the Hallstatt scabbard understood the same knowledge as whoever carved *both* patterns on the tunic of Viracocha 1,100 years later. Which in turn means that the Hallstatt Celts acquired their super-knowledge from a Supergod, who must have been the King of Hochdorf (whose number was 999) who died in around 550 BC.

The Secrets of the Swastika Panels

But surely, if the chalice was engraved 450 years after it was made, it could never have carried the implied instruction for the centre crystal to *virtually* spin, to emulate the spinning Sun (and radiate light) at the time it was manufactured.

Figure 60 shows that the lower foot-cone panels are variously patterned; (a) and (c)—two identical pairs—carry a Celtic continuous-line knot-work pattern whereas (bi) and (bii) are covered in swastika and reverse-swastika patterns. The patterns on the mesh-mat panels (d), examined in figure 48, differ, calling for closer examination and the consequential release of encoded information. In the same way, panels (bi) and (bii) differ from each other, calling for closer examination. Generally speaking, the swastika symbol is constructed of six lines and therefore the number 6 will be used to demonstrate the mirror-imaging principles that follow (although any other non-symmetrical number could be used).

The Secrets in the Swastika Panels

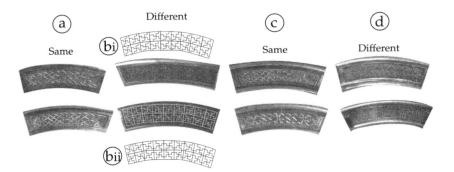

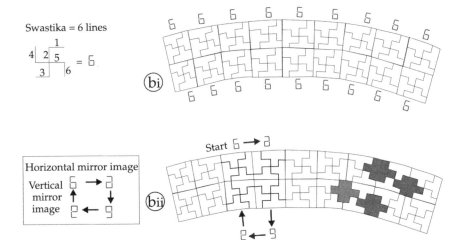

Figure 60. The lower foot-cone panels are variously patterned: (a) and (c)—two identical pairs—carry a Celtic continuous-line knot-work pattern; (bi) and (bii) are covered in swastika and reverse-swastika patterns. The patterns on the mesh-mat panels (d) differ, calling for closer examination and the consequential release of encoded information (previously analysed in figure 48). In the same way, panels bi and bii differ, calling for closer examination. The swastika is made up of six lines. (bi) shows each swastika to be identical to its neighbour. However, (bii) shows that adjacent squares carry mirror-imaged swastikas, both vertically and horizontally. Closer examination of (bii) reveals the same rotating algorithm obtained in figure 59c. This means that the chalice contained the encoded information to enable the quartz crystal to *virtually* spin (and radiate light) even before it was carved with the maze-like pattern on the upper foot-cone, which, in turn, means that King Arthur (or Merlin) likewise decoded the swastika panels and then engraved the same algorithm in a different way—using the maze-like pattern—to obtain the same result. Moreover, the original *swastika* pattern specifically refers to the revolving Sun on its axis, whereas the maze-like pattern of the Hallstatt scabbard and Viracocha is, initially, much more obscure and easier to overlook. The (bii) pattern results in a series of crosses [(bii), in-filled with grey].

The swastikas featured in (bi) are each identical to its neighbour. However, in the panel labelled (bii), adjacent squares carry mirror-imaged swastikas, both vertically and horizontally. Closer examination of the (bii) arrangement reveals the same rotating algorithm obtained in figure 59c. This means that the chalice contained the encoded information to enable the quartz crystal to *virtually* spin (and radiate light) even before it was carved with the maze-like pattern on the upper foot-cone. That, in turn, means that King Arthur (or Merlin) likewise decoded the swastika panels and then engraved the same algorithm in a different way—using the maze-like pattern—to obtain the same result. Moreover, the original swastika pattern specifically refers to the revolving Sun on its axis, whereas the maze-like pattern of the Hallstatt scabbard and Viracocha is, initially, much more obscure and easier to overlook. The (bii) pattern also results in a series of crosses [(bii), in-filled with grey].

The Secrets of the Yellow Rim and the Nails

Adding a ring of brass to the lip (figures 61a and 61c) has softened the rim of the bowl. A groove is moulded into the brass ring to provide an imperfect (sloppy) fit with the metal rim of the bowl. The ring is then held in position by three tapered brass nails equally spaced (figure 61b) around the rim and the bowl, which are then bent inwards towards the bowl. The distribution of the nails (figure 61b) accords with the geometric angles of an equilateral triangle (666), the number of the body. When the three nails are removed, the ring can be removed from the rim (figure 61c). The ratio of the length of the dimensions of the curiously 'not-quite-square' chalice now change, reducing from 178 mm x 185 mm to 176.7 mm x 179.7 mm [the width decreases by more than twice the change in the height]. Thus by removing the three nails the chalice becomes more 'square', enabling the release of more virtue and knowledge. The reason for removing the nails and the golden rim was discussed earlier, in chapter 2, and is provided here again for easy reference:

> Esotericists, like the Shamans, possess supernatural powers allowing them to function in one of two worlds at will, the physical or the spiritual. Thus, through instruction received from the

Brotherhood, the soul can leave the body at will to experience what is today called an 'out-of-body experience'. It is believed that their temple exists in the spiritual dimension above and away from the profane. It is as though the intellectual body hitches itself to the spiritual and in so doing experiences consciousness free of physical or emotional restraint. This capability is not open to lower initiates but only to the higher adepts who have progressed through disciplined study of the sacred sciences, years of devotion and probation.

Temporary evacuation of the soul from the body results from a three-fold technique obtainable only by disciplined meditation and ritual, which teaches men how to function away from the physical body at will. They teach that the spiritual nature, the soul, is attached to the physical form at certain points, symbolised by the [three] nails of the Crucifixion. Through initiation they are taught to *withdraw the nails*, enable the divine nature of man to come down from the cross *and thereby release their own soul* from their body into another dimension. Out-of-body experiences are possible only once the emotional, intellectual and physical bodies are at peace and equilibrium which in turn is achieved through meditation and ritual.

During an out-of-body experience the soul leaves the body through a mythical silver thread that, with practice, extends from the navel. The journeying soul can leave the body safely, providing the higher intellect holds this umbilical cord tight to provide a return path to the body. The practice is dangerous, as breakage of the silver thread precludes its return to the body. Should this happen, then the initiate would die. Ecclesiastes, in the Bible, says this:

> . . . Man goeth to his long home and the mourners go about the streets: or ever the silver cord be loosed *or the golden bowl (halo)* be broken . . . then shall the dust return to the Earth as it was; and the spirit shall return to God who gave it. (*Ecclesiastes* XII, 5–7)

Moreover, the squared-off version of the chalice (the square) now represents the Earth and the circular bowl the Sun *inside* the Earth, or the Sun *on* Earth (the Son of God on Earth), commemorating the visit of Jesus.

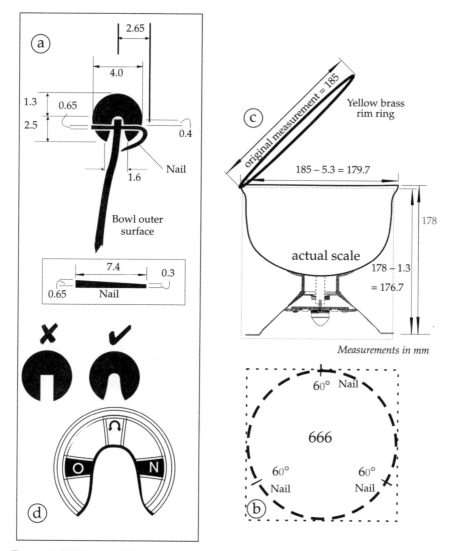

Figure 61. (a) The rim of the chalice has been softened by adding a ring of brass to the lip. A groove is moulded into the brass to provide an imperfect fit with the bowl. The rim is held in place by three tapered brass nails equally spaced (b) around the rim and the bowl and then bent towards the bowl. The distribution accords with the geometric angles of an equilateral triangle (666), the number of the body. When the three nails are removed, the ring can be removed from the rim (c). The ratio of the length of the dimensions of the curiously 'not-quite-square' piece now change, reducing from 178 mm x 185 mm to 176.7 mm x 179.7 mm [the width decreases by more than twice the change in the height]. Thus by removing the three nails the chalice becomes more 'square'. This describes the esoteric pracitise of removing the nails of the Crucifixion, enabling the divine nature of man (the soul, or halo—the brass rim ring) to be released from the body (666) (see main text). (d) The reason for the unusual profile of the groove in the ring and the reason for the wedge-shaped nails now become clear.

The reason for the unusual profile of the [sloppy] groove in the brass rim ring now becomes clear (figure 61d): the gold-plated brass ring represents a ring of light, a halo, and the unusual profile cut deliberately contains the shape of a human head—the two together referring to a halo around the profile of a human head. Each of the three tapered nails, in this scheme, is thus driven through the head of Christ (through Christ) confirming that the three rim nails (spaced at 60° intervals) represent the nails driven into Christ on the Cross, on Earth (666). At the same time, the nails through the head draw attention to the wounds to the head caused by the crown of thorns that Christ wore at the Crucifixion.

The Secrets of the Handle Escutcheon Plates

Each handle (plate 23) is made of cast silver, heavily decorated with inlaid enamelled panels fixed to the bowl by two rivets at the top and two below that are concealed by four tiny semispherical blue glass studs. The escutcheon plates are fixed to the bowl beneath each of the handles. Each plate carries four filigree panels and three large subconical enamel studs (figure 62). The complex shape of these studs raises suspicion because the bowl girdle studs (figure 51) are finished with a gently convex sectioned-arch shape. If a bowl girdle stud were fired at a body, it may well cause bruising. If a subconical bullet-shaped stud were fired at a body, it would penetrate. The subconical stud immediately becomes *aggressive*. Together, the arrangement of the three escutcheon studs takes the shape of an upside-down equilateral triangle (999) which must represent the soul, or godly, energy.

We now note that the *foot-cone* of the chalice is also subconically shaped. The three studs must therefore represent the aggressive nails hammered into Christ at the Crucifixion, one in each hand and one through the *foot* (feet). The top two are positioned beneath each of the handles, because that is where the studs (the nails) belong, in the hands. The handles are shaped to take one thumb from each hand. Lifting the cup, in this way, forces the palms to embrace the subconical studs, sending the studs (the nails) into the palms of the hands. By raising the cup to the mouth in this way, the recipient participates in a *virtual* Crucifixion and drinks the blood of Christ. By drinking from the

The Secrets of the Subconical Studs

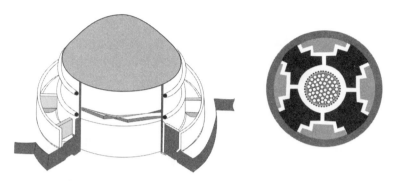

Figure 62. The escutcheon studs are subconically shaped, like the foot-cone. When the thumbs are placed through the handles of the cup and the palms embrace the bowl, the bullet-shaped studs dig into the palms, simulating the nails of the Crucifixion. The triangular arrangement of the three studs refers to the arrangement of nails used in the Crucifixion—one in each hand and one in the foot (-cone). The pattern on the studs takes the shape of a cross with dots in the centre (a cross punctured with holes).

cup the Apostles thus participated in a virtual Crucifixion and drank the blood of Christ at the Last Supper.

Close inspection of the Viracocha vase of Tiahuanaco shows the shape of the handles to be identical to those on the Ardagh Chalice, similarly enabling the lifting of the cup using the thumbs inside the handles, suggesting that the Viracocha vase was the Holy Cup of its day—a later ceramic version of the Holy Grail, left behind by Viracocha in around AD 500. It also means that whoever designed the Ardagh Chalice (the Holy Grail) must have made the Viracocha vase, supporting the fact that Viracocha and Jesus were one and the same spiritual energy.

The subconical studs on the chalice originally contained rings of amber in the channels around the mount, associating the studs with electromagnetic energy, the soul and the Sun.

The Derrynaflan Hoard

The Derrynaflan hoard, consisting of a large silver chalice (figure 63), a silver paten, a hoop (that may have been a stand for the paten), a copper alloy strainer-ladle, and a copper-alloy basin, was found on the

The Derrynaflan Hoard

Figure 63. The Derrynaflan hoard including chalice, wine strainer, paten (with inner ring) and bowl.

monastic site of Derrynaflan, County Tipperary, in 1980, in a covered pit by a man using a metal detector.

The chalice is a two-handled ministerial vessel which some compare to the Ardagh Chalice, although it is much more Byzantine in style. It has filigree decoration around the bowl but the decorative girdle differs substantially from the construction of the Ardagh Chalice.

The paten, described as a communion plate, is a highly polished concave silver plate with a diameter of 370 mm (14.5 inches). The top and sides are heavily decorated with twenty-four bronze stud mounts with enamelled studs and filigree panels. The sides are covered in knitted silver and copper wires that carry filigree panels interspersed with decorative square stud mounts and studs. The paten was made to sit on a rim, raising it 30 mm (1.25 inches) off the resting surface, enabling the paten to be lifted without crushing the sides.

The wine strainer-ladle was made by adding a pierced-metal plate to a long-handle ladle. The ladle carries a semispherical rock crystal at the handle end.

At a glance the quality and craftsmanship appear comparable to that of the Ardagh Chalice and it is tempting to suggest that they may have originated in the same workshop. But the Derrynaflan pieces contain none of the esoteric knowledge that is to be found in the Ardagh Chalice. The bowl girdle is much simpler than that of the Ardagh Chalice and although it carries twelve decorative studs, they are made of simple square amber pieces set in square mounts, rather than enamelled glass. The bowl girdle panels are manufactured differently—they are much simpler, manufactured using a simple flat backplate decorated with wire, not fabricated from an embossed openwork plate supported by a backplate. The handles are lighter in construction, and smaller—less likely to accommodate a thumb. It too has an escutcheon plate, beneath the handles, but again the structure is lighter and the three amber studs are simple and semispherical, rather than complex and subconical, meaning that although it could be used to drink from, it could never be used to emulate a *virtual* crucifixion.

The foot-cone is not subconical in shape. The foot flange accommodates a continuous ring of filigree that is punctuated with four square and four semispherical amber studs. Above this, on the shoulder of the cone, runs a shoulder girdle decorated with filigree wire panels punctuated by eight square amber studs. It has clearly been made by someone wishing to copy a work of quality without the necessary intellectual input required to encode esoteric knowledge into the design—the sunspot cycle could never be calculated using just two squares (4, 4) and one octagonal (8) shape.

The bowl lip, or rim, has been spun into shape; it does not carry a separate rim ring, or halo. Indeed everything about it is of a different *nature* from the Ardagh Chalice. But perhaps it was made by the same hand and meant to be that way, to paint a distinction between the real thing and imitations, which, although valuable, beautiful, and useful, belong in a different league altogether.

It is tempting to imagine the 19.2 cm (7.5-inch) Derrynaflan chalice was used at the Last Supper, to ladle the wine into the Ardagh Chalice. The volumetric capacity of both chalices is about the same. The ladle could have made a difference by straining wine kept in the 'impure' Derrynaflan chalice into the 'purified' Ardagh Chalice. If it was, it might have accompanied the Holy Grail on its journey. But if it was used to simply strain wine, then the Derrynaflan chalice would never have been touched by Christ (only by a ladle) nor would Christ have drunk from it, meaning that it never held the Eucharistic blood of Christ. There are other major differences that set the two pieces apart: the Derrynaflan chalice does not carry the names of the Apostles; it has not been engraved, suggesting a pedigree going back to before AD 453, and it does not contain the super-science of the Sun or the higher orders of spirituality.

The Copycat Monks

For the Ardagh Chalice to be the Holy Grail it must clearly be much older than current expert opinion believes it to be—AD 26 rather than AD 700—and herein lies the crux of the enquiry.

Nowadays, dating of organic antiquities can be established using the carbon 14 dating method. But the method is confined to organic material. The Ardagh Chalice and the Tara brooch do not contain any organic material, apart from amber, which is known to be millions of years old and therefore irrelevant for purposes of dating the manufacture of the pieces. In cases such as this, archaeologists look for organic compounds found near the artefact from which a 'date-by-association' can be obtained—for example, charcoal from an old fireplace. Dating of the charcoal then sets a minimum age for dating the non-organic artefact. But there are no accompanying organic materials to help date the pieces by association [notwithstanding the fact that the Ardagh Chalice was found together with four brooches which, as previously discussed, bear no esoteric resemblance to the Tara brooch; they are simply cheap seventh- or eighth-century copies of the Tara brooch which was revered by clerics]. This said, it is perfectly understandable that archaeologists should choose to date the chalice by association with the pretenders with which it was found and likewise understandable that the date could be so far removed from the truth.

To further substantiate their argument the experts fall back on the similarities in the style of the Ardagh Chalice, the Tara brooch and illuminated manuscripts, maintaining that the similarities demand that they must all be from the same period: insisting, for example (as we have already heard) that the insular majuscule text on the chalice is *identical* to that used in the Lindisfarne Gospels of AD 698 and therefore that the date is common to them all. And who could dispute that dozens of similarities can be found among the chalice, the Tara brooch and the illuminated manuscripts?

But association is a double-edged sword that begs the question of which came first, the chicken or the egg, the chalice or the manuscripts? Did the illuminated manuscripts inspire the production of the chalice and the Tara brooch? Or did the chalice and the Tara brooch inspire the production of the manuscripts?

The insular majuscule engraving on the chalice is not *identical* to that in the Lindisfarne Gospels as experts claim. It is rough and crude, as though to suggest that it might have been carved with a nail.

Generally speaking (in an engineering sense) any prototype model (or manuscript) is crude and unsophisticated. Subsequent models become more refined over time until the near-perfect finished product emerges ready for the market. The insular majuscule text in the Lindisfarne Gospels is neat, refined and near perfect, suggesting that the chalice came first and that whoever compiled the manuscript had plenty of writing practise before the manuscript was ready.

The evidence does not end there. The illuminated manuscripts contain other glaring similarities that are just *too obvious* if the official line is followed: consider the geometric shapes from the illustrations in figures 46, 47, 48, 50, 51, 60, 61 and 62. A few of these geometric line drawings are reproduced in figure 64 alongside corollary pattern designs from the books of Kells and Lindisfarne. The comparison is revealing and begs the question 'why would anyone create a manuscript containing such oddly specific geometric shapes, shapes that are all found prolifically in the Ardagh Chalice'? There would be no point in picking geometric shapes out of thin air, filling them with Celtic designs and including them in the most valued manuscripts ever written. The fact that they used the shapes is evidence that they had a *reason* for using them, because they *revered* them. The reason they revered them was that the shapes are found in the most important relic of the Christian Church, the Holy Grail. It was not the other way round. Can you imagine the most senior monk in a scriptorium

Examples of a three-dot marker [subconical escutcheon studs] found in the Book of Kells

Escutcheon subconical studs

Angel

Angel

St. John, Book of Lindisfarne

Figure 64. Comparison of geometric shapes found in the Holy Grail (from line drawings illustrated in this chapter) to similar shapes found in the illuminated manuscripts (after George Bain, *Celtic Art*). The appearance of the chalice inspired monks at Lindisfarne and Iona to copy the shapes and styles that appear on it.

instructing his artisans to '*manufacture a chalice* containing all of the peculiar shapes found in the manuscripts—that had been chosen from thin air'? It defies belief.

And there is more anachronistic evidence: peacocks feature prolifically in the illuminated manuscripts, ostensibly because of the belief that the peacock symbolised the purity of Christ. The association apparently arose from the belief that peacock meat does not putrefy with age.[42] St Augustine put the belief to the test by including roast peacock on the menu at a dinner in Carthage. Following the meal he ordered some of the meat to be set aside. After thirty days there was no bad smell and even after a year the meat had simply become dried out and desiccated.

If the monks copied the design of the chalice (and the Tara brooch) into the manuscripts, it seems likely that they copied the entwined bird heads from the Tara brooch (plate 21e) into their manuscripts, mistakenly believing them to be peacocks (figure 64, lower rectangle), unaware of the astronomical significance of the vulture and its association with the constellation of Orion and resurrection, the central theme of Christian teaching. This error, if it is one, supports the view that the birds were copied into the manuscripts because they [seem to] appear on the Tara brooch. But there is no need for a peacock to appear as a metaphor for the purity of Christ on the Tara brooch; that role is already fulfilled by the presence of the stag and the 144,000 (representing the number of the pure destined for Heaven). A peacock on the Tara brooch would be surplus to requirements whereas vultures convey an important astronomical function on the brooch. Again, this suggests that the ostensible peacocks were lifted from the Tara brooch, rather than that the Tara brooch vultures were copied from the manuscripts.

And in regard to unnecessary duplication, the manufacturer of the chalice would have no reason to encode information to enable the quartz crystal to spin (the swastika panels) and then again encode the same information, in a different way, in the maze-like carving on the upper foot-cone, supporting the assertion that whoever carved it did not manufacture it.

There is no scientific reason why the Ardagh Chalice cannot be the Holy Grail used by Christ at the Last Supper:

- The super-science of the Sun and the higher orders of spirituality were passed on to the Celts from the King of Hochdorf as early as 550 BC.
- The champlevé style of enamelled studs in bronze mounts first appeared in around 400 BC in the Basse Yutz flagon.
- The appearance of Cernunnos the stag, as Christ, appears in the Gundestrup Cauldron c. 100 BC and on the Tara brooch.
- The style of the brooch and chalice contains similarities of the La Tène III period, which extended from 150 to 50 BC.
- There is no reason why the Ardagh Chalice and the Tara brooch could not have been designed and manufactured under instruction from the miracle-maker Jesus, just as there is no reason why the treasures of Tutankhamun could not have been designed or manufactured under instruction from the boy-king, the 'Son of God', and no reason why Mayan transformers could not have been designed and manufactured by Lord Pacal—the former Christian-Jew who reincarnated at Tiahuanaco and engraved the Holy Grail maze pattern onto the Viracocha vase.[43]
- There is no reason why the treasures could not have been carried to England by Joseph of Arimathea.
- There is no reason why the treasures could not have been found by King Arthur, in accordance with the legends.
- There is no reason why King Arthur could not have decoded the esoteric knowledge contained in the Tara brooch, persuading him to believe that he had found the Holy Grail.
- There is no reason why Arthur, under the guidance of Merlin, could not have engraved the Grail to authenticate its provenance.
- There is no reason why the Grail and the brooch could not have been passed on to monks for safekeeping.
- There is no reason why monks could not have taken their treasures to the island monasteries—inspiring them to produce the illuminated manuscripts in the style of the Holy Grail and the Tara brooch.

If we accept the evidence of our enquiries, then we are relieved of our intellectual anxieties. We understand why we are born, why we die, why this has to be. We understand who Jesus was, why he came to Earth and the true meaning of what he left behind. We understand what Heaven is, what Hell is. We understand how to get to Heaven and how to avoid returning to Hell.

Conclusion

The Ardagh Chalice must be the Holy Grail referred to in the Arthurian legends. It was designed by Jesus to contain and convey the super-science of the Sun and the higher orders of spirituality:

- The 354 pieces correspond with the length of the Druidic year, last believed to have been used in AD 70, suggesting that the cup was manufactured before that time.
- The absence of one of the twelve decorative bowl-rim studs prophesied the betrayal of Jesus by Judas Iscariot and at the same time announced to the initiated the encoding of esoteric information; the 354 pieces of the chalice [together with the eleven or twelve bowl-rim studs] refer to the 365-day solar year and the 366-day solar leap year.
- The presence of two solar crosses on the bowl associates the cup with the Sun, light, God and the halo of Jesus.
- The absence of the first and last panels in the bowl-ring girdle reveal that Jesus was the first and last, the Alpha and Omega, and Venus, the evening and morning star.
- The absence of the name of Mathius in the engraved names of the Apostles around the bowl implies that whoever carved the chalice was unaware that Judas Iscariot was replaced by Mathius, suggesting that seventh-century clerics did not engrave the cup.
- The inclusion of the name of Paul suggests that whoever carved the chalice believed that Paul, not Mathius, took the place of Judas Iscariot.
- Grammatical errors in the names suggest that whoever carved the chalice was not an educated cleric, thus excluding educated seventh-century monks.
- The names of the Apostles on the chalice appear in Latin whereas the names of the Apostles in the Lindisfarne Gospels appear in Latinised Greek, suggesting that the engraving of the chalice and the writing of the illuminated manuscripts were carried out by different people.

- The rim of the bowl is softened by a gold-plated brass ring. A cross-section of the ring reveals a groove shaped like a human head. The surrounding brass ring forms a golden halo around the head. The halo [the brass ring] can only be removed by withdrawing the three tapered nails that hold the rim to the bowl, revealing the esoteric practise of releasing the divine nature of man from the body.
- The escutcheon studs are subconical in shape, enabling the holder of the cup to participate in a *virtual* Crucifixion.
- The decorative mesh-mat wire panels in the lower foot girdle explain that the body and soul are knitted together during this lifetime on Earth and that both are brought together by God.
- The decorative swastika panels convey virtual movement upon the foot-cone quartz crystal, causing it to virtually spin and thus radiate light in accordance with the legends.
- The arrangement of stones in the foot-cone can be used to calculate solar magnetic cycles.

The La Tène and Byzantine styles of the chalice show that it was manufactured in the eastern Mediterranean during the time of Christ and carried to Britain by Joseph of Arimathea following the Crucifixion. The chalice was part of a haul containing the Tara brooch that [eventually] passed into the hands of Sir Galahad, one of King Arthur's Knights of the Round Table.

In AD 453, Arthur broke the esoteric code of the Tara brooch and in so doing realised the pedigree of the chalice. To celebrate the discovery, Arthur's artisans engraved the chalice with the names of the Apostles [including St Paul] together with esoteric information supporting the provenance of the Holy Cup: two complementary dragon heads that depict the tau cross and an interlaced maze-like pattern that circumscribes the foot-cone, which conceals the esoteric number 99999 . . . the number of God incarnate on Earth—but only to he who looks at the Sun and sees it spinning on its axis [only to he who understands the super-science of the Sun].

- Only King Arthur could have recognised the pedigree of the chalice after breaking the code of the Tara brooch by withdrawing the sword from the stone and becoming one of the 144,000, making him the King that was and the King that will be.

- The decorative mesh-mat wire panels in the lower foot girdle explain that the body and soul are knitted together during this lifetime on Earth and that both are brought together by God.
- The large spinning centre quartz crystal emulates the spinning Sun, meaning that the chalice must (intellectually) radiate light, confirming efficacy upon the Arthurian legends that show King Arthur worshipping the Grail that radiates light. Arthur must have broken the esoteric codes of the swastika panels, and to celebrate the discovery [of the holy chalice that radiates light] he must have carved the same information into the chalice in a different way, using the maze-like pattern on the upper foot-cone.
- Only Arthur, under the guidance of Merlin, could have carved the chalice with the Viracocha and King of Hochdorf maze-like pattern that circumscribes the foot-cone.
- The chalice is engraved with two conjoined dragons, the mark of the Crucifixion of Christ and the insignia of Merlin, mentor of King Arthur.
- In the Arthurian legends King Arthur is also pictured worshipping the Grail, which is flanked by two dragons, and two dragons are engraved on the chalice.
- Only Arthur, under the guidance of Merlin, would have wished to carve the chalice with two dragons.

Similarities in style between the illuminated manuscripts and the chalice arise from the fact that the chalice and the Tara brooch were passed to monks for safekeeping after Arthur died in around AD 453. In AD 698 the monks took their precious treasures to the newly established monasteries at Lindisfarne and Iona where, overawed with what they possessed, they copied the revered style of the chalice and brooch into newly created illuminated manuscripts. The appearance of the Grail and the brooch in around AD 453 inspired the production of crude inferior look-alikes. Acquisition of the relics by monks in around AD 698 led to a second wave of good-quality, sophisticated look-alikes, like the Derrynaflan hoard, that flooded the market after that time.

In around AD 802, fleeing Vikings, the monks took the chalice, the brooch and their illuminated manuscripts across the Irish Sea to the monastery at Kells. Later, again fleeing from Viking raids, the brooch and chalice became separated. They were hidden from hostile incursions by monks and eventually lost, before their rediscovery in 1850 and 1868.

Today the Holy Grail is kept in the National Museum of Ireland in Dublin, together with the Tara brooch and the Rinnagan Crucifixion plaque.

CHAPTER SIX

The Secret of the Grail

The First Picture of God

The most remarkable feature of the Grail, revealed by our analysis, must be its association with light (electromagnetic energy) which in turn associates it directly with God, as no other known artefact does. He who beholds the light in the Grail is the one who understands the secrets of the maze-like engraving around the foot-cone and the reverse swastikas in the mesh-mat panels, knowledge of which enables the construction of an intellectual mechanistic model that sets the quartz crystal in motion. As the crystal virtually spins, the 666 of the body is converted into the 999 of the soul.

The Grail, with its maze-like pattern and reverse swastikas in common with the Hallstatt scabbard, the Viracocha tunic maze-like pattern, and the spiral arrangement on the Rinnagan Crucifixion plaque all break down the spiritual conversion process into definitive steps beginning with 666 and ending with 999, explaining that the purpose of physical life is to purify the soul within.

The same message was left by Lord Pacal; plate 4 shows Lord Pacal in his emanation as 'the beast', the stag, when the Mural of Bonampak transparencies are juxtaposed at 66.6°. Figure A27 shows Lord Pacal as the feathered snake, again as the beast on Earth, but only when the transparencies are set to 66.6°.

And the mosaic mask has more to reveal: when the transparencies are set at 99.9° (plate 24), a complex series of pictures (hitherto unpublished) emerges, showing the head and face of a man—the small man with the hat from Peru encountered earlier.

Figure 65 analyses the geometric significance of a series of shapes located either side of the small man's hat. The angular relationship between the shapes is given by the schematics a–c; the arc represents the disc of the Sun. An oblique line next to the Sun is set at 23.5° to the horizontal (the horizon), meaning that the line must represent the Earth which is tilted at 23.5° on its axis (figure 65b). When the Earth-lines are levelled they each intersect with a corresponding tiny circle positioned either side of the Sun discs. Figure 65d demonstrates that the two tiny circles must represent the planet Venus because the line of the brim of the hat intersects the circles at 177°, the angle by which Venus is tilted on its axis. The man with the hat is thus positioned between the rising morning star and the setting evening star, meaning that the man with the hat must be the Sun, God.

The small man with the hat shown in plate 24a (box framed) was found in the tomb of Viracocha Pachacamac, at Sipan in Peru. Figure 66 shows a crab covering the face of the small man in the composite sketch. Markings on the crab correlate with markings on the 60-cm- (two-foot-) high golden anthropomorphic crab-man found in the tomb of Viracocha (plate 5d), which is also sketched in figure 66e. The face of the bat god covers the face of the crab.

The ancient belief that the soul leaves the body through a hole at the top of the head was illustrated earlier by the Chinese jade burial suit of Prince Liu Sheng (plate 21g), and plate 24 shows the soul of the small man leaving a hole in his head. Indeed the picture becomes more complex—an eagle catches the soul in its open beak as it soars through the air.

The circular soul doubles as a halo for another character immediately below the beak [the triangular-shaped face has been coloured red to help identification]. Here stands a Christlike figure, as though prostrate on the cross, with ankles pinned together [indicated by the tiny red circle just above the feet] carrying the compasses of the Freemason. The compasses are composed of the same lines previously described as Earth-lines in the figure 65 analysis. They were set at 23.5° to the horizontal and by default at 66.5° (90° − 23.5°) to the vertical. The Christlike figure thus carries each leg of the compasses at 66° to himself. Earlier,

The Mosaic Mask of Palenque
The First Picture of God (II)

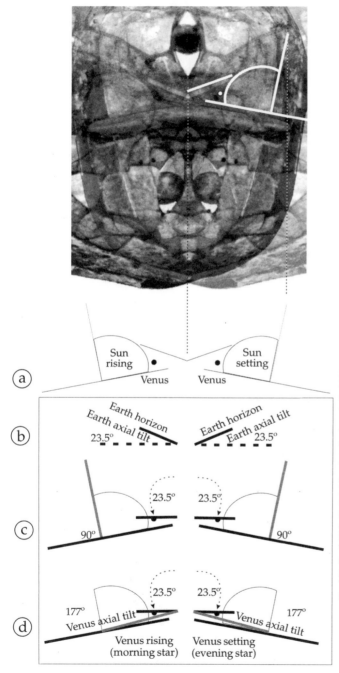

Figure 65. Composite scene from the mosaic mask of Palenque (see also plate 24). The small man carries a geometric line arrangement either side of his hat (highlighted in bold white on the composite picture). The line arrangement is reproduced in the schematics below. (a) Line arrangement as it appears on the composite. The arc represents the disc of the Sun. Venus is shown either side of the Sun in its various manifestations as the morning star and the evening star. (b) The line above Venus is tilted at 23.5° to the horizontal, indicating that the line represents Earth. (c) Adjusting the Earth-line by 23.5°, Venus rises and falls above and below the Earth's horizon. The line shown at 90°, is a reference line; when the line is moved counter-clockwise by 90°, it aligns with the 'Venus-line'. (d) When the Venus-line is now rotated clockwise by 177° [the angle by which Venus is tilted on its axis], it touches the Earth horizon line. This elaborate explanation confirms that the tiny circles either side of the Sun discs represent Venus, meaning that the man between the discs must be the Sun, God. This must therefore be the first picture of God.

The Mosaic Mask of Palenque
The Man Who Was Venus

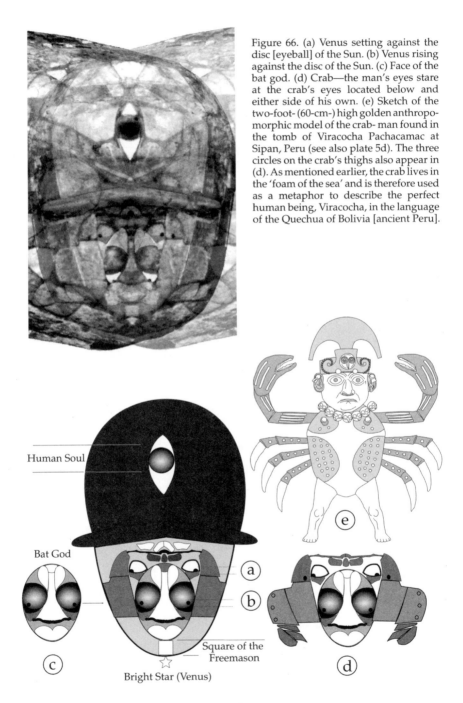

Figure 66. (a) Venus setting against the disc [eyeball] of the Sun. (b) Venus rising against the disc of the Sun. (c) Face of the bat god. (d) Crab—the man's eyes stare at the crab's eyes located below and either side of his own. (e) Sketch of the two-foot- (60-cm-) high golden anthropomorphic model of the crab- man found in the tomb of Viracocha Pachacamac at Sipan, Peru (see also plate 5d). The three circles on the crab's thighs also appear in (d). As mentioned earlier, the crab lives in the 'foam of the sea' and is therefore used as a metaphor to describe the perfect human being, Viracocha, in the language of the Quechua of Bolivia [ancient Peru].

Human Soul

Bat God

Square of the Freemason

Bright Star (Venus)

figure 42 showed Christ carrying the compasses of the Freemason set at 66° and showed the compasses formed by the spindles on the spinning wheel to be set in the same way.

Figure A26 shows a 'spider chamber' found in the tomb of Viracocha. The spider spins a silver thread which, like the analysis undertaken in figure 42, associates Viracocha with the mythical silver thread, the cable-tow that tethers the soul to the body during out-of-body sojourns. This explains why spiritual types (priests, clerics, orthodox Jews, etc.) all wear a hat when praying: to prevent the soul from leaving through the ostensible hole (spiritual gateway) we are told is located in the top of the head—should they become too close to God through prayer—before their time is up. The small man wears a hat to demonstrate the same principles.

The eagle with outstretched wings in plate 24 not only carries away the soul of the small man but also carries away the Christlike figure and his compasses (in its claws). At the same time the small man acquires wings, his spirit soars and he flies away with the eagle. The square of the Freemason appears on his chin together with a five-pointed star. All of this tells us that Lord Pacal, the Viracochas and Jesus were each, in his turn, the virtuous who became God, a bright star in the Heavens.

Moreover, this remarkable series of pictures explicitly acknowledges that 'God created man in his own image' (Genesis I, 27). Plate 24 therefore shows the first.ever picture of God and explains that man can become God, but only when man transforms the 66.6° into the 99.9°—the same message as the Grail. It seems, also, that the small man represents a picture of God on Earth, a Supergod. That this is the case is confirmed by further analysis provided by figures 65 and 66.

Whom Does the Grail Serve?

The answer to Perceval's question of 'Whom does the Grail serve?' should by now be clear. The Grail was the cup left behind by Jesus following his life on Earth. It is a tangible representation of everything he taught about the super-science of the Sun and the higher orders of spirituality.

The Theory of Divine Reconciliation (figure A19) explicitly recognises that God wishes to grow because more God is 'more love' and therefore 'more good'. But by 'making man in his own image' we learn that God cannot grow except through using living organisms as a conduit to accommodate spiritual growth. The Grail, that is to say the esoteric knowledge contained in the Grail, therefore, serves God.

Jesus sacrificed his life to convey the important message to the living of the day, and to those who would live later. Like Lord Pacal he ensured that his Holy Cup would be passed on, generation after generation, touching all who understood the esoteric knowledge.

We have already heard of how, during the Last Supper, Jesus introduced the cup to his Disciples:

> . . . And as they were eating bread Jesus blessed it and gave it to the Disciples and said, take eat, this is my body . . . and he took the cup and gave thanks and gave it to them saying drink ye all of it . . . for this is my blood of the New Testament which is shed for many for the remission of sins. (*Matthew* XXVI, 26–28)

What happened later is seldom mentioned: knowing that the end was near, Jesus went with his Disciples to pray on the mountain. During the collective prayers he withdrew—within earshot of the Disciples—for private prayer during which he enigmatically referred to the legacy he would leave behind for others:

> Father; if thou be willing remove this cup from me. (*Luke* XXII, 42)

> O my Father, if it be possible, let this cup pass from me, not as I will but as your will. (*Matthew* XXVI, 39)

In so doing Jesus introduced the esoteric nature of the Grail to his Disciples, who were thereafter charged with its safekeeping.

The Celtic swastikas, spirals, knot-work, numbering system, Excalibur, the Grail and the illuminated manuscripts all convey the exact same information found in the treasures of the world's sun-worshipping civilizations: the soul really can become a star.

Decoding the Viracocha Transformer

The best accounts of Peruvian mythology come from Spanish chroniclers around the time of the conquest in AD 1532. One of these, Cieza de Leon, a native Peruvian, from the age of thirteen, spent ten years living among the indigenous Indians of the new colony. Eventually, gaining their confidence, he was able to share in the legends of their ancestors. His book, the *Crónica del Perú*, was published in 1550, at the age of thirty-two:

> Before the Incas ruled or had even been heard of in these kingdoms these Indians relate a thing more noteworthy than anything else. They say that there suddenly appeared, coming from the south, a white man of large stature and authoritative demeanour. This man had such great power that he changed the hills into valleys and from the valleys made great hills, causing streams to flow from the living stone. When they saw his power they called him Maker of all things created and Prince of all things, Father of the Sun. For he did other still more wonderful things, giving being to men and animals; by his hand very great benefits accrued to them. This is the story that the Indians themselves told me and they heard it from their fathers who in turn heard it from the old songs which were handed down from very ancient times.
>
> They say that this man travelled along the highland route to the north, working marvels as he went and they say they never

saw him again. They say that in many places he gave men instructions on how they should live, speaking to them with great love and kindness, admonishing them to be good and to do no damage or injury one to another, but to love one another and show charity to all. In most places they call him Viracocha. In many places they built temples to him and in them they set up statues in his likeness and offered sacrifices before them. The huge statues in the village of Tiahuanaco are held to be from those times. (Cieza de Leon, *Crónica del Perú*, Part II, Ch. 4)

They narrate further, that, leaving the place where this occurred, he came to the coast and there, holding his mantle, he went forth amidst the waves of the sea and was seen no more. And as he went they gave him the name Viracocha, which in their language means 'foam of the sea'. (*Crónica del Perú*, Part II, Ch. 5)

When we examine the myth, the historical accounts, from this and other sources, we learn that a legendary white god named Viracocha journeyed from the ancient city of Tiahuanaco, by the waters of Lake Titicaca in the Bolivian highlands, and travelled the length of Peru performing miracles.

In *The Lost Tomb of Viracocha* I showed that Viracocha actually lived and walked the lands of Peru more than 1,500 years ago after tracing his journey from Tiahuanaco to his treasure-filled tomb in the Huaca Rajada, a mud-brick pyramid complex near the small Mochica town of Sipan on Peru's northwest coast. The tomb had been discovered earlier, in 1990, by archaeologist Dr. Walter Alva, director of the Bruning Archaeological Museum, who never made the connection between the occupant of the tomb and the stories of the Incas.

Archaeologists named the man in the tomb the 'Old Lord of Sipan'. His tomb was stocked with all kinds of treasures that would in time reveal his true identity; one particularly striking piece was a 60-cm-(2-foot-) high gilded copper anthropomorphic figure (plate 5d) sporting the face of the occupant of the tomb, attached to the body of a large crab, a creature that lives both on land and in the sea, in between the land and the sea, in the 'foam of the sea', the translation of which becomes 'Viracocha'.

Soon it became clear that here, in the long-lost pyramids of Sipan,

The Lands of Lord Pacal and Viracocha

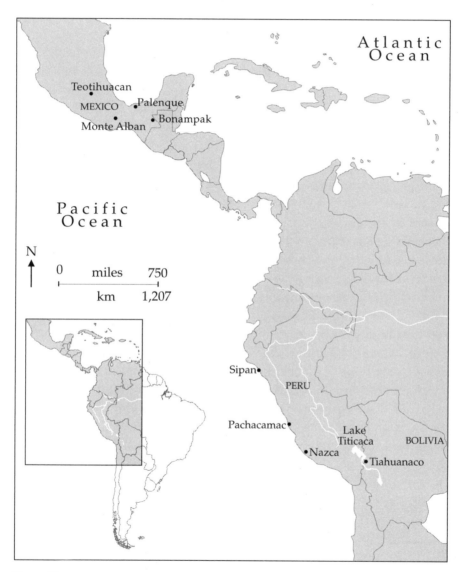

Figure A1.

lay the bones of Viracocha, the legendary white god who had side-stepped the annals of history. The story of the white man with the beard, revered throughout South America, was not just a myth after all.

The Secrets of Tiahuanaco

Bolivian archaeologist Arthur Posnansky was one of the first academics to question the foundation date of the ancient city of Tiahuanaco (figure A2), located 4,000 metres (13,000 feet) high in the Bolivian altiplano (the high plain). Sedimentation and lake-level samples allowed him to set down the development of the site into five epochs, or periods. The first period corresponded with the geological upheaval that elevated the altiplano from the ocean floor; the second, to the melting of the glaciers, the consequential over-filling of Lake Titicaca (with glacial meltdown) and then the subsequent partial emptying of the lake caused by tectonic movement. These were followed by a third period that saw the advent of enchased, or polygonal, stone blocks, similar to those used by the later Incas; a fourth period, exemplified by the use of dried mud-brick; and a fifth and final period when the city was taken over by the Incas, from around AD 1300 to 1538.

After surveying the site in considerable detail, Posnansky noticed that the lateral angles, between the cornerstones of one of the temples (figures A2 and A3), the Kalasasaya (the Temple of Standing Stones), and a partially buried observational lava block that once marked the location of the monolithic stone Gateway of the Sun (figure A3a), measured 23° 8′ 48″, a figure very close to the present-day angle of tilt of the Earth on its axis (the obliquity of the Earth).

Further investigation showed that the Sun would rise above each corner of the Kalasasaya entranceway at the time of the solstices, 21st December and 21st June, were it not for a slight discrepancy: the Sun would have risen exactly above the corners had the tilt of the Earth amounted to 23° 8′ 48″, which it did not; the tilt of the Earth when he measured it was 23° 27′, much the same as it is today. Posnansky therefore was convinced that the Earth had tilted, albeit very slightly, since the site was constructed in antiquity.

In 1958 Bolivian archaeologist Carlo Ponce Sangines sank more than 500 shafts into the ground around Lake Titicaca searching for

Tiahuanaco, Bolivia

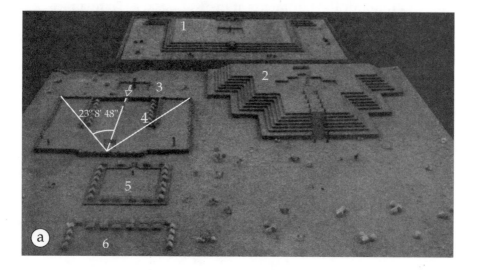

Temple of the Kalasasaya

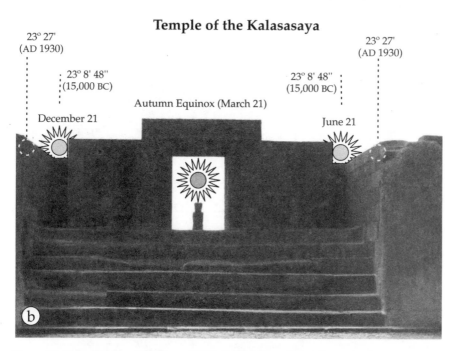

23° 27'
(AD 1930)

23° 27'
(AD 1930)

23° 8' 48"
(15,000 BC)

23° 8' 48"
(15,000 BC)

Autumn Equinox (March 21)

December 21

June 21

Figure A2. (a) Aerial view of Tiahuanaco, Bolivia (reconstruction): 1. Kanta, 2. Akapana, 3. Temple of Stone Heads, 4. Kalasasaya, Temple of the Standing Stones; the lateral angles shown, according to Professor Arthur Posnansky in 1914, enumerate astronomical information (see main text), 5. Putuni, 6. Kerikala. (b) Kalasasaya stairway [viewed from the direction of the white arrow in (a)]; Posnansky also noticed that the Sun would rise above the statue of Viracocha in the centre of the Kalasasaya stairway at the time of the southern hemisphere autumn equinox and above the corners of the stairway at the time of the solstices.

191

Astronomical Alignments at the Kalasasaya, Tiahuanaco

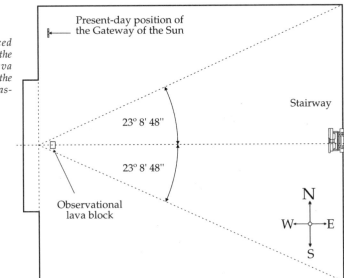

(a)

Posnansky noticed that the angle from the observational lava block to each of the cornerstones measured 23° 8' 48''.

Present-day position of the Gateway of the Sun

23° 8' 48"

23° 8' 48"

Stairway

Observational lava block

N
W — E
S

(b)

Sun's magnetic field shown in a northeasterly direction

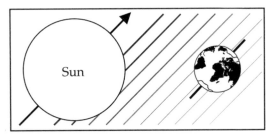

Sun

(c)

Sun's magnetic field shown in a southeasterly direction

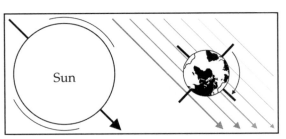

Sun

Figure A3. (a) and (b) The Sun and Earth's magnetic fields are mutually coupled. Analysis of sunspot activity shows that the Sun's magnetic field shifts direction after 3,740 years, five times every 18,139 years (one long cosmic cycle). Sometimes, in a worst-case scenario, the Earth flips on its axis, realigning its magnetic field to that of the Sun. When this happens, catastrophic destruction frequents Earth.

more clues buried in the layers of strata. He divided the development of Tiahuanaco into three phases using the latest (1940s) carbon 14 dating methods: the 'Formative', 200–1 BC; the 'Urban', 10–AD 400; and the 'Imperial', AD 400–AD 1300. Sangines uncovered five separate towns each on top of the other, successively destroyed by earthquakes and volcanic eruptions.

In the 1950s the scientist Immanuel Velikovsky pointed out that science was at a loss to explain how coal deposits could have developed in the ice-cold tundra of the Antarctic where no trees grow, how fossilised palm trees could have established themselves at Spitzbergen in the arctic circle, which for months of the year is deprived of daylight, and how perfectly preserved long-haired wooly mammoths, discovered under layers of Siberian permafrost with buttercups clenched between their teeth and undigested food in their stomachs, could possibly have survived in an area where no food grows.

Velikovsky was convinced that the Earth, at some time in the past, must have tilted on its axis, not gradually, but instantly, each time by a massive amount, causing catastrophic calamity across the globe. Areas once positioned at the poles would have been repositioned at the equator and at the same time the hot equatorial regions would have flipped over into the polar regions, instantly freezing mammoths. Massive tidal waves would have swept across continents burying forests under miles of mud; mountains would have been levelled; while sea-level plains would have been lifted high into the skies, which would account for the presence of large quantities of seashells in places like Tiahuanaco, 4,000 metres (13,000 feet) above sea level.

[Some researchers claim that this can never happen; after all, the ice caps are known to be millions of years old, proving that the caps (and therefore the Earth) could never have moved in the past—because if they had moved, they would have melted and new caps would have formed. But this objection may be overcome as follows: ice ages on Earth are characterised by the increase in the size of the polar caps. No one understands how ice ages are caused. As Immanuel Velikovsky points out, ice caps are made from fresh water. More rain or snow is therefore required to make more ice. But if temperatures *fall*, then there is *less* evaporation of water from the world's oceans. Less evaporation means *less* cloud, *less* rain and *less* snow, meaning that ice caps cannot grow when temperatures *fall*. Conversely, when temperatures *increase*, there is more evaporation, but the warmer temperatures cause the ice caps to melt and *shrink*, not grow. Velikovsky pointed out that the only way ice caps could be made to *grow* would be for the Earth to heat up *from the inside*. That would cause the oceans to evaporate more easily. Rain and snow would increase, increasing the size of the ice caps. That is where Velikovsky ended his enquiry. But taking this mechanism one step further: if the Earth heats up from *within*, then the polar caps will become slushy at the interface with the planet (underneath the polar cap). When the Earth tilts off its axis, the ice caps will be left behind as the Earth beneath slides on a layer of slush. Thus the Earth can still tilt off its axis and the polar ice cores will retain their true age going back millions of years, because the polar caps would remain stationary with respect to space. That this has happened in the past is borne out by the presence of massive stones and boulders that today litter open fields around the world. Geologists maintain that they have been *deposited* by *melting* glaciers but it is much more likely that the moving Earth, beneath the caps, dragged the boulders into position. Moreover, when the Sun's magnetic field twists and the Earth does *not* twist off its axis, the Sun and Earth's magnetic fields will be misaligned. The misaligned magnetic fields will cause electrical currents to flow in the Earth's molten magma core. The Earth will increase in temperature and the scenario above will be set into motion. It is also interesting to note that such a phenomenon would increase pressure within the core, causing increasing volcanic activity and the blowing of super-volcanoes.]

We know, from studying the treasures of the Maya and the super-science of the Sun, that the Sun's twisting magnetic field (figure A3) causes Earth-tilts (commonly referred to as pole-shifts). It seems that the ancient Tiahuanacos, in drawing our attention to the change in the tilt of the Earth, were attempting, at Tiahuanaco, to tell modern man that their own civilisation was destroyed when the Earth tilted on its axis. This is a clue to understanding the meaning of the bas-relief carving featured on the lintel of the Gateway of the Sun at Tiahuanaco (figure A4). Decoding of the sun shield of Monte Alban (plates 2 and 3) and analysis of the decoding (figure 9) revealed the southern point of the Star of David poking into the mouth of the Viracocha bas-relief carving.

Gateway of the Sun, Tiahuanaco, Bolivia

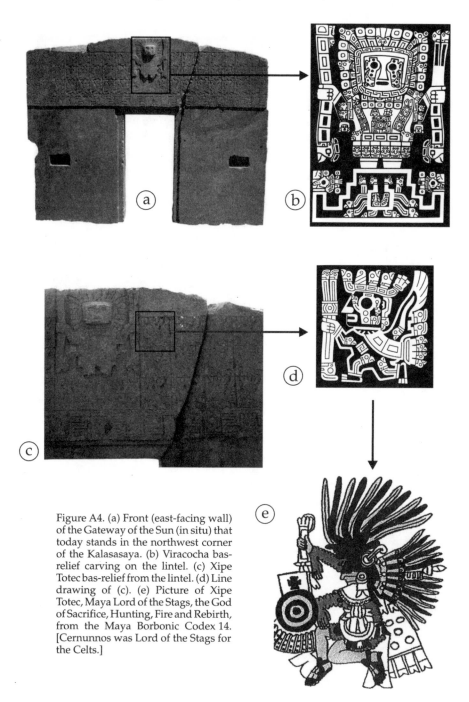

Figure A4. (a) Front (east-facing wall) of the Gateway of the Sun (in situ) that today stands in the northwest corner of the Kalasasaya. (b) Viracocha bas-relief carving on the lintel. (c) Xipe Totec bas-relief from the lintel. (d) Line drawing of (c). (e) Picture of Xipe Totec, Maya Lord of the Stags, the God of Sacrifice, Hunting, Fire and Rebirth, from the Maya Borbonic Codex 14. [Cernunnos was Lord of the Stags for the Celts.]

195

Cracking the Code of the Viracocha Transformer (I)

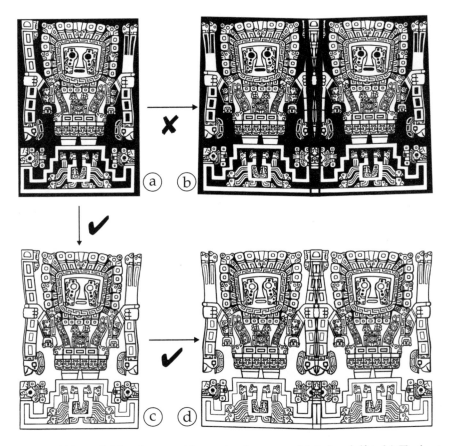

Figure A5. The top left-hand corner of the carving shows a semicircle (one *half* circle). The front side of the gateway also carries 48 other carvings [of Xipe Totec, Lord of the Stags]. These clues are in themselves astronomically insignificant. However, we note that there are 96 microcycles of magnetic activity in one *whole* sunspot cycle (figure A11). This suggests that half of the available information may be missing. By making a transparent facsimile of the Viracocha carving, the available information is doubled and now becomes astronomically significant (there are two semicircles in one Sun, and 2 x 48 = 96 microcyles of magnetic activity in one sunspot cycle). The first step in the decoding process is to overlay one half semicircle on its transparent facsimile, as shown in (b), above. However, this Peruvian 'transformer', unlike the Mayan transformers, contains a built-in 'decoding inhibitor'. Attempts to decode the carving in this condition are defeated because the black areas obscure the underlying line patterns, as in (b). We note from (a) that creatures with a long body and the profile of a bird's head hang upside down from each of the hands of Viracocha. The body of each contains rectangles. Some of the rectangles are in-filled with black, others in-filled with white. This is an instruction which tells us to convert the black solid areas of the bas-relief carving into a line drawing: *'turn the black rectangles into white rectangles'*, as in (c). Now when we attempt to decode the transformer by overlaying the two semicircles, as in (d), a composite design appears which shows that Viracocha is, like Lord Pacal of Mexico and Tutankhamun of Egypt, the feathered snake (appendix 3).

196

Cracking the Code of the Viracocha Transformer (II)

Aztec (Mexico)

Nazca (Peru)

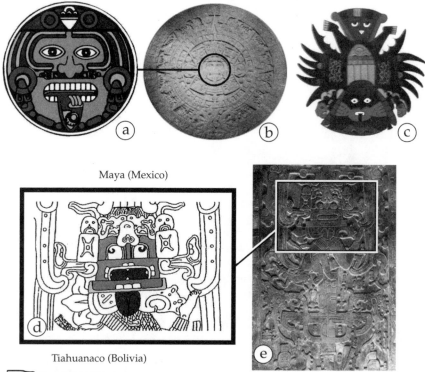

(a) (b) (c)

Maya (Mexico)

(d) (e)

Tiahuanaco (Bolivia)

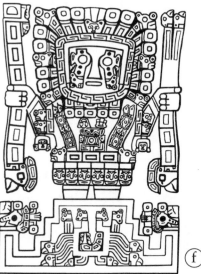

(f)

Figure A6. Representations of the Sun God from various American Indian tribes: (a) from the Aztec calendar of Mexico (b); (c) from Nazca textiles, Peru; (d) from the Mayan Lid of Palenque (e); (f) Viracocha carving from Tiahuanaco, Bolivia. Viracocha differs from the others in that the extended tongue is missing. The tip of the Star of David in plate 2 and figure 9g provides the missing tongue, inviting the onlooker to search for a tongue. One finger is missing from each of the hands of Viracocha.

Cracking the Code of the Viracocha Transformer (III):
The Secrets of the Viracocha Statue

Figure A7. Statues from Tiahuanaco conceal secret instructions. The facial markings of this one from the Kalasasaya are similar to those on the Viracocha carving found on the Gateway of the Sun, suggesting that this statue is another representation of Viracocha. However, we note that the hands of the Viracocha statue correctly carry five fingers, unlike the Viracocha carving on the Gateway of the Sun, which has one finger missing from each hand. (i) The Viracocha statue carries a figure of a male in his right hand and a figure of a female (ii) upside down, in his left. This tells us to, firstly, *make an image* (male) *of Viracocha* (the Viracocha transformer from the Gateway of the Sun), *then make another image,* this time *the* (opposite), *mirror image* (female). Finally, we are instructed to *turn the mirror image* (female) *upside down.* When these instructions are followed, another secret message is revealed (figure A8).

Cracking the Code of the Viracocha Transformer (IV)

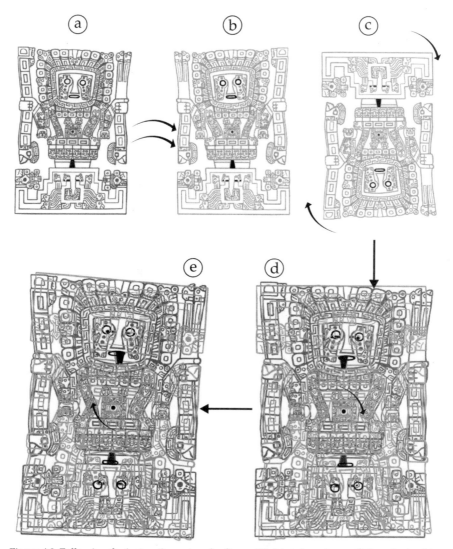

Figure A8. Following the instructions given by figure A7: (a) *make an image of Viracocha* (male); (b) *make another image, the opposite of the Viracocha image* (female); (c) *turn the second image* (female) *upside down.* Now, by using the Mayan transformer decoding process, the two images are overlaid (d). The missing tongue from the Viracocha bas-relief is now restored (located). Rotating the transparencies back and forth (d) and (e) about the epicentre (the circle located in the centre of the composite arrangement), the tongue of Viracocha waggles alternately from left to right. At the same time Viracocha closes each eye alternately. We again note that the Viracocha carving has one finger from each hand missing. The message here is that the observer should *stand behind the doorway of the Gateway of the Sun raising one finger of each hand* so that one finger frames either side of the doorway (figure A9). The angle of the Sun can now be measured through the doorway using parallax error derived by alternately opening and closing each eye.

Decoding the Viracocha Transformer (V)

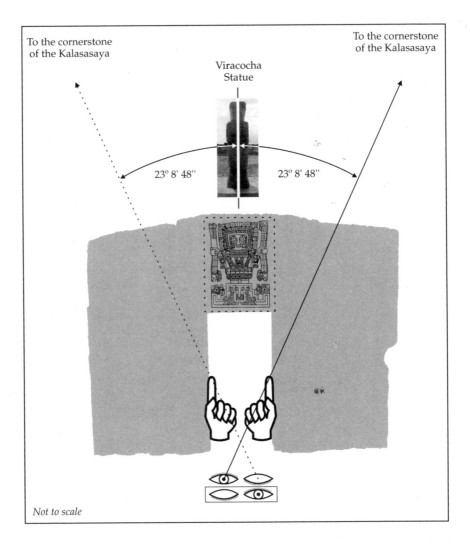

Not to scale

Figure A9. The Viracocha Transformer, when decoded, calls for the observer to stand behind the Gateway of the Sun in the Kalasasaya at Tiahuanaco. The lateral angle from the centre of the gateway to each of the cornerstones of the Kalasasaya can then be measured using parallax error derived from alternately opening and closing each eye (measured against raised index fingers) as shown above. This is the reason the Viracocha Transformer carries only three fingers and a thumb—the message being *'using one finger from each hand...'*. The measured angle of 23° 8' 48" corresponds to the tilt of the Earth on its axis at the time Tiahuanaco was built. This angle varies from the tilt of the Earth, measured as 23° 27' in 1930. In 1914 Professor Arthur Posnansky believed that the Kalasasaya contained astronomical alignments and obtained the same information using surveying instruments. He proposed consequently that Tiahuanaco dated as far back as 15,000 BC.

Looking more closely at a line drawing of the bas-relief (figure A5c), it becomes clear that the tongue of Viracocha is missing, which is highly unusual. The Sun God featured throughout South and Central America is almost always shown with his tongue poking out of his mouth (figure A6a–e).

The statue of Viracocha that stands in the middle of the Kalasasaya, just beyond the gateway, provides the next clue in helping to understand the meaning of the Viracocha bas-relief line drawing. The statue carries a male figure in his right hand and a female figure in his left (figure A7).

Following the instructions leads us to arrange the Viracocha transformer transparencies as shown in figure A8, revealing the secret message that Viracocha encoded into his bas-relief carving (figure A9): the Earth was destroyed on previous occasions when it tilted on its axis.

APPENDIX TWO

Secrets of the Ancients

Why and How They Encoded Their Secrets into Their Treasures

In *The Mayan Prophecies*, *The Supergods*, *The Tutankhamun Prophecies*, *The Lost Tomb of Viracocha* and *The Terracotta Warriors* I explained how the 'sun-king' leaders of the ancient Maya, Egyptians, Peruvians and Chinese possessed a scientific understanding of a very high order, one that modern man is only now beginning to grasp. They taught their people that the Sun controls fertility on Earth, that it controls personality determination (Sun-sign astrology) and that solar magnetic reversals bring periodic catastrophic destruction to Earth, erasing each civilisation in turn from the annals of history. These Supergods taught that the soul is imperishable, everlasting and, for the pure, destined for the stars; rebirth on Earth awaits the rest.

The mechanics of the reincarnation process imply that the super-knowledge, which takes many lifetimes to accumulate, could be acquired more quickly if individuals were able to build upon previous knowledge with each successive incarnation. But a new brain and heart, each incarnation, precludes such gains. So the purification process takes many more lifetimes than it otherwise might. To overcome this the ancients encoded their super-knowledge into their treasures. Rediscovery of the same knowledge, in the next incarnation, would enable a higher starting level of purification, giving the soul a better chance, they believed, of transmigration and transmutation into a star the next time around.

But how could the knowledge be 'written down' so as to guarantee its transmission over vast epochs of time? Throughout history, nations and languages have been wiped out by conquering armies and political regimes eager to impose their own beliefs on defeated nations. Ideas and cultures are lost through ideological succession. Natural disasters, floods, fire and earthquake likewise erase all evidence of earlier civilisations. Solar-inspired catastrophe cycles that periodically cause the Earth to tilt on its axis likewise defeat the transmission of knowledge.

Thus, it was important to preserve the ancient knowledge for themselves, to help them get to Heaven next time around. At the same time, it was also important to deny non-spiritual people access to the holy knowledge, meaning that if they were to preserve and safeguard it for themselves, they had to encode it.

Encoding Information Using Pictures

There are two preferred ways to 'write down' knowledge for posterity without the use of words. One way of encoding information is through the use of pictures: one picture tells a thousand words and all pictures are common to all people. Lord Pacal encoded his sacred knowledge into his Mayan transformers using pictures and mirror images of those pictures which when laid one upon the other reveal hundreds of other pictures. Plates 2, 3, 4, 5b, 6–13 and 24 show a few examples.

Encoding Information Using Numbers

Another way to encode information is by using numbers. The cultural common denominator, the number 10, is common to all mankind, because all of mankind has 10 fingers. Lord Pacal chose to use numbers in his encoding of solar magnetic cycles into the pyramid clues at Palenque, figure A17, and also to draw parallels with biblical quotations; plate 5b (detailed in figure A10) shows Lord Pacal wearing the esoteric number 144,000, mentioned in Revelation, on his forehead. The numbers they chose to convey astronomical and spiritual information are set down in figure 12.

Figures A11 to A17 show that the spiritual leaders of the Maya, Egyptians, Peruvians and Chinese all encoded the super-science of

The 144,000 Message
of Lord Pacal

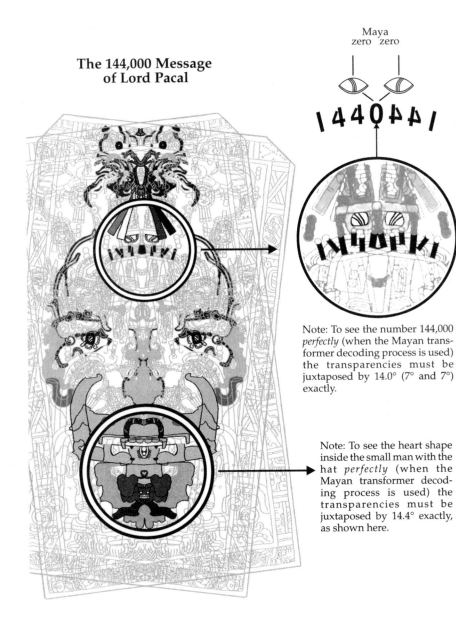

Maya
zero zero

Note: To see the number 144,000 *perfectly* (when the Mayan transformer decoding process is used) the transparencies must be juxtaposed by 14.0° (7° and 7°) exactly.

Note: To see the heart shape inside the small man with the hat *perfectly* (when the Mayan transformer decoding process is used) the transparencies must be juxtaposed by 14.4° exactly, as shown here.

Figure A10. In the Bible those with 144,000 written on their foreheads represent the chosen few who will enter the Kingdom of Heaven. In this decoded picture, from the Amazing Lid of Palenque, Lord Pacal carries the number 144,000 on his forehead *(above, top, circled)* only when one transparency is inverted and overlaid onto the other, juxtaposed by 7° and 7° (7, 7). The perfect heart shape, contained within the composite picture of the small man with the hat *(bottom, circled),* can be completed only when the transparencies are each juxtaposed by 14.4° (7.2° and 7.2°). These messages taken together tell us that only the pure of heart will become one of the 144,000, like Lord Pacal.

The Sunspot Cycle Message of Lord Pacal

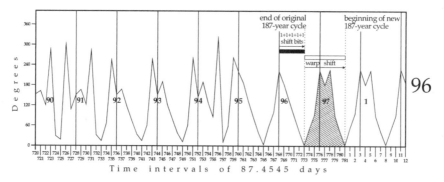

Figure A11. The computer-calculated version of the sunspot cycle shows that 96 microcycles of magnetic activity take place on the Sun every 187 years (the 97th cycle leads to an even longer cycle of 18,139 years). The 96-cycle sequence was known by ancient sun-worshipping civilisations who encoded the secret super-science of the Sun into their treasures. *(Note: To save space the first 89 microcycles are not shown).*

96

Figure A12. (a) The Palace at Palenque. (b) Tablet of 96 glyphs from the steps of the Palace at Palenque. (c) The Pyramid of Inscriptions, Palenque, burial place of Lord Pacal and his tombstone, the Lid of Palenque (figure 54b).

205

The Sunspot Cycle Message of Tutankhamun

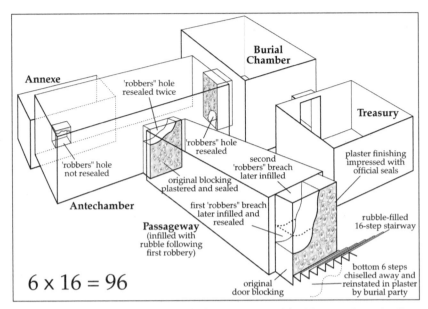

$$6 \times 16 = 96$$

Figure A13. According to archaeologists, the bottom 6 steps of the 16-step stairway leading to Tutankhamun's tomb were chiselled away by the burial party to 'permit access of larger pieces of furniture' into the tomb. The steps, originally stone, were reinstated in plaster by the same burial party. But why would a burial party seal a tomb and then repair a broken stairway before filling in the stairway with rubble behind themselves? This would simply invite others to use the steps in the future, to gain access to a solid wall. The 6 and the 16 are astronomically significant: $6 \times 16 = 96$, the number of magnetic cycles in one sunspot cycle.

999 in the Tomb of Viracocha Pachacamac

Figure A14. The coffin lid was tied down by 9 copper straps along each edge (9,9,9,9), a number unique to the Supergods. The vertical edges, down each corner, likewise carried the same number of straps (9,9,9,9). He was accompanied by eight others, nine (9) in all. This was no ordinary man. Like the other two sunkings, Lord Pacal of Mexico (9,9,9,9,9) and Tutankhamun (9,9,9,9,9) of Egypt, this man was a Supergod, later revered by the Incas.

206

The 9 9 9 Message of Viracocha Pachacamac

Figure A15. The lid of the coffin of Viracocha Pachacamac was tied to the sides by 3 sets of copper straps (3, 3, 3), 9 in all, along each side (9, 9, 9, 9). The corners were likewise tied together, and to the floor of the coffin, with the same number of straps, 9 at each corner (9, 9, 9, 9). The tomb was the final resting place of the Viracocha Pachacamac and eight companions, 9 in all. The corner brackets of the King of Hochdorf's carriage were pinned to the carriage platform by 9 nails (9, 9, 9, 9) and 9 dinner plates were stored on the carriage.

The 9 9 9 Message of Tutankhamun

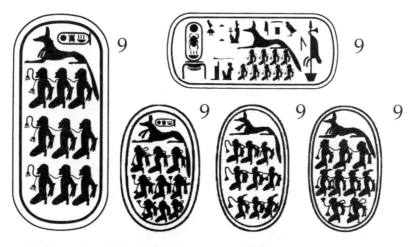

Figure A16. Door seals and object seals from the tomb of Tutankhamun showing the so-called 'prisoners', groups of 9 individuals (9, 9, 9, 9, 9) bound by rope around the neck and arms. Each rope terminates with a lotus flower, the epitome of sun worship, suggesting that the 'prisoners' were in 'divine captivity' on Earth. [The taking of prisoners was also a metaphor for 'thou shall not kill']. Tutankhamun was also buried in 9 coffins, one inside the other.

The 9 9 9 Message of Lord Pacal

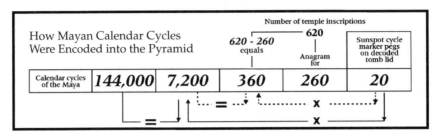

How Mayan Calendar Cycles Were Encoded into the Pyramid		Number of temple inscriptions		Sunspot cycle marker pegs on decoded tomb lid
		620	620	
		620 - 260 equals	Anagram for	
Calendar cycles of the Maya	**144,000**	**7,200**	**360**	**260**	**20**

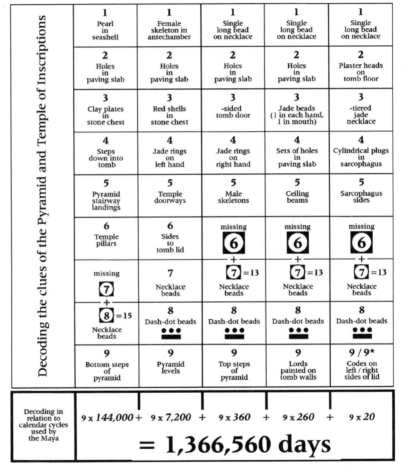

	1	1	1	1	1
	Pearl in seashell	Female skeleton in antechamber	Single long bead on necklace	Single long bead on necklace	Single long bead on necklace
	2	**2**	**2**	**2**	**2**
	Holes in paving slab	Holes in paving slab	Holes in paving slab	Holes in paving slab	Plaster heads on tomb floor
	3	**3**	**3**	**3**	**3**
	Clay plates in stone chest	Red shells in stone chest	-sided tomb door	Jade beads (1 in each hand, 1 in mouth)	-tiered jade necklace
	4	**4**	**4**	**4**	**4**
	Steps down into tomb	Jade rings on left hand	Jade rings on right hand	Sets of holes in paving slab	Cylindrical plugs in sarcophagus
	5	**5**	**5**	**5**	**5**
	Pyramid stairway landings	Temple doorways	Male skeletons	Ceiling beams	Sarcophagus sides
	6	**6**	missing **6**	missing **6**	missing **6**
	Temple pillars	Sides to tomb lid	+	+	+
	missing **7**	**7** Necklace beads	**7** = 13 Necklace beads	**7** = 13 Necklace beads	**7** = 13 Necklace beads
	+				
	8 = 15 Necklace beads	**8** Dash-dot beads •••	**8** Dash-dot beads •••	**8** Dash-dot beads •••	**8** Dash-dot beads •••
	9	**9**	**9**	**9**	**9 / 9***
	Bottom steps of pyramid	Pyramid levels	Top steps of pyramid	Lords painted on tomb walls	Codes on left / right sides of lid

Decoding in relation to calendar cycles used by the Maya	9 x 144,000 +	9 x 7,200 +	9 x 360 +	9 x 260 +	9 x 20
			= 1,366,560 days		

Figure A17. Lord Pacal encoded the number of the Supergods 9, 9, 9, 9, 9 into his treasures in the Temple of Inscriptions, Palenque. The number of objects in the tomb cleverly construct a numerical matrix that conceals information: 9 multiplied by the Mayan calendar cycles of time, in days, amounts to 1,366,560 days; the 'Birth of Venus' for the Maya. Moreover, 1 + 3 + 3 + 6 + 6 + 5 + 6 + 0 = 9, the number of a Supergod. They were attempting to convey the fact that Lord Pacal was the spiritual 'rebirth of Venus' (Jesus).

the Sun and the higher orders of spirituality into their treasures, using numbers, for rediscovery next time in their next incarnation on Earth should they fail to make it to Heaven this time around.

Studying these numbers, it becomes clear that the ancients were trying to explain that the purpose of this physical life on Earth is for each individual to purify the soul within, as a pre-requisite for entry into the kingdom of Heaven. This is achieved when the aspirant successfully converts the body, the beast (666), into godly energy, the soul (999), which the scriptures tell us can only be done through 'loving our neighbour'. Love purifies the heart, which in turn purifies the soul.

How the Soul Gets to Heaven

In 1915 the physicist Albert Einstein published his General Theory of Relativity containing his equation $E=mc^2$, which means that *energy* equals *mass* multiplied by the *speed of light* (c) squared. This means that energy can be converted to mass. The Bible teaches that God is Light, which modern science recognises as electromagnetic energy (E).

The Bible also teaches that God made man in his own image, which is revealing because man can only grow to a certain size; to grow further he must throw away a sperm. Likewise a woman, to grow further, must throw away an egg.

Christianity also teaches that God is good and God is love. The only thing better than God, therefore, must be more God. By making man in his own image God reveals that he cannot grow, at least not without throwing a piece of himself away. And it seems that this is precisely what must have happened when the physical Universe was created. In the beginning, God threw away some of his energy (E) (for the sake of explanation, say about 5%). The energy converted into mass, the physical Universe. In moving across Einstein's equation, the (+) (for example) energy must change its sign to (−), a simple rule of algebra. This tells us that the physical Universe must therefore be the opposite of God, which means that the physical Universe and everything in it, including the Earth, must be Hell. It must also mean that everything in the carbon-based Universe, including trees, flowers and physical bodies must be the Devil (666), which we have already determined to be the opposite of God (999). So when Christianity says bad souls go to Hell, it simply means that bad souls return to the carbon-based Earth, which is Hell. This in turn means that all of the world's religions explicitly recognise the reincarnation process.

But surely, by sacrificing himself in such a way, God has not grown, he has reduced in size—by 5%.

The Mechanism of Soul Transmigration

In the beginning, when God sacrificed (say) 5% of himself, the energy exploded with what physicists today refer to as the 'big bang'. Time began when the Universe began, things (events) began to happen (transpire): some things before other things and some things after other things, unlike previously when the only thing that existed was light.

With time, evolution of species began. Human bodies evolved. Brains evolved. In the human womb, the heart pumps blood around the body and the brain becomes electrically active. The voltage of the brain, being opposite to the voltage of God, attracts more electromagnetic energy (imagine a bubble of electromagnetic energy) directly from God as it develops in the womb. This energy, the soul, attaches to the body and stays with the body until the voltage of the physical body falls to a lower value, when it is too weak, too sick, to hold on to it. In between times (during the lifetime of an individual on Earth) the voltage of the soul (when it is entombed within the body) is able to either increase or decrease.

Humans are composed of the physical body; the soul (the spiritual body); the mind (the intellectual body); and the heart (the emotional body). These four 'bodies' live in distinct worlds which conform to different rules. For example, in the physical world, if I have one dollar and you have one dollar and we exchange them, then we each finish up with only one dollar, which seems to prove, at least in the physical world, that we cannot get something for nothing. But the other worlds are not the same. For example, in the intellectual world, if I have one idea and you also have one idea and we exchange them, then we both finish up with two ideas. In the intellectual world we can double our intellectual wealth at no cost. It seems that in the emotional world, if I love you, then my soul voltage will grow. If my soul voltage grows, then when it leaves my body it will be attracted back to God and God will grow. Conversely,

The Three Worlds

Figure A18. Some of the stories from the Amazing Lid of Palenque explain that the souls of those who die at childbirth, in battle and in sacrifice migrate to the Paradises, various destinations of the dead, to enjoy heavenly bliss, presumably before proceeding to the God World, the place where God resides. Some pictures show how the soul leaves the body for either rebirth in the stars (the heavens and the God World) or rebirth on Earth (reincarnation). Others describe the journey of the soul into the underworld or through purgatory, the place where the heart is purged of sin. The Maya also believed that there were nine levels to the underworld through which the departed soul had to travel prior to moving on, either to the God World or to reincarnation on Earth. (It seems that perfectly purified souls fast-track through the Soul World to the God World and that impure souls suffer in the underworld (purgatory) for their earthly sins before acquiring the energy to reincarnate on Earth for another chance of soul purification.)

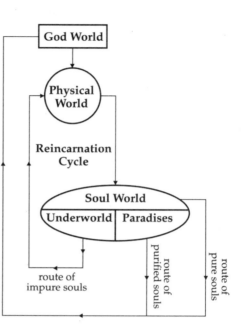

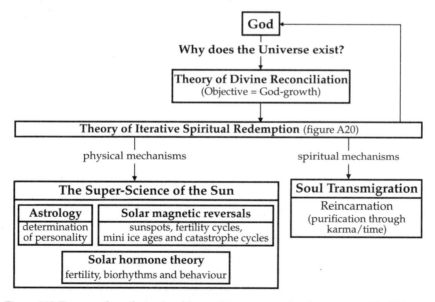

The General Theory of Existence

Figure A19. Treasures from the tombs of the sun-kings suggest that the purpose of the Universe is to accommodate God-growth (in accordance with the Theory of Divine Reconciliation, as detailed in the main text). Figure A20 resolves the Theory of Divine Reconciliation and the Three Worlds hypothesis into a working model.

The Theory of Iterative Spiritual Redemption

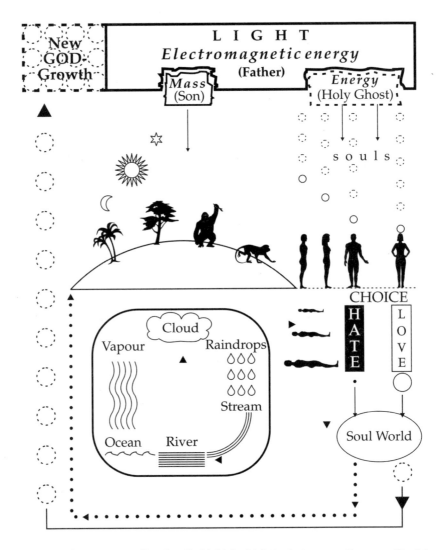

Figure A20. The scriptures tell us that God is Light. Light is electromagnetic energy. Einstein tells us that $E = mc^2$, which means that energy (E) can be converted into physical mass (m) and mass can be converted into energy. The equation tells us that the release of energy, when mass is converted, is proportional to the speed of light squared (c^2). This suggests that in the beginning God sacrificed a part of himself, creating the physical Universe (the Son). Physical bodies then evolved to attract discrete packets of electromagnetic energy (souls) away from the source of energy (God). The journey of the soul is analogous to that of a raindrop, which is reborn many times. Purification comes through love and sacrifice. Purified souls return to the creator. As a result, the creator grows. Bad souls return to Earth, attempting purification once again.

if I hate you, then my soul voltage will fall, and I will return to Earth to a lower-voltage body. The important thing to remember is that the destination of my soul depends on me, what I think and do to you. Nothing you can do can send my soul to Heaven or to Hell.

An interesting observation emerges from this type of analysis: if I encourage *you* to hate *me*, then I could effectively send *you* to Hell, because *your* soul voltage will fall, which is another reason why this sacred knowledge had to be encoded and kept secret. Imagine the chaos on Earth if people began sending their adversaries to Hell. Few, if any, would get to Heaven, thereby confounding the divine objective of the Universe which is to accommodate God-growth, through mankind, as a spiritual conduit. The good news is that if *you* do hate *me*, then *my* heart will suffer and because suffering purifies the heart *my* soul voltage will increase, meaning that if *you* hate *me*, you send *my* soul to Heaven.

The physical Universe continues to perplex modern-day physicists. Surprisingly, nothing has been learned about gravity, the force that makes things fall to the ground, the same force that holds the Universe together, since Isaac Newton first defined it in the third part of his *Principia*, in 1687. It is hard to believe that no one knows what causes it. No one knows why in this, our twenty-first century, objects fall to the ground.

And yet physicists are quite sure that by counting the planets and stars they can calculate a figure for the total amount of gravity that should be present in the Universe. But when they do the calculation the figure obtained is much less than the figure needed to hold the Universe together. To overcome this, physicists pretend that there are more planets and more stars out there than actually exist. They call the missing stars and planets 'black matter' because it cannot be seen. This may seem absurd, but it does at least mean that their calculations are correct. Similarly, when they calculate the rate of expansion of the Universe they discover that their figures are in fact much lower than they should be, meaning, they argue, that there must also be 'dark energy' out there, making the Universe expand more quickly than it actually does.

It has never occurred to them to consider that 95% of the energy in the Universe, God, did not convert to physical matter when the Universe began or that God might be holding the Universe together.

The Sun as the Feathered Snake

The Sun as the Feathered Snake

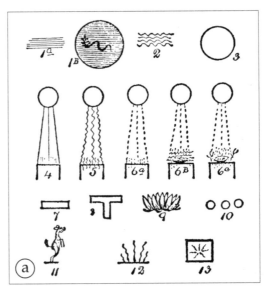

Figure A21. (a) Sketches of the 25,000-year-old lost Tibetan Naacal tablets, made by the explorer James Churchward during his stay in a Tibetan monastery in the 1930s. They show the sinking of the legendary island of Lemuria caused by adverse solar radiation patterns; increased levels of radiation led to the overheating of the landmass, causing the release of subterranean gases and the sinking of the land itself. One of the sketches (labelled as 1ᴮ) shows a feathered snake-like mark across the face of the Sunóthe earliest known depiction showing the Sun as the 'feathered snake'.

Figure A22. (a) Schematic of the the neutral sheet of the Sun illustrated as a feathered snake. The feathered snake of the Sun was worshipped and depicted in carvings and paintings throughout Egypt (b) and Mexico (c).

Tutankhamun, the Feathered Snake of Egypt

Figure A23. Tutankhamun carried the vulture (feathers) and a snake on his forehead. His beard was fashioned as the body of a snake which ended with the tail feathers of a bird.

215

Viracocha, the Feathered Snake of Peru

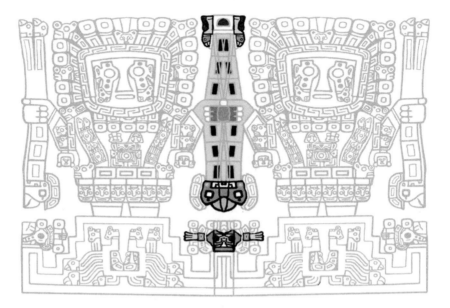

Figure A24. The Viracocha transformer from the Gateway of the Sun, Tiahuanaco, showing Viracocha as the feathered snake.

The Feathered Snake of Viracocha

Figure A25. Viracocha as the feathered snake, featured on the golden spider chambers from his tomb at Sipan c. AD 500.

The Feathered Snake Drawings of Nazca

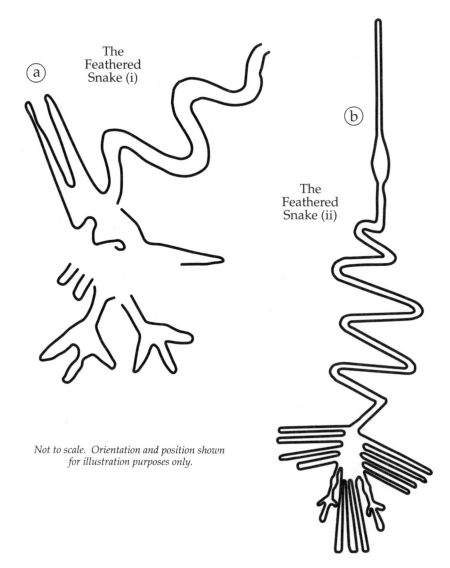

The
Feathered
Snake (i)

The
Feathered
Snake (ii)

*Not to scale. Orientation and position shown
for illustration purposes only.*

Figure A26. Two of the Nazca line drawings made by the legendary white god Viracocha as he walked the lands of Peru performing miracles in around AD 500. These two depict his signature: the feathered snake.

Lord Pacal, the Feathered Snake of Mexico

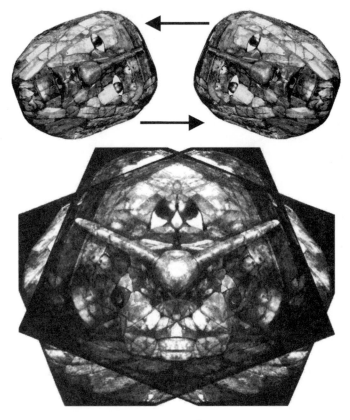

Figure A27. Lord Pacal as the feathered snake, from the decoded mosaic jade mask found in his tomb at Palenque c. AD 750. The picture is revealed only when the transparencies are each rotated by 66.6° (the number from Revelation [666]) and overlaid as shown.

Calculation of the Sunspot Cycle Using Sacred Geometry

The 'sacred shapes' encoded into Gothic architecture by the Freemasons, the solar cross, the pentagon, hexagon and octagon, may together be used to calculate the duration of the sunspot cycle without the use of a computer. In revering these shapes they were attempting to convey the hidden super-science of the Sun which affects every aspect of our lives.

Figure A11 shows the computer-calculated version of the 187-year sunspot cycle. Figure A28a shows how 6 microcycles of solar magnetic activity amount to one 11.5-year hypothesised cycle (6 x 8 bits [time intervals of 87.4545 days] = 700 days [48 bits]). This relationship can be simply represented by a hexagon (figure A28b) whose sides are each of 8 bits (700 days) in duration (or, as in the case with the Holy Grail, an octagon with sides 6 bits in length).

The hexagon, or octagon, can be placed on top of the microcycle series and rolled over one side every 700 days, or two sides every 1,400 days, etc. (figure A29). One complete revolution of the hexagon would amount to 6 microcycles, 48 bits: one 11.49-year hypothesised cycle. All that would be needed is some sort of calendar to keep track of the accumulation of the periods of 700, 1,400, etc., days.

This is all very well until the hexagon encounters the first magnetic microcycle containing a shift bit—which occurs when the 11.49-year cycle and the 187-year cycle cross over and interfere with each

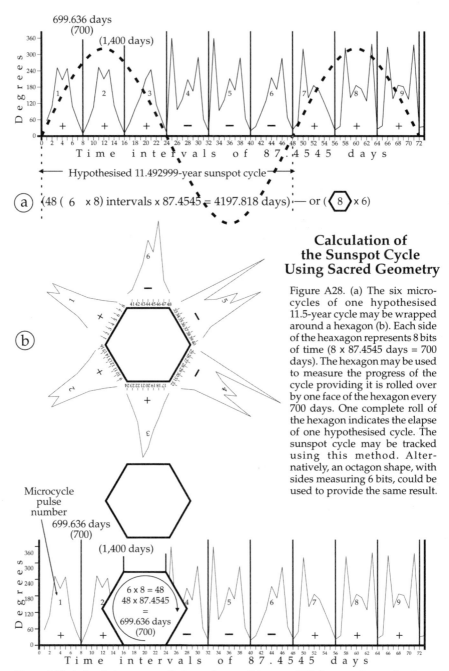

Calculation of the Sunspot Cycle Using Sacred Geometry

Figure A28. (a) The six micro-cycles of one hypothesised 11.5-year cycle may be wrapped around a hexagon (b). Each side of the heaxagon represents 8 bits of time (8 x 87.4545 days = 700 days). The hexagon may be used to measure the progress of the cycle providing it is rolled over by one face of the hexagon every 700 days. One complete roll of the hexagon indicates the elapse of one hypothesised cycle. The sunspot cycle may be tracked using this method. Alternatively, an octagon shape, with sides measuring 6 bits, could be used to provide the same result.

Figure A29. A simple hexagon, rolled over by one side every 700 days, can be used to keep track of sunspot cycles. One complete revolution of the hexagon amounts to one complete sunspot cycle of 11.4929 years.

220

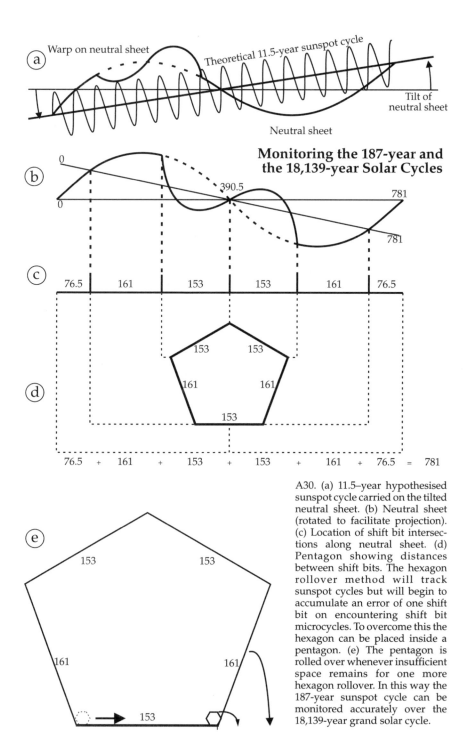

Monitoring the 187-year and the 18,139-year Solar Cycles

(a) Warp on neutral sheet

Theoretical 11.5-year sunspot cycle

Tilt of neutral sheet

Neutral sheet

(b) 0

390.5

781

0

781

781

(c) 76.5 | 161 | 153 | 153 | 161 | 76.5

(d) 153 153

161 161

153

76.5 + 161 + 153 + 153 + 161 + 76.5 = 781

(e) 153 153

161 161

153

A30. (a) 11.5–year hypothesised sunspot cycle carried on the tilted neutral sheet. (b) Neutral sheet (rotated to facilitate projection). (c) Location of shift bit intersections along neutral sheet. (d) Pentagon showing distances between shift bits. The hexagon rollover method will track sunspot cycles but will begin to accumulate an error of one shift bit on encountering shift bit microcycles. To overcome this the hexagon can be placed inside a pentagon. (e) The pentagon is rolled over whenever insufficient space remains for one more hexagon rollover. In this way the 187-year sunspot cycle can be monitored accurately over the 18,139-year grand solar cycle.

Monitoring the 187-year and the 18,139-year Solar Cycles Using Stonehenge

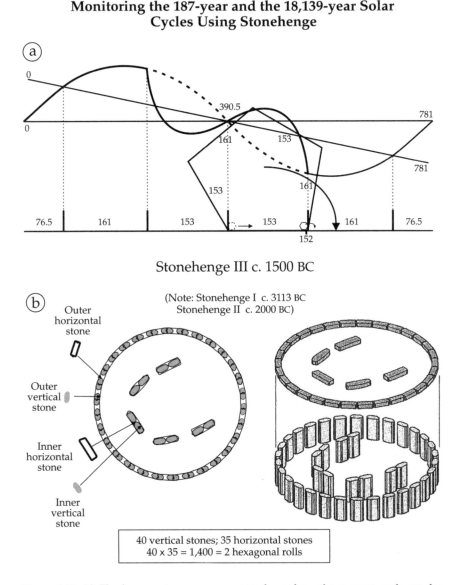

Figure A31. (a) The hexa-pentagon arrangement shows how the sunspot cycle can be monitored using hexagons (or octagons) in conjunction with a pentagon. These shapes were encoded by the Gothic Masons in their cathedral architecture during the mediaeval period. This formed the basis for sacred geometry, the geometric shapes built into the architecture of churches throughout Europe. (b) Stonehenge can be used to track the sunspot cycle: The trilithon arrangements (three-stone arches on both the outer ring and inner horseshoe ring) at Stonehenge are made up of 40 vertical stones and 35 horizontal stones (in total). If one stone is marked each day, then all stones would be marked after 1,400 days (40 x 35). The marking of stones could be used as a calendrical accumulator in conjunction with the hexa-pentagon method of sunspot calculation.

other [meaning that the microcycle is 9 bits long instead of 8]—five such shift bits occur during the 187-year cycle and are shown (in A30c) dropping from the waveform figure A30b. From this point on, the simple hexagon will begin to accumulate a one-bit error with every shift bit encounter. Figure A30d shows that the distances between shift bits may be expressed by an irregular pentagon with sides of 153, 153, 161, 153 and 161 (781 in total).

The shift bit de-synchronisation, using the hexagon method of sunspot cycle measurement, may be overcome by placing the hexagon inside the irregular pentagon (figure A30e). The hexagon is rolled over as before. Because 153 and 161 are divisible by 8 'remainder 1', the rolling hexagon will eventually run out of space to roll over. Whenever this happens the pentagon rolls over (taking the hexagon with it). The de-synchronising shift bit is hence 'skipped', maintaining synchronism between the hexagon and the sunspot cycle (figure A31a). The same applies to an octagon rollover sequence.

A simple calendar, like that in figure A31b, could be used to keep track of the accumulation of days: each day one stone, either vertical or horizontal, is marked, on the arrangement of 40 vertical and 35 horizontal stones (40 x 35 = 1,400 = two sides of the hexagon). The hexagon is rolled over two faces once all 1,400 have been marked.

Notes

Chapter One

1. In *Critias* and *Timaeus* c. 355 BC.
2. The Greek statesman c. 638 BC.
3. From the Greek word Keltoi—the 'secret people'.
4. The language derives from four main groups of a branch of Indo-European and is spoken in most of Europe. Gaelic and its close relatives Lepontic, Noric and Galatian were once spoken in a wide arc from France to Turkey and from the Netherlands to Italy and Celtiberian, once spoken in Spain, are now long obsolete. The third in the group, the Brythonic, or P-Celtic, is spoken by the Welsh, Cornish, Bretons and Gauls [of France] whereas the Goidelic, or Q-Celtic, is spoken by the Irish [Gaelic, from the association with the French, Gaul], the Scots and the Manx of the Isle of Man. The extinct and the contemporaneous are often classified as two branches, but competing schemes prefer different combinations.
5. Deoxyribonucleic acid—the giant molecule that makes the building blocks of biorganisms.
6. The Germanic invaders who conquered much of Britain between the 5th and 7th centuries and who pushed the Celts westwards across Britain.
7. Believed to have been compiled in the monastery of Inisfallen between 1056 and 1092. The monastery was established in around AD 650 on the 23-acre island of Innisfallen [the modern-day spelling differs slightly] in the lower Killarney Lake, County Kerry, Ireland. The transcript of the Annals, up to 1092, is believed to have been used at a monastery at Lissom and compiled from earlier documents maintained at the monastery of Emly. It was probably continued at Lissom until between around 1130 to 1159 when it was passed to South Munster, probably Inisfallen.
8. Northwest of the Black Sea between the Carpathian Mountains and the River Don.

9. There were five sons of Míl altogether: Éremón, Donn, Ír, Éber and another (the name of the fifth does not appear in the translation because of damage to the original manuscript). Éber was born in Egypt, Donn was born in Scythia and Ír and Éremón, the youngest two, were born in Spain.

10. The Annals state that the 'Scotti' were converted to the Christian faith [in AD 433]. *The Encyclopaedia of Ireland* [under the heading of 'Scotland, links with'] says that later 'an expedition led by the three sons of Erc from Irish Dal Raida (in County Antrim, Ireland) founded the Kingdom of Argyll (now Scotland) in around AD 500'. Hence the origin of Ir-land (after Ír the son of Míl) and Scotland (after Scotta, the Pharaoh's daughter).

11. So named after *hall,* the Celtic word for salt, and *statt,* the Celtic word for place.

12. *The Tutankhamun Prophecies* sets out in detail just how the twent-eight-day solar radiation cycle correlates with variations in fertility hormones.

13. Paleomagnetic evidence, from Pearson and Cox (*Climate and Evolution,* 1978), and tree ring data from Bucha, 1970 [both documented in *The Mayan Prophecies*], suggest that the Sun's magnetic field shifted in 3113 BC and again in around AD 620 (1,366,040 days after the 3113 BC shift). It appears that the magnetic twist of AD 620 was of insufficient strength to tilt any of the planets off their axis but did result in adverse radiation from the Sun that deleteriously affected the Earth (see main text).

14. Areas around the Earth's equator are struck by more perpendicular solar X-rays and are hence more affected.

15. • They were all born through an Immaculate Conception.
   • Buddha's mothers name was Maya. Maya was the name of the architect of Tutankhamun's tomb, and also the name of his wet-nurse. The word Maya means 'illusion' in ancient Sanskrit.
   • Maya was a culture that flourished in Mexico c. 100–750 AD and Lord Pacal, the priest-king leader of the Maya, taught that this life was illusion.
   • Krishna is the Greek word for the 'anointed one' and Christ anointed (baptised) others.
   • Jesus is known as the Son of God [from the Tibetan Chi, (godly energy) and the Greek Zeus, the creator God, Chi Zeus, the Son of God who died c. 32 BC. [The Bible says: ' . . . the angel of the Lord appeared unto Joseph in a dream saying . . . Mary shall bring forth a son and his name shall be Chi Zeus', *Matthew* I, 20–21]; the name Tut-ankh-amun translates into 'the living image of God'—the Son of God—and Ch'in Shi Huangdi, the first emperor of unified China, was known to his people as the 'Son of Heaven'.
   • Stories left behind by Lord Pacal (from the Mural of Bonampak) say that

he was the Lord of Sacrifice who died on a cross-made from two pieces of wood. Jesus died on the cross at Easter and the Roman Catholic word for Easter is Paschal.

- Viracocha is the Quechua word for 'foam of the sea', a metaphor for the perfect human being. A person in 'the foam of the sea' is simultaneously in contact with all of the Earth's elements of earth, air, fire and water: the earth, beneath the feet; the air; the fire (the Sun) that shines on the face; and the water. Any movement towards the sea causes loss of contact with the earth. Any movement towards the land causes loss of contact with the water. Hence, a person reaches perfection only in the 'foam of the sea'. A 60-cm- (2 foot-) high golden anthropomorphic figure of a crab-man (plate 5d) was found in the tomb of Viracocha at Sipan in Peru. The crab is a creature that lives on the land and in the sea, in the foam of the sea.
- The Brahmans, of India, believe Heaven to be a 'milky ocean' (foam of the sea) which is why they believe the cow to be sacred.
- All of the Supergods—Krishna, Tutankhamun, Buddha, Ch'in Shi Huangdi, Jesus, Viracocha (and Viracocha Pachacamac) and Lord Pacal —performed miracles.
- When they died they all became Venus.

16. The Indian Vedas (divine knowledge of the Brahmans) tell of the Indian holy trinity: Brahma (the Holy Ghost, or spirit), Vishnu (the flesh, incarnate on Earth) and Siva (the father). Vishnu is said to have incarnated on Earth nine times, the eighth time as the Hindu God Lord Krishna and the ninth as Lord Buddha. The Vedas are believed to have been written by the Indo-Aryans prior to their entering India in around 1500 BC. The four main Vedas are: the Rig-Veda (hymns and praises); Yajur-Veda (prayers and sacrificial formulae); Sama-Veda (tunes and chants); and Atharva-Veda of the Atharvans, the officiating priests at the sacrifices. They are all written in an old form of ancient Sanskrit.

17. Stories from the sun shield of Monte Albania (plate 3c) show Lord Paccar reincarnating as Venus.

18. The 'bright' star refers to the bright star in the dark night sky (the evening star) as against the 'morning star' that competed with the rising sunlight and hence was less bright.

19. The plural for 'fibula', used to describe a safety-pin-style cloak fastener.

20. When found the carriage was crushed, requiring extensive restoration and reconstruction.

21. The formal period in pre-history during which bronze was most favoured for metalworking.

22. Previously featured in *The Lost Tomb of Viracocha* and *The Terracotta Warriors*.

23. The technique is often compared to the later technique of cloisonné, the ornamental craft in which metal strips are soldered into a pattern on a metal surface and the resulting compartments (cloisons) filled with coloured enamel and then fired.

24. *Encyclopaedia of World Mythology*, Octopus, 1975.

25. *Encylopaedia of Myths and Legends*, Arthur Cotterell, Cassell, 1989.

26. Governed Britain AD 78–85.

27. In *Natural History*, published in around AD 50, the Roman scholar Pliny the Elder (AD 23–79) describes the pagan oak tree ritual '. . . clad in white robes, the priest climbs a tree and with a golden sickle cuts a sprig of mistletoe'. *Pharsalia* [c. 48 BC], Loeb, 1962.

28. The Universal Law of action and reaction.

29. The National Museum of Ireland has dozens of examples like these.

Chapter Two

30. Who may have been one and the same as King Menes.

31. See *The Tutankhamun Prophecies*: 'The Mystery of the mixed-up meat'.

32. Asher, Benjamin, Dan, Ephraim, Gad, Issachar, Judah, Mandasseh, Naptali, Reuben, Simeon, and Zebulun.

33. The body of books accepted by the Church.

34. *The Times* (review article), April 10, 2004.

35. An Island Dependency of the U.K. located in the Irish Sea.

36. Fifty days after the Jewish festival of Passover [the eight-day spring festival that commemorates how the Angel of Death *passed over* Jews houses, so that only the Egyptian firstborn sons were killed—which is seen as divine retribution, following the Pharaoh's edict that all male Jewish infants should be killed].

37. *The Ultimate Encyclopaedia of Mythology*, Arthur Cotterell, Hermes House, 1999, p. 13.

38. Bede's *Ecclesiastical History of the English People*. Ed. B. Colgrave and R. A. B. Mynors (Oxford 1969), IV. 4.

Chapter Three

39. So-called because the first letter of each column was often 'illuminated' in red, *ruber* (Latin).

40. Easter, commemorating the crucifixion of Jesus, coincides with the Jewish festival of Passover. The so-called Easter Controversy refers to the dispute concerning the preferred dating of the Easter festival. The Jews calculate

the date of Passover as occurring on a full moon. Christians knew only that the Crucifixion coincided with Passover and that it occurred at some time after the spring equinox (the 21st March) and on a Sunday. In order to ascertain a date for Easter, the Christians therefore had to synthesise the days and dates of Passover, the full moon, the spring equinox and the day of Sunday. This means that Easter Sunday falls on the first Sunday following the full moon that follows the spring equinox, meaning that Easter falls on a different date every year. The Irish Celts had their own way of doing the calculation but fell into line in AD 632. Northumbria (Lindisfarne) conformed in AD 664, Iona in AD 716 and the Welsh Church by AD 768.

41. However, an account from Prosper of Aquitaine's reliable *Chronicon* of AD 431 says that 'Pope Celestine ordained Palladius sending him to the Irish believers in Christ as their *first* Bishop. . . . Later writers, such as Muirchu, anxious to respect Palladius, yet wishing to present Patrick as the *first* Bishop, imagined Palladius failing in his task, being succeeded by Patrick, hence the dating of Patrick's arrival [as Bishop] at AD 432'. (quoted from The *Encyclopaedia of Ireland*, Gill & Macmillan, 2003)

Chapter Five

42. Isidori Hispalensis *Episcopi Etymologiarum sive Originum*, ed. W. M. Lindsay, 2 vols., Oxford, 1911, Vol. 2 lib XII vii.48.

43. These Supergods knew of their impending death, as a passage from the Popol Vuh implies: 'They were endowed with intelligence; they saw and instantly they could see far, they succeeded in seeing, they succeeded in knowing all that there is in the world. When they looked, instantly they saw all around them, and they contemplated the arch of the heavens and the round face of the Earth. The things hidden (in the distance) they saw all, without first having to move; at once they saw the world. . . . Great was their wisdom'. (*The Popol Vuh*, Delia Goetz and Sylvanus G. Morley, University of Oklahoma Press, 1947)

Bibliography

Adès, Harry, *Celtic Art*, Paragon, 1999.

Aidey, Dr. W. Ross, *'Cell Membranes, Electromagnetic Fields and Intercellular Communication'*, Basar, E. (ed.), from a paper presented at the International Conference on Dynamics of Sensory and Cognitive Processing in the Brain, Berlin, August 1987.

Ashe, Geoffrey, *A Guidbook to Arthurian Britain*, Longman, 1980.

Bain, George, *Celtic Art—the Methods of Construction*, Dover, 1973.

Banck, Johanna, *Feine Tüche Für Den Fürsten*,Theiss Verlag, 2002.

Barber, Elizabeth Wayland, T*he Mummies of Urumchi*, W. W. Norton and Co., 1999.

Berresford Ellis, Peter, *The Ancient World of the Celts*, Constable & Robinson, 1998.

Bettany, G. T., *The World's Religions*, Ward Lock & Co., 1890.

Biel, Jörg, *Experiment Hochdorf*, Archäologische Denkmalewr in Hessen 51, 1994.

———, *Das Rätsel der Kelten vom Glauberg*, Theiss Verlag, 2002.

———, *Der Fürst*, Theiss Verlag, 2002.

———, *Der Keltenfürst von Hochdorf*, Theiss Verlag *1998*.

Capon, E., and MacQuitty, W., *Princes of Jade*, Sphere, 1973.

Cavendish, R., *An Illustrated Guide to Mythology*, W. H. Smith, 1984.

Coghlan, Ronan, *The Encyclopaedia of Arthurian Legends*, Vega Books, 1991.

Cotterell, Arthur and, Rachel Storm, *The Ultimate Encyclopaedia of Mythology*, Hermes House, 1999.

Cotterell, Arthur, *Myths & Legends*, Cassell, *1992*.

Cotterell, M. M., *Astrogenetics*, Brooks Hill Robinson & Co., 1988.

———, *The Amazing Lid of Palenque*, vol. 1, Brooks Hill Perry & Co., 1994.

———, *The Amazing Lid of Palenque*, vol. 2, BHP & Co., 1994.

———, *The Mayan Prophecies*, Element, 1995 (coauthored).

————, *The Mosaic Mask of Palenque*, BHP & Co., 1995.

————, *The Mural of Bonampak*, BHP & Co., 1995.

————, *The Supergods*, Thorsons, 1997.

————, *The Lost Tomb of Viracocha*, Headline, 2001.

————, *The Tutankhamun Prophecies*, Headline, 1999.

Dix, Gregory, *Jew and Greek—A Study in the Primitive Church*, New York: Harper & Bros., 1953.

Egerton Sykes, *Dictionary of Non-Classical Mythology*, J.M.Dent and Sons, 1952.

Eysenck, H.J., and, D. K. B. Nias, *Astrology: Science or Superstition?* Maurice Temple Smith, 1982.

Finlay, Ian, *Celtic Art*, Noyes, 1973.

Ghezzi, Bert, *The Times Book of Saints*, HarperCollins, 2000.

Gibbon, Edward, *The History of the Decline and Fall of the Roman Empire*, ed. J. B. Bury, 7 vols., London: Methuen, 1896–1900.

Goetz, D., and, S. G. Morley, *The Popol Vuh* (after Recinos), Wm. Hodge & Co., 1947.

Green, Miranda, *The Gods of the Celts*. Sutton Books, 1986.

Herm, Gerhard, *The Celts*, Weidenfeld and Nicolson,1976.

Hessisches Landesmuseum Darmstadt, *Katalog der Glauberg–Funde*,1980.

His Majesty's Special Command (translation), *Holy Bible*, Eyre & Spottiswoode, 1899

Hitching, F. The World Atlas of Mysteries, Wm. Collins & Son, 1978.

Horton, Fred L. Jr., *The Melchizedek Tradition—A Critical Examination of the Sources to the Fifth-century A.D. and in the Epistle to the Hebrews*, Cambridge University Press, 1976.

Hubert, Henri, *The History of the Celtic People*, Bracken Books, 1993.

Hutchinson, *Encyclopedia*, Helicon, 1998.

Jordan, M., *Encyclopaedia of Gods*, Kyle Cathie, 1992.

Lafferty, P., and, J. Rowe, (eds.) *The Hutchinson Dictionary of Science*, Helicon, 1996.

Laing, Lloyd, and Jennifer Laing, *Art of the Celts*,Thames and Hudson, 1992.

Lalor, Brian (ed.), *The Encyclopaedia of Ireland*, Gill Macmillan, 2003.

Legge, James, *The Chinese Classic*, vols. I–V, University of Hong Kong Press, 1960.

le Plongeon, Augustus, *Sacred Mysteries among the Mayas and the Quiches 11,500 Years Ago*, Macoy, 1909.

Mallory, J. P., and, Victor H. Mair, *The Tarim Mummies*,Thames and Hudson, 2000.

Mac Airt, Seán (ed.) *The Annals of Inisfallen*, Dublin Institute for Advanced Studies, 1988.

Moon, Peter, *The Black Sun*, Sky (New York) 1997.

Moore, Hunt, Nicolson and Cattermole, *The Atlas of the Solar System*, Mitchell Beazley, 1995.

Morley, S. G., *An Introductiion to the Study of Maya Hieroglyphs*, Dover, 1915.

MacNeill, Eoin, *Celtic Ireland*, Dublin: Martin Lester Ltd, 1921.

McLeish, Kenneth, *Myths and Legends of the World*, Blitz Editions, 1996.

Musurillo, Herbert (ed.), *The Acts of the Christian Martyrs*, Oxford Clarendon Press, 1972.

Osborn, Eric, *The Beginning of Christian Philosophy*, Cambridge University Press, 1981.

Parker, Geoffrey, *The Times Atlas of World History*, HarperCollins, 1978.

Pearson, R., *Climate and Evolution*, Academic Press, 1978.

Peterson, Roland, *Everyone Is Right: A New Look at Comparative Religion and Its Relation to Science*, California: De Vorss & Co, 1986.

Philip's *Atlas of the Celts*, George Philip Ltd, 2001.

Pierpaoli, Walter, and William Regelson, with Carol Colman, *The Melatonin Miracle*, Simon & Schuster, 1995.

Posnansky, Arthur, *Tihuanacu, the Cradle of American Man*, New York: J. J. Augustin, 1945.

Powell, Neil, *The Book of Change: How to Understand the I Ching*, Orbis, 1979.

Poynder, Michael, *Pie in the Sky*, Rider, 1992.

Price, Glickstein, Horton and Bailey, *Principles of Psychology*, Holt Rinehart and Winston, 1982.

Raftery, Barry (ed.) *Atlas of the Celts*, Philips, 2001.

Reiche, Maria, *Nazca Peru, Mystery of the Desert*, Hans Shultz-Severin, 1968.

Reinhard, Johan, *The Nazca Lines: A New Perspective on Their Origin and Meaning*, Editorial Los Pinos, 1985.

Roys, Ralph R., *The Book of Chilam Balam of Chumayel*, University of Oklahoma Press, 1932.

Rutherford, Ward, *Celtic Lore*, Thorsons, 1993.

Ryan, M. (ed.) *Treasures of Ireland*, Royal Irish Academy, 1983.

Schweitzer, Albert, *The Quest of the Historical Jesus*, trans. William Montgomery, New York: Macmillan, 1961.

Sharkey, John, *Celtic Mysteries*, Thames and Hudson, 1975.

Swami Shri Purohit, *The Geeta*, Faber & Faber, 1935.

Sykes, Egerton, *Dictionary of Non-Classical Mythology*, J. M. Dent, 1952.

Talbot Rice, David, *The Dark Ages*, Thames & Hudson,1965.

Thomson, W. A. R., *Black's Medical Dictionary*, A. & C. Black, 1984.

Thorpe, Lewis (trans.) Geoffrey of Monmouth (c. 1136), *The Kings of Britain*, Penguin, 1973.

Von Hagen, W., *The Ancient Sun Kingdoms of the Americas*, Thames and Hudson, 1962.

Wallace, P. F., and Raghnall Ó Floinn (eds.), *Treasures of the National Museum of Ireland*, Gill & Macmillan, 2002.

Warner, R. (ed.), *Encyclopaedia of World Mythology*, BPC, 1970.

Wegener, G. S., *6,000 Jahre und ein Buch*, Oncjken Verlag Kassel, 1958.

Welker, H. A., P. Semm, R. P. Willig, W. Wiltschko, L. Vollrath, 'Effects of an artificial magnetic field on seratonin-N-acetyltransferase activity and melatonin content of the rat pineal gland', *Exptl. Brain Res.* 50:426–531, 1983.

White, J., *Pole Shift*, Virginia Beach: ARE Press, 1993.

Willis, Roy (consultant), *Dictionary of World Myth*, Duncan Baird, 1995.

Willis, Roy (ed.), *World Mythology—The Illustrated Guide*, Piatkus, 1993.

Zaczek, Iain, *The Art of the Celts*, London: Parkgate Books, 1997.

———, *Chronicles of the Celts*, Collins & Brown, 1996.

Index

Note: Page numbers in **bold** refer to black-and-white illustrations. Numbers preceded by CP refer to the color plates.

Books of Related Interest

The Tutankhamun Prophecies
The Sacred Secret of the Maya, Egyptians, and Freemasons
by Maurice Cotterell

The Lost Tomb of Viracocha
Unlocking the Secrets of the Peruvian Pyramids
by Maurice Cotterell

The Terracotta Warriors
The Secret Codes of the Emperor's Army
by Maurice Cotterell

The Grail
The Celtic Origins of the Sacred Icon
by Jean Markale

King of the Celts
Arthurian Legends and Celtic Tradition
by Jean Markale

Mabon and the Guardians of Celtic Britain
Hero Myths in the Mabinogion
by Caitlín Matthews

The Mystery of the Grail
Initiation and Magic in the Quest for the Spirit
by Julius Evola

Walking the Maze
The Enduring Presence of Celtic Spirit
by Loren Cruden

Inner Traditions • Bear & Company
P.O. Box 388
Rochester, VT 05767
1-800-246-8648
www.InnerTraditions.com

Or contact your local bookseller